GUNS AND CONTROL

A NONPARTISAN GUIDE TO UNDERSTANDING MASS PUBLIC SHOOTINGS, GUN ACCIDENTS, CRIME, PUBLIC CARRY, SUICIDES, DEFENSIVE USE, AND MORE

GUY SMITH

FOUNDER, GUN FACTS PROJECT

Skyhorse Publishing

Skyhorse Publishing books may be purchased in bulk at special discounts for sales promotion, corporate gifts, fund-raising, or educational purposes. Special editions can also be created to specifications. For details, contact the Special Sales Department, Skyhorse Publishing, 307 West 36th Street, 11th Floor, New York, NY 10018 or info@skyhorsepublishing.com.

Skyhorse® and Skyhorse Publishing® are registered trademarks of Skyhorse Publishing, Inc.®, a Delaware corporation.

Visit our website at www.skyhorsepublishing.com.

10 9 8 7 6 5 4 3 2 1

Library of Congress Cataloging-in-Publication Data is available on file.

Cover design by 5mediadesign

Print ISBN: 978-1-5107-6007-3
Ebook ISBN: 978-1-5107-6008-0

Printed in the United States of America

Dedicated to Rosie, Charlie, and Michael. Just thinking of you makes me smile.

Also dedicated to the hundreds of Gun Facts volunteer researchers who have helped to make dispassionate discussions possible through great data and their hard work.

Contents

Contents

Foreword
By Lt. Col. Dave Grossman, US Army (ret.)

You hold in your hands the single best scientific, statistical analysis available on the issue of guns and gun control. If you truly desire "just the facts" and not propaganda on this critical subject, then *this* is the book for you.

As you read through this book, you will begin to understand the Herculean task that Guy Smith has set for himself in assembling this body of data. Allow me to explain some complexities about guns and violence to illustrate why Guy's distillation is important.

First is the subject of media violence and its impact on violence in our society. This topic was just too far outside Guy's scope in writing this book. Guy has done a great job covering the subject of "media contagion" (his suggestion that we are really looking at "competition killers," instead of mass murders, is brilliant), and we both recommend my book, *Assassination Generation*, for more information on that aspect of the subject.

Additionally, I co-authored the book *Control: Exposing the Truth About Guns* with Glenn Beck (which made the *New York Times* Best Sellers list), and I think we did a good job of covering the nexus between media violence and violence in our society. It would make a great companion to this book, if you would like more information.

One other aspect of the complexity associated with the task that Guy Smith has set for himself is the impact of medical technology holding down the murder rate. Over any period of time, the murder rate (the raw number of dead people) completely under-represents the problem, because the medical community is saving ever more lives.

In 2002, Anthony Harris and a team of scholars from the University of Massachusetts and Harvard published a landmark study in the journal *Homicide Studies* which concluded that medical technology advances since 1970 have prevented approximately three out of four murders. That is, if we had 1970s-level medical technology, the murder rate would be three or four times higher than it is today.

One medical expert told me that he believes tourniquet use alone, in the last decade, may have cut the murder rate in half. Today, every cop and EMT carries a tourniquet on their person, whereas ten years ago none of them did. If a cop slaps on a tourniquet and saves a life, he has also prevented a murder. If twenty police officers a day (among the half-million on duty, between the three shifts, working in these violent times every day) slap on a tourniquet and prevent a murder, then we have cut the murder rate roughly in half.

The aggravated assault rate is a better measure, but that data is easy to "fudge." Where do you draw the line between aggravated assault and "simple" assault? It can be like "grade inflation" in our schools.

When we compare money over any period of time, we talk in terms of "inflation adjusted dollars." And when we look at murders over any period of time, we need to speak in terms of "medically adjusted murders." If we did this one thing, it would completely change how we view the problem of violent crime in our nation, and around the world.

Unfortunately, that UMass/Harvard study is just one data point. Until we begin to track "medically adjusted murders" like we do "inflation adjusted dollars," it will be very hard to calculate this aspect into the hard statistical data that Guy has integrated in this singular, remarkable book.

The point of my missive is to demonstrate what a superb job Guy Smith has done in compiling the available facts and data in this specific area. Parsing out the media violence issue, setting aside the impact of medical technology for future researchers, and focusing with laser precision on taking what is available, Guy has given *you*, the reader, the information that you need to come to intelligent, informed conclusions on this critical subject.

In the end, facts are facts, and facts are important. *That* is something we can all agree on.

Our society cannot have an adult conversation about guns, crime, violence, and gun control unless we work with real, true, solid data. Information. Facts. And *this* book is the place to find those precious commodities

Whatever your position on these critical subjects, I implore you to not just read, but *study* this book. The solution to our nation's problems cannot be found in emotions. But the facts to be found in this book can aid us greatly in the worthy endeavor of leading our nation to a better and safer place. *That* is something else we can all agree on, and Guy Smith has given us an invaluable resource to assist in that endeavor.

—Dave Grossman
Author of *On Killing, On Combat,*
and *Assassination Generation*

Foreword

By David T. Hardy, Former Associate Editor of the *Arizona Law Review*

A RECENT FAD HAS BEEN to announce that we need to have a "serious conversation" about firearms violence and gun control. The truth is that we have been having that conversation, at a very serious level, for nearly half a century. Serious criminological work on that issue began in the 1970s, with major contributions by professors of criminology and statisticians—David Bordua, Alan Lizzotte, Gary Kleck, and John Lott, among others. All these concluded that few, if any, forms of gun control were associated with lower rates of violence.

One might ask, after half a century of research and publication, what could Guy Smith add to the issue?

The answer is (with all due respect to his predecessors): He is very, very, readable. His predecessors were technical authors, writing largely for an audience of the same. Their creations were scientific, technical, and usually quite long. We read them (as, alas, I am sure they read my own efforts) for work, not for enlightenment.

In contrast, Guy's book is something that an intelligent reader can understand, without setting aside a week to read and imperfectly grasp. Reading it is a pleasure rather than a duty. That makes *Guns and Control* exceptional—no, make that unique—in the field of criminology and gun control.

That readability makes it useful both to readers and to friends they may wish to inform. If a person wants a serious conversation on gun control, this book should be the starting point. Unless the points Guy Smith makes can be answered, it will also be the ending point.

—David T. Hardy
Former Associate Editor
of the *Arizona Law Review*

Introduction

complexity, n. The mother of reinvention

TO PRACTICALLY PLAGIARIZE *The Hitchhikers Guide to the Galaxy*, let's say that guns and gun control policy are complicated. Really complicated. You just won't believe how vastly, hugely, mind-bogglingly convoluted gun policy is. It is nitpicky, muddled by vastly different and constantly changing laws, warped by cultural variations (national and regional), muddied by political opportunists, lied about by politicians, and driven by fear on all sides. In short, an intellectual mind-bender of galactic proportions.

I'm here to help you wrap your brain around the topic without it bursting in the process.

For more than twenty years, I have traversed and explored the gun control sciences. It started as many intellectual pursuits do, with the observation of something that did not make much sense to me. Most science does not begin with a shout of "Eureka!" but with someone like me muttering, "Well, that's odd."

In my younger years, the nightly news often contained gut-wrenching accounts of homicides, followed instantly by representatives of gun control groups decrying the society-ending plague of guns. But in the non-rural, high-tech county in which I lived, nobody could recall the last time anyone—aside from a burglar—was shot. Indeed, I was twenty years old before the first shooting death occurred in my hometown, and that was by a police officer in an indisputable act of self-defense from a crazed, knife-wielding attacker. In other words, what I witnessed in real life was utterly different than what the evening news portrayed.

One of the worst things that can happen to someone with an education and career experience in research design is to have their interest piqued, for it drags them off into ever-deepening quests for more data, more complex analysis, and the eventual realization later in life that it is unwise to start relaying acquired knowledge at social gatherings. Starting with one small statistical datapoint and the associated misinformation on the topic of guns and homicides, I dug deeper, and deeper, and deeper. This minor bit of insight unleashed a massive time-suck, an insatiable monster of curiosity. Secondary research soon led to primary research. This quickly led to my hard drive being overwhelmed with national crime databases and international suicide stats. It evolved to email contacts with criminologists, participation in forums with constitutional scholars, and an ever-increasing education in propaganda analysis.

It also led to a humorous marital moment. My wife (God rest her soul) emerged from the bedroom one Saturday morning to discover me feverishly *rat-a-tatting* on my computer keyboard, the dual monitors decorated with spreadsheets and data visualizations. When she asked what I was doing at my desk at eight o'clock on a Saturday morning, I sheepishly replied, "I'm doing multivariate regressions on FBI supplemental homicide tables." Fortunately, she just smiled in that special way spouses of geeks do instead of filing for divorce.

Over time, I found an audience that craved unpolluted insight about guns and gun violence. It started with the humble objective of identifying and debunking bad information on the topic of gun control policy in an effort to get politicos to quit lying (I failed). Over time my activities expanded to publishing both the bad and the good information that was available, distilling the critical data, and explaining it for clarity (I succeeded). Ultimately, I stitched together far-flung pools of data, incorporated analysis, and visually presented the realities about guns and gun control in order to expand public perspective (I kinda excelled).

The process taught me a few undeniable things:

THE FIELD AIN'T FOR WIMPS: Gun policy covers a lot of turf. It may not contain as many disciplines as global climatology (quite seriously, that field has everything from astrophysics to zoology), but it does have quite a few—criminology, statistics, sociology, psychology, mental health management, cultural studies, and more. If you want to understand who is being dishonest in gun control debates, watch to see which of these topics they avoid discussing.

NUMBERS REALLY, REALLY, REALLY MATTER: Start talking to the average voter about population-proportional statistical variations of, well, anything, and their eyes will glaze over before they faceplant into the carpet. Yet such numbers are critical to understanding some of the most basic issues surrounding gun control policy, and are even more so in gaining uncluttered perspective. That has been a big part of my job—distilling and then presenting the realities of guns and gun control without having to first force-feed black coffee into my audience.

PEOPLE LIE AND OFTEN USE NUMBERS TO DO SO: Gun control is ideology-driven politics, regardless of which side of the debate one might reside on. Some politicos have openly and routinely fed the public ample amounts of bovine byproduct in order to push an agenda, and they have done so using an amazing array of substandard stats based on inappropriate data sources, abysmal methodologies, and outright misdirection.

NOTHING IS CONSISTENT: I often have to discuss cultural attitudes as a contributing factor to gun misuse, and thus what polices might work. My favorite joke while speaking to audiences is that if you take one thousand National Rifle Association (NRA) members and put them in a room full of guns, the only death will be from boredom after listening to them yammer on and on about which makes, models, calibers, grip styles, and finishes they like best. But if you take one thousand members of competing inner-city street gangs and put them in a room full of guns, nobody is getting out alive. Likewise, throughout gun studies there is little consistency across regions, nations, cultures, laws, limits, or restrictions. This inconsistency is used by various groups to misarticulate reality and push their proposals into law.

THIS BRINGS US BACK TO the reason this book is in your hands. Getting your brain around all that complexity via web research would be perilous. Relying on seemingly trustworthy sources, such as medical schools that routinely commit criminology malpractice, would lead to less understanding, not more. Forget about the policy groups, be they pro- or anti-gun, for the meager art of omission is sufficient to create ignorance disguised as education and lead you away from practical insight.

This book exists so you can come to grips with the subject of guns and their control without hourly trips to Starbucks. It will explain the varied topics that are in perpetual debate, examine what is reliably known and not well known, provide high-level perspective, and dive into detail where appropriate. It will also expose many places where the politicians and policy groups have managed to muddy our intellectual waters in order to frighten voters and, in the process, ease them past critical thinking.

Illuminate, triangulate, illustrate, and in the process, create a better-informed voter.

A note about data used in this book

The reader will notice a startling lack of "studies" being cited throughout this tome, but instead will see ample tables and charts presenting pure data from nearly pristine sources like the Federal Bureau of Investigation's (FBI) Uniform Crime Statistics, the Centers for Disease Control's (CDC) mortality and injury databases, and summaries of those sources by the Bureau of Justice Statistics.

There are a few reasons for me being so downright strict in my data selection. Foremost, the raw data from these sources is often complete, inarguable, and very illustrative of reality. Whereas some artful research studies creatively use data to portray fiction, the raw data is untainted by intellectual dishonesty. Another advantage is that you do not have to take my word about anything since the same data from the same sources is available through any web browser. You can go look up the details yourself and it isn't hard at all. Lastly, politicos with agendas will have a really hard time denying the presentations herein. They will anyway, but when asked "what is your objection to the FBI's Uniform Crime Reporting data?" their argumentative nature rapidly abates.

But, alas, not all answers can come from these sources. I do have to rely on a handful of surveys and studies to bring clarity. For example, the FBI can tell us how many gun murders there were last year, but those statistics say nothing about how guns get into the hands of street gang members. When looking for added clarity, I rely primarily on work done by criminologists. It is their field of expertise, as opposed to, say, a pediatrician. In some instances, I have used survey data, such as those concerning gun ownership or defensive gun use rates. Surveys are direct data acquisitions and do not rely on mathematical adjustments, so despite problems with surveys in general (which I disclose herein), they add quality insight for your benefit.

In short, I wanted to provide you, the astute and rational reader, with the real numbers, unfiltered, unadjusted, and un-politicized.

A note about policy

If you expect to find proof points about gun control policy, either for or against, or if you expect me to tell you what legislation is or is not advisable, you will be disappointed.

Don't get me wrong. After studying guns, violence, and policy for over twenty years, I have more than a few opinions. But you don't need anyone's opinions, even mine. What you need is the data presented in simple terms so you can wisely make your own policy and politician choices. The NRA and Everytown for Gun Safety will gladly give you plenty of opinions. I give you the straight dope so you can decide while being fully informed.

A note about funding

The Gun Facts project has none.

The Gun Facts project is slightly poorer than a frugal monk. When I formalized the project, I set a rule against accepting money from policy organizations. We have been offered money by a national gun policy outfit, and we have also been offered lucre from the largest state affiliate of a different national gun policy organization. We turned them both down—and it hurt because their combined cash would have more than quadrupled the Gun Facts project's annual donations. All of Gun Facts's operating capital comes from fans. The average one-time donation is less than twenty dollars. Some donors make an automatic monthly contribution, but the average recurring tithe is under ten dollars.

In short, we are always close to broke. But the alternative is to accept money from groups on a mission. That could open the gateways of Heck and tempt them into dictating the outcome of our research or censoring our analysis and publishing. It would also allow some large swath of the public to disbelieve anything we say because we are "in the pockets" of "the gun lobby" or "the gun control lobby."

Who needs those headaches?

A note for nitpickers

Before complaints can be filed, understand a few things about this book:

- Every book takes time to write. For a complex subject like this, that duration can be long. If the data presented is not up-to-the-minute inclusive, this is one possible reason.
- Not all data sources are consistent. As you will see in one chapter, the FBI online tools for extracting crime data changed, and not for the better, making some data extracts possible only through 2014. And detailed tables concerning crime were available for 2017 but not 2018. Aside from these calamities, I tried in all cases to use the most recent data on which I could lay my digital hands.
- Even old data can be useful. When showing perspective on an issue, historical data is often quite sufficient. If one maps robbery data

between countries from 1980 through 2005, odds are extremely good that—in the absence of an observable trend—2006 through today is likely similar.

- In many instances I report simple regression results. Unless otherwise mentioned, all regressions achieve a 95 percent confidence level and probability values (p-values for the statistically savvy) ≤0.05.
- I do not present multivariant analysis for multiple rational reasons. These reasons include (a) that high-level information is what the public at large desires, (b) this takes huge amounts of time which publishing deadlines disallow, and (c) since I am not trying to prove or disprove any point, simple regressions are sufficient to increase understanding of most topics.

CHAPTER 1

Gun Availability

You cannot commit a gun crime without a gun.

Fifty-four percent of counties in the United States have zero murders, much less gun homicides.

GUNS AND THEIR AVAILABILITY ARE a classic coin metaphor. Guns are indeed used to commit crimes. They are also used to prevent crimes. They can contribute to accidental deaths but are unlikely to do so if precautions are taken.

The problem with modern discussions about the mere availability of guns is that all competing factions see it as a one-sided coin, an object that has never existed. To understand how private ownership of guns affects society, you have to flip the coin . . . repeatedly.

The critical take-aways

- There is weak correlation between guns per capita and homicides
- Gun violence is strongly associated with specific geographies and subcultures
- Few guns used for crime come from retail sources, but many come from underground networks

Availability and confounding variables

I have a long-running joke I give when speaking to audiences:

> *Last time I checked, the annual NRA convention was about seventy thousand members. These are people that own guns and know how to use guns. They are in a confined space with lots of guns. But nobody gets killed. Now, take seventy thousand garden variety street gang members and put them into the same building with the same stockpile of guns. You'll need plenty of mops and buckets to clean up the blood.*

The point of this exaggerated contrast is to demonstrate that the mere availability of guns is not deterministic to their misuse. Other factors are at play. In this particular and silly comparison, there is a clear difference in the cultural values of the two groups. NRA members are largely "law and order" types. Street gang members have little or no respect for any law, and from crime statistics, no respect for gun laws. Two heavily armed groups but with very different cultural norms produce two very different outcomes. Likewise, comparing the homicidal tendencies of the United States, which has the highest per capita gun ownership rate in the world, with the Falkland Islands or Yemen (the second and third gun ownership *rate* countries[1]) would present equally confusing results.

Despite these complications, looking at countries around the world provides both insight and statistical landmines. To get a handle on all these gruesome details, let's look at dead people.

Criminologists who have explored guns and policy tend to focus most ardently on homicides. The reason is that there is little debate over whether a person is dead from one country to another, whereas the definitions for assault, robbery, rape, and other acts of violence vary quite a bit. That being said, an "honor killing" might be ignored in Afghanistan and thus not be tallied in crime statistics, but the same act would earn a court-ordered lethal injection in Texas. By and large, however, the major classifications for what constitutes a homicide are consistent across borders and the United Nations Office on Drugs and Crimes tries to keep global definitions and the resulting data aligned as much as is humanly possible.

If the availability of guns was a major factor in public endangerment, then in theory—and with all other factors being equal—the countries with the highest rate of private gun ownership should have the most bloodshed. But all other factors are far from being equal.

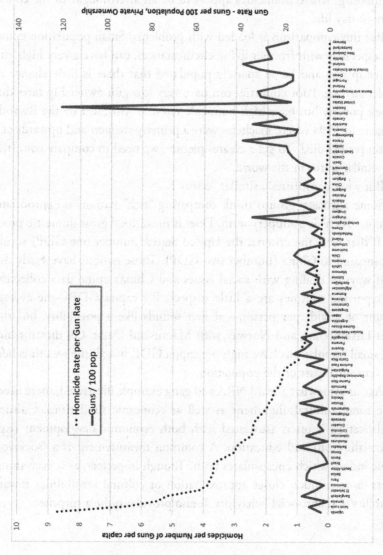

Ownership rate: Small Arms Survey 2017; Homicide rate: United Nations Office on Drugs and Crime

The huge spike in gun ownership rates on the right side of the chart is the United States. The homicide rate (murders per one hundred thousand people) per gun ownership rate for each country is plotted from the highest—Uganda at 31,262% the rate of the United States—to the lowest—Luxembourg, where homicides appear to be an afterthought in the course of day-to-day life.

But this comparison is loaded with problems. Small population countries, especially with frontier living circumstances, can have a very high gun ownership rate and be so sparsely populated that there is little chance to murder anyone. Poor countries can have very low gun ownership rates due to their poverty but have high homicide rates, as witnessed by the Rwanda Massacre in 1994 where machetes were a primary weapon and upwards of a million people died. To get a clearer picture, we need to compare countries with similar status in the world.

But what constitutes a similar "status"?

Some advocacy groups think comparing "rich" nations is appropriate. It is not. "Rich" is a slippery term. Does it mean total gross domestic product? If that were the criteria, the United States (number one GDP) would be compared to China (number two GDP). Those nations have vastly different ways of dealing with social issues and China's crime data collection and reporting routines are a little suspect. Per capita GDP—the average amount of wealth per person—at first sounds like a possibility, but this mixes Luxembourg and Norway with Macau and Qatar. Oil dictatorships with small populations have high per capita GDP, but all the wealth is held by a very small part of the population.

As our somewhat absurd NRA and gang example illustrated, there needs to be some cultural alignment as well as economic similarities. Cultural sophistication is often associated with both economic development (e.g., industrialization) and education. A common measurement is a "socioeconomic index" which encapsulates both. Though imperfect, as is everything, it gets us to a much closer approximation of cultural sensibilities toward sociability and antisocial behaviors. It also provides quite a surprise.

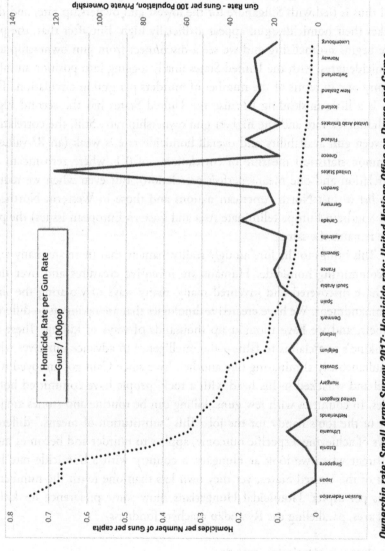

Ownership rate: Small Arms Survey 2017; Homicide rate: United Nations Office on Drugs and Crime

Looking at just the top 25 percent of nations on the socioeconomic index,[2] we again see some things that are surprising and not surprising at all. It is predictable that the modern and dictatorial Russia heavily restricts private gun ownership and also has a higher homicide rate per owned gun than all contenders. Japan has some of the strictest gun control in the world, and thus is tied with Singapore for the lowest gun ownership rate, and this makes their homicides/gun appear artificially high. But after that, the picture begins normalizing and we see a disconnect from gun ownership and homicide rates, with the United States finally logging into position number twenty-one in terms of the number of murders per gun in circulation. This too is a little misleading because the United States has the second highest homicide rate and the highest gun ownership rate. Still, the correlation between gun availability and overall homicide rate is weak (an R^2 value—common statistical measure of correlation—of 0.1, where zero means no correlation and one means perfect correlation). But even when we reduce this list to just North American nations and those in Western, Northern, and Southern Europe (eliminate Asia and Eastern European issues) the picture remains the same.

This brings to the fore an ugly reality, namely that there are many ways of committing homicide. Humans are inventive creatures and over time we have discovered and invented many, many ways of violating the sixth commandment. We have created technologies that are taking us to different planets, and we have thought up thousands of ways of killing. These are mankind's two claims to fame—the intelligence to advance ourselves while simultaneously eliminating one another. Ever since Cain got annoyed with Abel and whacked in his head with a rock, people have committed homicides. In countries with few guns, killing can be routine and stones are just one of the tools handy for the job. This "substitution of means," different ways of achieving a specific outcome, applies to murder and becomes more apparent when we look at Hungary, a country with a homicide rate half that of the United States, yet they own less than one tenth the number of guns per capita. Homicidal Hungarians show some preference for knives and axes, paralleling the Rwandan machete fondness.

The other side of the coin—prelude

Guns can be used offensively and defensively. I devote a complete chapter to that side of the coin, but defensive gun uses (DGUs) are worth mentioning now due to the confusing homicide comparisons above, and the other confusing violent crime statistics later.

One criminologist[3] gathered together a dozen surveys and studies conducted by various academics, polling companies, and news organizations. The average number of American DGUs per year was slightly below two million. This criminologist's own study concluded there were 2.5 million DGUs, and his estimate wasn't even the highest of the group. A deeper dive into survey respondents also produced an estimate that four hundred thousand of these DGUs prevented death or serious injuries. This illuminates one open and eternal question about guns, namely how many murders are prevented using a gun when compared to how many murders are committed with them. Another highly unsettling question explored in the DGU chapter is if a lack of guns might be an endangerment to any subsegment of a population, in particular to women. But for now, we'll focus on the availability of guns and the harm they can cause.

Where is the gun violence and who is doing it?

As we dive specifically into American use and misuse of the available gun supply, we'll see that our NRA vs. gang duality is not misplaced. Much of American gun play is highly isolated. In fact, one research organization discovered that in their year of study, 54 percent of counties in America had no homicides whatsoever and that 2 percent of US counties had 51 percent of the nation's homicides.[4] This agrees with original research done by the Gun Facts Project where we found:

1. The top twenty cities for homicides …
2. Had 7 percent of America's population, but …
3. Produced 21 percent of its murders

Whenever you see a massive skewing of the location for homicides, we can begin to explore what variables are at play. Since 72 percent of American homicides in 2017 involved guns, this will tell us much about the nature of guns and their use in violence—homicides, assaults, and robberies.

A big note about gun ownership rates

One bedevilment in the gun research is knowing how many guns there are. This applies to the national stockpile. It applies to state-level estimates. It applies to even rough guesses about how many households have one or more guns.

The fact is nobody knows for certain. Some people think the lack of gun registration in America is a bug, others think it is a feature. For our purposes, it is a minor nightmare but one we can work around.

Until recently, two of the three major tracking polls (Gallup, ABC, and Pew) that measured household gun ownership noted that the level of ownership had been more or less steady for a couple of decades. The third poll showed a declining rate of household ownership. When it was discovered that the third poll was surveying everyone, not just registered voters, they adjusted their process and came to the same conclusion as the other two polls.

This lack of precision has led to no end of confusion for the public, and the confusion will not abate soon. Most trending polls that ask people about their gun ownership have two problematic issues:

SAMPLE SIZE: Everyone is on a budget, and polling companies survey as few people as possible to keep costs under control while maintaining reasonable statistical confidence. But when your survey 1,500 people in fifty-one jurisdictions (fifty states plus Washington, D.C.) that is roughly thirty people per state, which is statistically insubstantial.

HONESTY: One study[5] noted that nearly 9 percent of respondents simply refused to answer questions about their gun ownership. Historically, women have reported household gun ownership rates at levels significantly lower than men do. Odds are that convicted felons who are prohibited from owning guns don't answer questions about gun ownership honestly. Nor would illegal immigrants. The point is that gun ownership rates estimated by surveys are approximations and given the common factors I just listed, possibly on the low side.

That the various surveys are in rough agreement about the rate of gun ownership provides moot comfort. The validity of gun ownership rates becomes a bit more dicey if we explore county-level data, because a reliable estimate of gun ownership in California includes the high rate of ownership in the central valley (largely rural and agricultural) and San Francisco (which has no public gun stores at all but had twenty-five firearm homicides in 2018). This concern properly noted, let's look at the top counties in the United States and their propensity toward murder. From this you will also get a sense about how various policy groups cherry-pick locations to study to suit their goals.

For our purposes, I averaged the state-wide household gun ownership rates from two different studies[6] to estimate gun availability and used county level data from the FBI's Uniform Crime Reporting databases for 2014 (the last year for which the FBI's older reporting system has data and made it possible to dump data by regions).

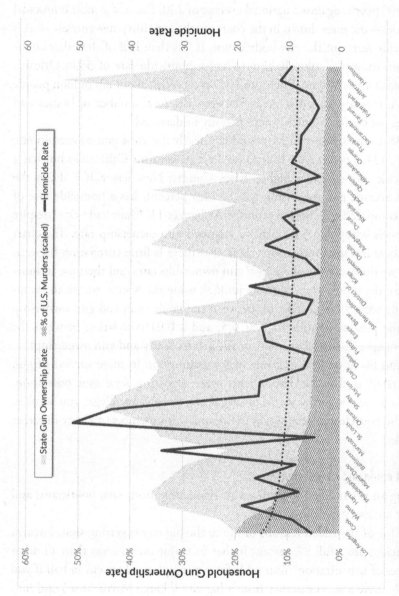

State gun ownership rates: Average of Behavioral Risk Factor Surveillance System (BRFSS) and YouGov survey; Crime: FBI Uniform Crime Reporting

In 2014, Los Angeles County—home to deep "gangsta" subcultures—led the nation in terms of total homicides. In that year, L.A. had a homicide rate double the average of all other counties in the US (5.4 incidents per 100,000 people against a national average of 2.8). But of the most homicidal counties—the ones shown in the chart are the top thirty-five entries—L.A.'s homicide *rate*, not the raw body count, is less than half of the other counties (for example's sake, Baltimore had a homicide rate of 34.0; Orleans, Louisiana 43.6; Wayne, Michigan 18.7, etc.). With about ten million people in L.A. County, this divergence between the *total* number of bodies and bodies per capita (homicide rate) is easily understood.

Baltimore County in Maryland has nearly the same gun ownership rate as L.A. (21.4 percent for Maryland; 19.8 percent for California) but has a homicide rate six times higher. Essex County, New Jersey, if it shares the state's average gun ownership rate of 11.3 percent, has a homicide rate of 15.1 compared to Jefferson County, Alabama's 11.7 homicide rate, despite Jefferson's whopping 53.1 percent assumed gun ownership rate. The chart and these instant comparisons show that there is little correlation between what we think are the likely *legal* gun ownership rates and their use in murder (for the more ardent statistics junkies; using the R^2 test, we see an exceptionally weak 0.08 correlation between homicide rates and gun ownership and the p-value is quite high at 0.5, and a 0.01 correlation between the percentage of national murders in any given county and gun ownership).

You likely noticed that one major assumption in these surveys of gun ownership is that the respondents were reporting *legal* gun possession. Welcome to the messy world of illegal gun possession, illegal gun sources, and the ever-clearer view of why NRA and Crips members are very different people.

Street crime and its gun sources

Living an urban lifestyle comes with risks, aside from rats, politicians, and other unsavory creatures.

One of the added hazards of life in the big city is getting shot. Firearm homicides are a full 97 percent higher in major metro areas than all other degrees of urbanization. Your odds for getting plugged are cut in half if you simply drive a short distance from a big city ("Large Metro Area") and into the adjoining suburbs ("Large Fringe Metro").

The reasons for this are manifold. First, there is simply more opportunity for both street crime and spontaneous violence, such as a fist fight erupting outside of a bar. In America, violent crime is about 23 percent higher in the

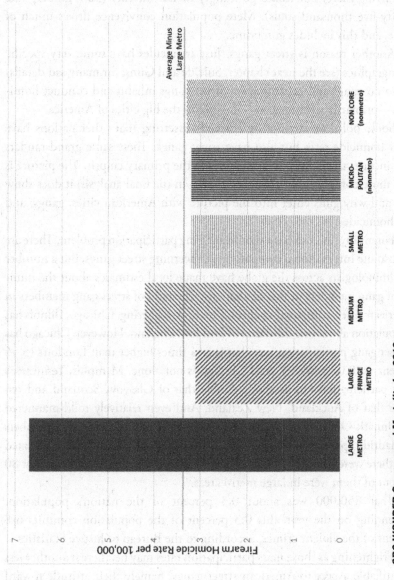

CDC WONDER Compressed Mortality for 2016

top 20 percent of cities (ranked by population) than the bottom 20 percent. Your typical ATM mugger or liquor store bandit thrives in Houston (robbery rate 205 incidents per hundred thousand people with over 2.3 million folks living there) but would go hungry in Carson City (32.7 robbery rate of fifty-five thousand souls). Mere population convivence drives much of crime, and this includes gun crime.

Another reason is street gangs. Just as suicides have some very specific demographics (see the next chapter, Suicide and Guns, for many sad details) so too do gangs and urbanization. Street gangs inhabit and conduct homicides—primarily with firearms—mainly in the big cities of America.

Some politicos counter by correctly asserting that other nations have lower homicide rates but also have street gangs. These same grandstanders then incorrectly blame gun availability as the primary culprit. The picture is a bit more complicated than that, though in the final analysis, it does show how and why guns enter into the picture with American cities, gangs, and gun homicides.

Foremost, America has a significant gang participation problem. There are no absolute international comparisons concerning street gangs, but a number of criminologists across the globe have made local estimates about the number of gang members in this-or-that city. The ratio of street gang members in American cities, compared to cities abroad, is staggering. Chicago, Illinois has a population about one third that of London, England. However, Chicago has a street gang participation rate that is 314 times higher than London's (5.56 percent vs. 0.02 percent). And Chicago is not alone. Memphis, Tennessee's gang participation rate is about double that of Glasgow, Scotland and ten times that of Auckland, New Zealand. And even relatively mild-mannered Cincinnati, Ohio has more than seven times as many street gang members as Madrid, Spain. Way back in 2012, the National Gang Center estimated that there were over 850,000 gang members in the United States and that 80 percent of them were in large metro areas.

That 850,000 was about 0.3 percent of the nation's population. Depending on the year, this 0.3 percent of the population commits 6-8 percent of the violent crimes, according to the Bureau of Justice Statistics.

Frightening as those mass participation rates may be, there is another less quantifiable aspect to American street gangs, namely their attitude toward violence. In the United States, street gang members commit homicides over amazingly trivial issues. *Ear Hustle* is a very popular podcast recorded in California's San Quinten Prison. In one episode, an inmate told his story about the murder that led to his incarceration. He was a member of one

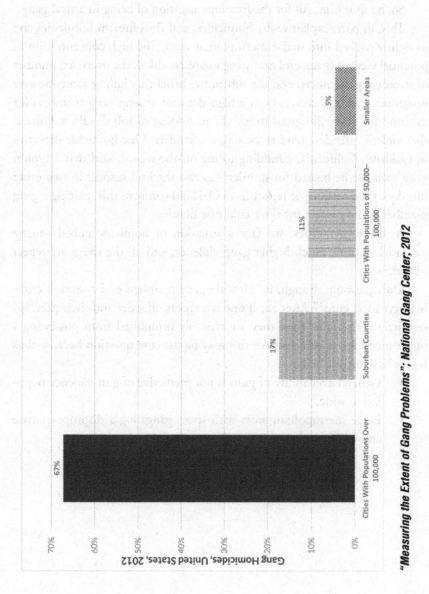

"Measuring the Extent of Gang Problems", National Gang Center, 2012

gang (let's say Gang-X). While in a bodega, another person came in and jokingly suggested that the future inmate was actually a member of rival Gang-Y.

So, he shot him. All for the frivolous assertion of being in a rival gang.

This, in part, explains why homicides, and thus firearm homicides, are so tightly packed into major metropolitan areas. The high concentration of potential victims (gang and non-gang members alike), the oversized number of street gang members, and the subculture belief that killing someone over insignificant things creates both a high demand among gang members for firearms and the willingness to use them. Adding to this deadly mixture is that violent offenders tend to be repeat offenders. One homicide detective in Oakland, California, confiding to me off-the-record, said that a typical gang member he busted for murder was also the lead suspect in two other murders. One newspaper report from Oakland confirms this, placing a gang member as the suspect for three cold case files.[7]

In the bigger cities, we face a situation of homicide cubed—many potential victims, much higher gang violence, and all the thugs are repeat offenders.

One question, though, is "How do gang members and common criminals get their guns?" After all, if one is a repeat offender and their previous conviction is serious, then they are typically prohibited from possessing a bullet much less a gun. Indeed, this may be the core question because thus far we have established:

- General availability of guns is not predictive of gun violence population wide.
- Large metropolitan areas with street gangs log a disproportionate amount of violent crime and gun crime.

A NOTE ON CONFOUNDING DATA

One problem with American criminology data is an adherence to "confirmation." When one rolls through the 2017 FBI Uniform Crime Statistics, they will see that only 6.4 percent of firearm homicides are ascribed to gang activity. You will also notice that more than 43 percent of homicides have "unknown" circumstances and 20 percent are specifically classified as "arguments." Another 12.7 percent did not have a classification (the data was blank).

I once asked a detective in Oakland, California about this (and if you are wondering why I know so many cops in Oakland, it comes from living there for over fifteen years). Barely paraphrasing, he told me:

> If I get called to a scene, and there is a body in an ally, face down with an entry wound in the back of the skull, and the victim is wearing Bloods colors in Crips territory, then I *know* this was a gang-related homicide. But without witnesses, I have to log it as "unknown." If witnesses reported hearing two men shouting at one another right before a gunshot was heard, then I can log it as an "argument" homicide. But it was likely an argument about gang conflicts.

The point, as we continue to explore this topic, is that we see the split between direct measurement and strict crime-scene analysis. One agency, using survey techniques, reports that gangs commit violence at a rate much higher than the general populace, but the overly-strict FBI data is under-reporting the reality.

The source of guns for all crimes is largely underground and changing the laws about how guns are retailed made this number grow.

Source of firearm			
Purchased or traded from—	1997– Before NICS	2004– After NICS	
	14.0%	11.3%	
Retail store	8.2%	7.3%	-0.9%
Pawnshop	4.0%	2.6%	-1.4%
Flea market	1.0%	0.6%	
Gun show	0.8%	0.8%	
Family or friend	**40.1%**	**37.4%**	
Purchased or traded	12.6%	12.2%	
Rented or borrowed	18.9%	14.1%	
Other	8.5%	11.1%	
Street/illegal source	**37.3%**	**40.0%**	**2.7%**
Theft or burglary	9.1%	7.5%	
Drug dealer/off street	20.3%	25.2%	
Fence/black market	8.0%	7.4%	
Other	**8.7%**	**11.2%**	

Firearm Violence, 1993–2011; Bureau of Justice Statistics, 2013

The Bureau of Justice Statistics (BJS) periodically studies where guns used in violent crimes come from. This tells us much about the availability of guns, but also how criminals go about getting them. Using the extreme NRA vs. gang comparison that opened this chapter, we might expect that criminals—including the street gang members causing the disproportionate number of violent crimes—would obtain their guns however they could, including from non-legal sources. Indeed, in all years where the BJS has been documenting crime gun sources, this has been the case with a *minimum* 40 percent of crime guns coming from completely unregulatable underground supplies. By contrast, only 9.9 percent came from gun stores and pawnshops.

But this doesn't tell the whole story. Another 37.4 percent of crime guns were acquired through "family or friends," also called "acquaintance transfers" by other law enforcement agencies. In here we have an unknown quantity of guns that were transferred to known prohibited persons. These illegal and intentional transfers may have been one gang member trading to another. It could be a family member knowing that it was illegal to give an ex-con cousin a spare pistol. It also includes the notorious, though statistically rare, "strawman" purchase, where a prohibited person convinces a friend or family member to buy a gun for them at a retailer.

This means the range of intentionally illegal gun acquisitions of crime guns goes from 40 percent to 77 percent. Even using just the lower percentage for perspective, the great gobs of crime guns are completely unaffected by legislation controlling retail access.

Before we continue with that not-so-amazing revelation, we should ponder the 2.3–2.7 percent shift of crime guns from trail to underground sources between 1997 and 2004. In 1998, just after the older data in the table above, the National Instant Check System (NICS) went live. This is the "background" check the federal government established to prevent criminals from buying guns at gun stores, pawn shops, or any licensed dealer, including your "gun nut" brother-in-law who buys and sells collectable pistols for fun and profit and has a Federal Firearms License (FFL) to make it all legal. The NICS system also affects gun stores and other FFL dealers who sell guns at gun shows—if you buy a gun from them at a gun show, you will go through a background check.

Between these two years of measurement, one before and one after NICS went into effect, a little less than 3 percent of criminal acquisitions stopped being made at retail outlets and started being made in underground markets. One could argue that all NICS did was move the problem from a point of traceability (sales records at gun stores) to completely untraceable black markets.

Another aspect of the underground gun markets is that many of the guns are "recycled." This tidbit is both important and frustrating. Guns are durable. So durable in fact that the lion's share of guns brought to "gun buybacks" are positively antique. I have watched the goings on at six gun "buybacks" and have seen people walk away with cash or gift certificates in exchange for firearms evidentially handed down from a great grandfather, a little rusty but still operational. This degree or durability means that once a gun leaks into the underground markets, it can have many "owners" in a relatively short amount of time. It also keeps the transaction price low, around $250 per gun, using a weighted average cost reported in one study of Chicago criminals.[8] The problem is that we really do not know how many times an underground gun passes from one owner to the next. If, as some criminologists suspect, a gun can have a dozen or more owners, then the need to add more guns to the underground market is small. As such, further restrictions on retail availability of guns might have a negligible effect on the number of guns used in crime.

Gun durability and the recycling of guns in underground networks also helps to explain the long amount of time between when a gun is sold at a licensed gun store and when it is recovered at a crime scene, and the short amount of time from when a street criminal acquires a gun and when they are caught with it. It takes almost forever for a gun to make the journey, but a thug caught with a gun got it very recently.

The Bureau of Alcohol, Tobacco, Firearms, and Explosives (BATF) often reports on the "time to crime," which is the amount of time between when a gun is sold by a federally licensed retailer (e.g., gun store, Walmart, Cabela's, etc.) and when it is recovered at a crime scene. In 2017, the average "time to crime" was 9.3 years. Our older study from Chicago, noted above, using BATF tracing data, showed that only 6.6 percent of crime guns were retailed within six months of use. In short, very few criminals acquire their guns at gun stores in general, much less buy them and use them shortly thereafter.

But the underground market is different. In black markets, criminals can find and acquire guns quickly enough and buy them at discounted prices. In one small and localized study,[9] the average time from when a criminal acquired a gun and when it was recovered was two months on average. That is 112 months from when the gun was sold at retail and only two months from when it was acquired off the streets. This helps illustrate that for the bulk of gun violence, moderating the retailing of guns has little to no effect. Criminals in poor neighborhoods do not travel to the closest Bass Pro Shop and pay full retail for a brand-new gun. Instead they exercise their local networks to find a ten-year-old gun—typically one with obliterated serial numbers and likely used by other criminals in other crimes—and buy it for a half to one third the price of new hardware.

A NOTE ABOUT TRACE DATA

A "BATF trace" is when a local law enforcement agency recovers a gun, then asks the Bureau of Alcohol, Tobacco and Firearms to identify the original owner, the person who bought the gun at retail. Though trace data is robust enough for getting your mind around some gun topics, BATF trace information has more than a few quirks which leads trace data to be of slightly flimsy value.

Foremost, not every gun traced is a crime gun. For example, one rural county with a very low population suddenly leapt up the charts one year in terms of traced guns. But the county did not have a crime spree. It did have an avid gun collector who passed away from old age, and the local authorities (for reasons unknown) decided to do a trace on every gun in his collection, which numbered in the hundreds. For the year in question, this county looked like the gun crime capital of America.

Likewise, not all gun crimes have a recovered gun. As I have already mentioned, guns are recirculated in underground markets and a homicide weapon can find a new owner after the killing is done. Other times a murder weapon is deposited in the nearest lake or river, never to be recovered or matched to a crime. And in other instances, the murderer keeps the gun but is never caught.

Like the FBI crime reporting system, there are many instances in which the crime associated with the traced gun has unknown circumstances. For 2017, 43 percent of gun homicides could not be categorized for any particular circumstance, which makes the associated tracing a half-empty glass.

All this said, BATF trace data still provides a clear enough lens into the misuse of guns to make headway in understanding the realities of guns and their control.

Some people of the political caste have hypothesized that active gun runners are buying guns in states where laws are not strict and transporting them into states where gun sales laws are much more so. However, the data shows this to not be the case. The BATF reports annually on what guns are traced and for what crimes they were confiscated. According to their 2017 report, only 0.6 percent of traced guns were recovered in "weapons trafficking" offenses. In fact, weapons trafficking is nineteenth on the list of crimes from which guns were recovered, far below the number one reason—prohibited persons being in possession of a weapon—which occurs forty-two times more often. This, of course, is incomplete as these are just the people who were caught trafficking guns. But the tiny number exposes the rather small fraction of crime gun movement that derives from intentional trafficking.

Where it gets most interesting is the source and destination states. The BATF annually documents the states in which crime guns were originally retailed and those in which they were later recovered. On average across all states, 65 percent of crime guns were originally retailed in the same state from which they were recovered, and most of the rest came from immediately neighboring states. It is this "adjacent state" effect that creates a distorted view about imported guns. About 11 percent of Americans move each year, and several estimates show that about only 40 percent of those folks move a hundred or more miles away. Based on the current US population and the pollster estimates of a 40 percent household gun ownership rate, this divides out to about 5,755,000 people in gun-owning households that relocate a fair distance away, but most relocate either in the same state or *neighboring states*. Thus, a gun legally purchased in State-X has a high probability of legally being relocated to State Y, and most of the time when it crosses state lines, it is to the next state over. Sometime after the household and the gun have relocated, the gun may be legally sold in State-Y. It is later on, after the gun was legally transported into another state, that these guns slip into the underground.

Buried in this data is one non-obvious quirk. Long ago, the Gun Facts project used the same BATF data from an earlier year (2013) and checked the to's and from's of each state, and then benchmarked each state using a gun control wish list published by the Brady Campaign to Stop Gun Violence (now renamed the Brady Plan). We were testing if the allegedly "strict" slate of laws favored by gun control groups had any bearing on the interstate transportation of guns. Much to our surprise, states with very strict gun control laws imported most of their crime guns from other states with strict laws, not from states with "lax" gun control laws.

This is not as sinister as it seems. Many states with stricter laws are in the same region. Since most people who relocate do so in under a hundred miles—those moving across state lines and bringing their guns with them, and later those guns leak into the underground market—it's probable that those guns end up in other nearby or neighboring strict-law states. For example, Connecticut, New Jersey, Maryland, New York, and Massachusetts are all nicely clustered in the far northeastern corner of the lower forty-eight,

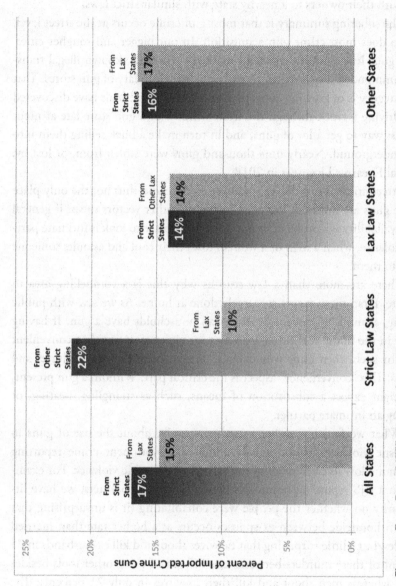

Firearms Trace Data, BATFE for 2013; Gun control state rankings, Brady Campaign 2013 State Scorecard; Top 10 strict and lax states, except Hawaii and these states also occupied five of the top six places on the Brady list of states with strict gun control. It is quite natural and normal for guns legally acquired in one of these five states, each with strict gun control laws, to relocate with their owners to a nearby state with similar strict laws.

The sobering summary is that most gun crime occurs at the street level, and so does most crime gun acquisition. In our bigger and rougher cities, older guns leak into underground markets—via theft, known illegal transfers, unintended illegal transfers, and even mass burglary of gun stores. That last category is of growing concern as enterprising criminals have discovered that driving a truck through the front window of a gun store late at night is a fast way to get a lot of guns, and in turn make a buck selling them into the underground. Nearly nine thousand guns were stolen from, or lost by, Federal Firearms Licensees in 2018.

Street crime is not the only source of crime and thus not the only place where guns are misused. We need to explore other vectors to see if general gun availability is a problem or not. One good place to look is intimate partner violence, when a man or a woman loses their cool and assaults someone close to them.

There are more than a few reasons why this is a compelling area to explore. First, these events are largely done at home. As we saw with public polling, around 40 percent of American households have a gun. If having a gun in the house was either a catalyst for violence or merely a convenient tool for such, then guns would figure into a lot of domestic injuries and deaths. This "convenience" aspect is the critical part. Without a gun present, we might expect a substitution of means, such as strangling, beating, or knifing an intimate partner.

What we find is a rather mixed perspective about the use of guns in domestic violence. Unfortunately, much of government crime reporting does not allow us to filter all of the aspects of domestic violence. For example, in a BJS report on homicides between intimate partners, we have little clarity on whether the people were cohabitating (it is unsurprising that firearm homicide between ex-spouses occurs at a higher rate than married couples, but a little surprising that ex-wives shoot and kill ex-husbands in 75 percent of these murders-between-exes instead of using other tools besides guns, whereas men shoot and kill their ex-wives in only 71 percent). The cohabitation element is important because the hypothesis is that having a gun around instigates or facilitates violence, so you would want to measure situations where the perpetrator and victim were in the same house. Otherwise, a murder would be more likely planned than spontaneous.

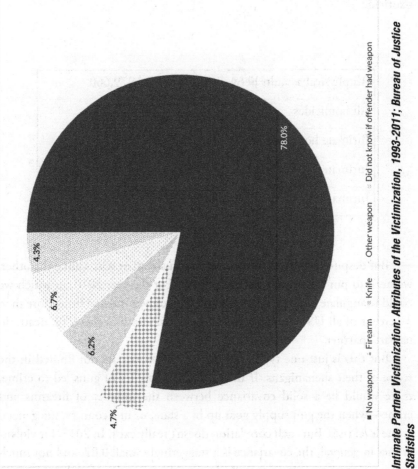

Intimate Partner Victimization: Attributes of the Victimization, 1993-2011; Bureau of Justice Statistics

■ No weapon ✦ Firearm ≋ Knife Other weapon ⋰ Did not know if offender had weapon

78.0%

4.7%

6.2%

6.7%

4.3%

Using the most recent BJS report[10] on *nonfatal* domestic violence, and the approximately 980,000 physical attacks between intimate partners (domiciled and otherwise), we see that gun play enters into the picture only a small portion of the time.

On the flip side, however, when it comes to the nearly 1,500 homicides between husbands and wives (to narrow the view to likely cohabitating couples), firearms dominate the means of choice for committing mariticide or uxoricide.

All physical assaults between intimates	979,660
All homicides	14,748
Intimate homicides	1,487
Intimate gun homicides	892
Intimate husband/wife gun homicides	461

But despite the horror of the idea of a husband or wife killing the other, we need to put this into some perspective. For the year 2010, in which we could triangulate all the data, the rough breakdown is that a little more than 3 percent of all US homicides were when a spouse shot their "till death do us part" partner.

But this is just one type of crime, and criminals are not limited in the scope of their shenanigans. If the general availability of guns led to crime, there would be a solid covariance between the number of firearms and crime—when the gun supply goes up in a state, or in a country, the general crime level rises. But such correlation doesn't really exist. In 2017, for violent crimes in general, the covariance is a staggeringly small 0.02, and not much larger for property crimes at 0.06. In specific categories of violent crime, it is high—0.12 for robberies and 0.19 for burglaries. Though it makes sense that robbers benefit from having guns as a tool of their trade, and for burglars to want to defend themselves from armed homeowners (or to steal homeowner guns), if the availability of guns encouraged crime, one would expect much more significant alignment. But we do not see such.

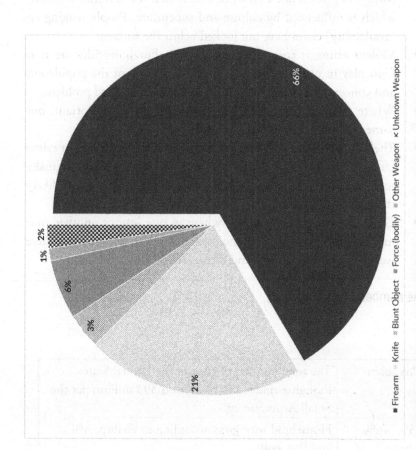

IIntimateI Partner Victimization: Attributes of the Victimization, 1993-2011; Bureau of Justice Statistics

■ Firearm ■ Knife ▧ Blunt Object ■ Force (bodily) ▨ Other Weapon ✕ Unknown Weapon

But that is just one side of the coin—the perpetration of gun violence against people, innocent and otherwise. We must ask if the net availability of guns has any social benefit. This more illuminating data on the availability of guns will be covered in the chapter on defensive gun uses.

The spin

- Misuse of guns is not a factor of availability. It is a factor of intent, which is influenced by culture and subculture. People making an "availability" claim have not looked below the surface.
- Violent crime is committed everywhere, but homicides are not. Gun play in order to kill is confined to subsets of the population and concentrated in larger cities. It is not a generalized problem.
- Where guns are acquired for criminal use is very important, but some policy groups do not discuss this.
- There is no "iron pipeline." BATF trace data shows that most crime guns are recovered from the same state where they were originally sold and most of the rest come from neighboring states, likely through legal migration.
- Guns are misused nearly everywhere in one way or another. You may live in a county with no homicides, but that doesn't mean there were not armed robberies and threats from hotheads.

By the numbers: gun availability

Unknown	The total number of guns in the United States, though estimated to be around 393 million per the Small Arms Survey.
43%, 46%, 42%	Household with guns according to Gallup, ABC, and Pew polls.
73%, 41%, 26%	Guns used in homicides, robberies, and aggravated assaults compared to other weapons.
197%	Firearm homicide rate for large metropolitan areas compared to the average of all other degrees of urbanization.

CHAPTER 2
Suicide and Guns

MY FRIEND PAUL COMMITTED SUICIDE. He used a gun.

I mention this not for pity, but to note that I have more than a passing interest in the subject of guns and voluntary exits from this world. Paul was a gun owner, though something less than a "gun enthusiast." At the time of his suicide, he was a year out of college, newly married, not a drug or alcohol abuser, had no mental health history, nor was he involved in activities statistically associated with suicide.

But Paul had a serious bump in his personal life and decided he couldn't cope. There was also two days between receiving the bad news and getting home to where his gun was. Being a smart and educated man, he could have devised any number of modes of suicide on the two day drive. It simply took facing the stark emptiness of this life-altering event before he made his final decision.

The question I asked then was, "Did having that gun lead to his suicide?" I have discovered this is a question many friends and family ask when someone they care about decides to pull their own plug.

The critical take-aways
- There is nearly no correlation between firearm availability and the rate of successful suicides.
- Firearm suicide rates are largely skewed to older white males in non-metropolitan areas.

- "Red flag" laws have not been effective in slowing homicides, and improvements in suicide rates appear to be tied to collateral mental health interventions.

In the United States, suicide by firearm is the most common mode, comprising about 50 percent of all suicides (suffocation is the second most common mode, racking up 23 percent of instance).[1] This is why criminologists guffaw when they see any of the gun policy organizations exaggerate by saying, "30,000 Americans died from gun violence last year." Criminologists know that in bad years two-thirds of these "gun violence" deaths are suicides.

This is not a trivial point. Accept for the moment that gun availability has no effect on the rate of suicides (which it does not, as I will demonstrate shortly). Does including suicides in "gun violence" numbers make rational sense?

Measuring the correlation between gun availability and suicide rates across American states is a bit of a folly. There are no precise statistics to know the average rate of gun ownership by state, which makes half of the measurement suspect. In fact, some criminologists believe the best proxy for gun ownership rates are state-by-state suicide rates. This leads to a chicken-and-egg circular analysis, whereby using a population measurement cannot also be used as an effect measurement. It would be akin to measuring the probability of being in an automobile accident by restricting the study population to just car owners.

International comparisons, however, are doable and insightful.

According to their website, "The Small Arms Survey (SAS) provides expertise on all aspects of small arms and armed violence." They have measured many aspects of international gun availability, from the number of people evading gun registration laws in their country (the "non-compliance rate") to the per capita private gun ownership rate in most countries. The World Health Organization (WHO), an offspring of the United Nations, logs many interesting facts about what ails and kills people around the globe, including details about suicide rates. It is easy work to contrast gun availability data by country from the Small Arms Survey with suicide data from the World Health Organization.

The correlation between private gun ownership and successful suicides is nearly nonexistent (an R^2 regression of 0.04—where "zero" means no correlation and "one" means perfect correlation—for our original 2006 study, though a spot check of current data shows no meaningful change). The United States has the highest private gun ownership rate, as is visible by the

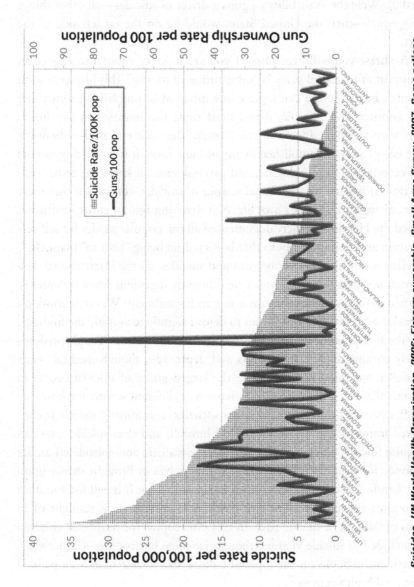

Suicides, UN World Health Organization, 2006; Firearm ownership, Small Arms Survey, 2007. Some nations get lost in the crowing of the index.

huge spike near the center of the chart, but is just slightly above average in terms of the percentage of the population that kills themselves (11.1 people per one hundred thousand residents, as opposed to an international average of 10.0). Were the availability of guns a driver of suicides—all other things being equal—then the United States would be on the far left side of the chart.

A phrase you will hear often if you are unlucky enough to engage an economist at a cocktail party is "substitution of means." This fifty-cent term describes how a person can replace one mode of accomplishing something with another. For example, if you need some fast money you can find a short-term gig, float a loan, or rob a bank. The same end goal—obtaining fast cash—can be accomplished in any of these ways. It is interesting to note that economists, criminologists, and psychologists all know the term "substitution of means." In the dismal science of suicides, this means that there are many ways to end one's own life. Not that long ago, an entire institution named the Hemlock Society documented all the popular modes for self-termination and published books that bordered on being "how to" manuals.

This is our first clue about guns and suicides. As the international data exposes, people around the world are diligently ingenious when it comes to planned dying. A lack of firearms is not an impediment. We could move on from this one clear fact, but I want to detour slightly to amplify the findings.

The first point of investigation revolves around culture. People predominately commit suicide from stress and depression, though medical issues are well represented and may drive the largest group of suicidal people to commit the act. Different cultures have very different norms for how one handles personal difficulties. In some societies, committing suicide is considered immoral and an insult to God himself, and thus suicide rates can be quite low. In other societies, suicide is ritualistic and considered an act of honor for people who have shamed themselves or brought shame upon their families. A cultural tidbit from Japan holds that it is evil for a mother to commit suicide but allow her children to survive, as is thought of in terms of "shinjū," a suicide pact. In this philosophy, the murdered children are included as suicide victims (though Japanese law codifies it otherwise). Indeed, entire books on the topic of culture and suicide have been penned by mental health experts.[2]

The subsequent theory then would be that similar cultures would have similar suicide rates. There is some proof of this for Americans.

My Canadian friends hate it when I say that the United States and Canadian cultures are more alike than different. Both countries have similar

Judeo-Christian and European origins. Both nations were frontier countries. The two nations routinely swap residents, entertainment, and all manner of cultural elements. One of the best rodeos in the world is in Calgary instead of Dallas. A punch line I like to use when speaking to audiences is that the only two meaningful differences between Americans and Canadians is that canucks are politer and Americans prefer beer with flavor (note to the Molson Corporation: try hops).

With such similar cultures you would expect the overall suicide rate to be similar. For the year in the previous chart, the American suicide rate was 11.1 and the Canadian rate was 11.4. Nearly identical, though frankly with the bleak winters in the western provinces, I'm surprised the Canadian suicide rate is that low. However, Canadian gun ownership rates are about one third that of America—same suicide rates, far fewer guns up north.

Another handy contrast is to compare the nation with the highest gun ownership rate (the United States) with the modern nation having the highest suicide rate (Lithuania in our 2006 review). I have no idea exactly what was so depressing about that country at that time, and certainly hope things have improved. But in that year more than three times as many Lithuanians committed suicide as did Americans. However, Lithuanians own about 2 percent as many guns per capita as Yanks.

This brings us back to culture and substitution of means. Suicidal Americans prefer guns. The equally suicidal Canadians lean toward poison. Chronically depressed Lithuanians hang themselves. Globally, suicide is a daily fact of life and seemingly immune to the presence or absence of guns.

It is the American adoption of guns as the primary means of suicide that creates confusion. That the rate of firearm suicide is high in America leads some people to mistakenly conclude that guns are contributory to suicide rates. I have encountered people with inherently anti-gun dispositions that claim that "guns make a successful suicide more likely." This is demonstrably untrue given that nearly gun-free Lithuanians are hugely successful when it comes to killing themselves. The same can be said for Russians (suicide rate of 31.7 in 2006), Sri Lankans (30.7), Hungarians (25.3), Japanese (24.7), Belgians (19.6), Finns (19.5), and on and on and on.

America's middling suicide rate, but its outsized firearm suicide rate, cause the two to be conflated unless one explores the global realities. Digging deeper into American suicides makes this even more clear.

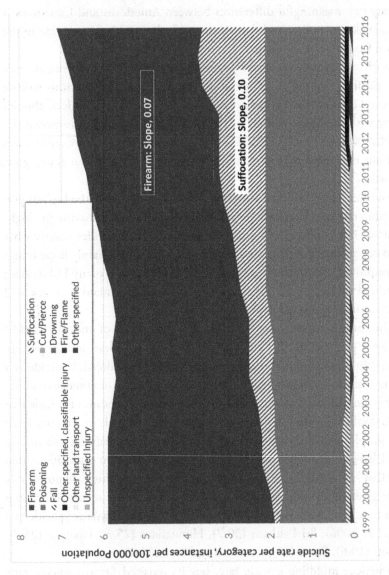

Firearm: Slope, 0.07

Suffocation: Slope, 0.10

Suicide rate per category, instances per 100,000 Population

1999 2000 2001 2002 2003 2004 2005 2006 2007 2008 2009 2010 2011 2012 2013 2014 2015 2016

Suffocation
Cut/Pierce
Drowning
Fire/Flame
Other specified

Firearm
Poisoning
Fall
Other specified, classifiable Injury
Other land transport
Unspecified Injury

Centers for Disease Control, WONDER database

Up until the Great Recession of 2008, the American suicide rate was relatively stable. Firearm suicides, though still the leading means for the act, dominated. Yet throughout the twenty-first century, the part of the suicidal population using guns remained steady and the number of people suffocating themselves went steadily upwards. According to the accumulated "Firearms Commerce" reports by the Bureau of Alcohol, Tobacco and Firearms (BATF), the supply of handguns—the primary firearm used for suicides—went up by sixty-six million since the year 2000, or by some estimates about a 71 percent increase in the supply. A tiny increase in the firearm suicide rate during this period, paired with a large increase in the handgun supply, is another indication of the lack of a cause-and-effect relationship.

But as a means that can be substituted, it is interesting that the rate of firearm suicides is steady. After all, if guns were a contributing factor to successful suicides, then the growing stockpile of guns would lead to a rising firearm suicide rate.

Comparison	Ratio
Men/Women	5.8
White/Black	2.6
Non-Metro/Metro	2.3
Later Life/Earlier	4.9

A natural question to ask is "who kills themselves with guns?" The basic answer is older, white, rural men. Men use firearms to commit suicide nearly six times more frequently than women. Whites are more than twice as likely than blacks to do so (though American Indians and Alaska Natives are even more prone to firearm suicides than whites). People in cities are half as likely to use a gun for a suicide as people in suburban or rural areas. And men in the second half of their lives are almost five times more likely to commit suicide with a gun than younger men.

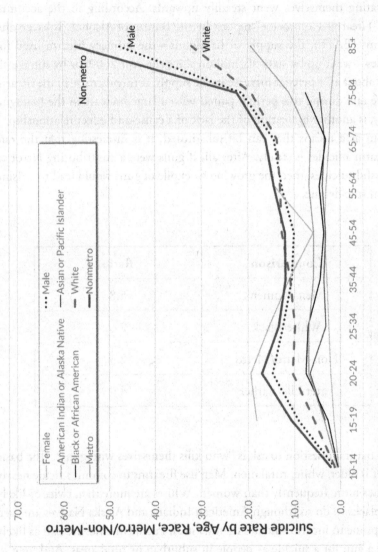

Centers for Disease Control, WONDER database, 2016

Older, white, non-urban men are the firearm suicide demographic. According to one survey,[3] whites are 53 percent more likely to own guns than blacks on a per capita basis. Men are more likely than women to do so, as well (though we note in passing there is a well-documented underreporting of household gun ownership by women, and that gun-owning women, as a market segment, have been growing steadily since the 1980s). But the largest divergence is location. As you would expect, men in rural areas own more guns than city dwellers, by a two-to-one ratio.

This also explains why there is a large amount of time between when a gun is purchased and a firearm suicide. Yes, some people do buy a gun (or even rent one at a shooting range) and kill themselves the same day. But various studies have shown that this is the rare instance, with the time between purchase extending from a few months to many years. One study[4] noted that nearly 75 percent of firearm suicide victims had household possession of a firearm for over five years. Unlike my friend Paul, suicides tend not to be rash events. People suffer with depression and suicidal thoughts for extended periods of time before making serious attempts at ending it all.

This is where we stumble into the temptation to generalize. Some of the generalization that *could* be made about older, rural men include that they are more socially isolated, they have a "stand on your own two feet" attitude, which includes not wishing to be a burden on others, and might encounter more serious economic disruptions as they age and are unable to provide for themselves. And as noted before, facing a serious health issue is a motivation for many suicidal people. The suicide rate for non-metro white males starts rising sharply at age sixty-five and continues rising past the Center for Disease Control's eighty-five-plus group (that last group has a firearm suicide rate more than three times that of the general population).

But again, are guns a factor? Perhaps only from a psychological basis. Stipulate for a moment that rural people, regardless of sex, have ready access to both firearms and poisons for rodent and other pests. Among age forty-five-plus rural whites of both sexes, we see a huge divergence in the means for suicides, with women opting for poison much more often than men, but men opting for firearms much more often than women. Even in some of the most suicidal and firearm-owning sub-populations in the United States, the idea that firearms drive suicides is inaccurate when we view the subcultural (in this case, male/female) attitudes. I mentioned this seeming anomaly to a woman I know who has no pro- or anti-gun bias, and she opined that women would not want to leave behind a mess for other people to clean up, and thus poisons were preferred among women.

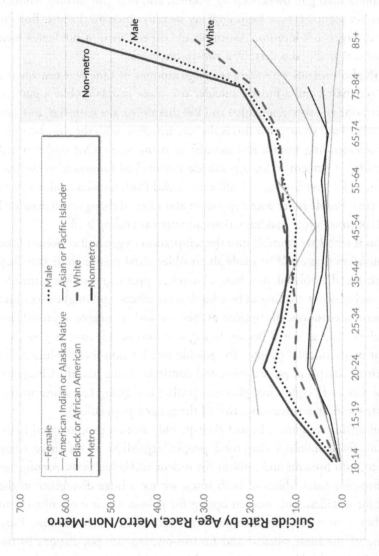

Centers for Disease Control, WONDER database, 2016

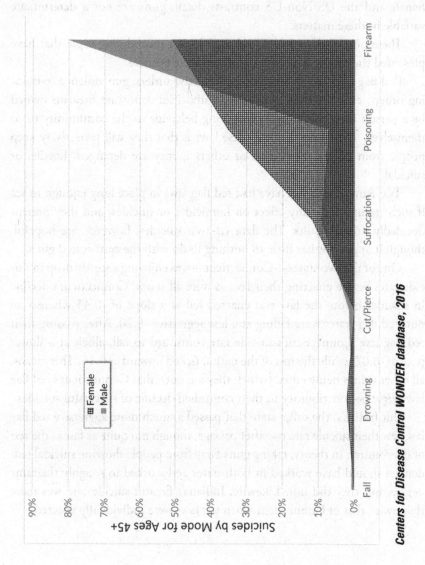

Centers for Disease Control WONDER database, 2016

It is the disproportionate rate of old, white, rural, male suicides with firearms that keeps escaping the attention of people who misread this as a gun availability problem. Stress, depression, and anxiety are the mental health issues that lead people to want to commit suicide, and as the male/female and the US/Non-US contrasts detail, guns are not a determinate variable in these matters.

These observations make "red flag" laws a meandering topic that have presented the public with one significant false positive.

Red flag laws (a.k.a. emergency protective orders, gun violence restraining orders, etc.) are those where the authorities confiscate firearms owned by a person demonstrating endangering behavior to the community or to themselves. The theory behind these laws is that they will proactively keep people from killing themselves or others if they are deranged, hostile, or suicidal.

Two American states have had red flag laws in place long enough to see if such statutes have any effect on homicides or suicides, and they present decidedly mixed results. The data vis-à-vis suicides, however, are hopeful, though it appears it has little to nothing to do with the confiscated guns.

One of the two states—Connecticut—was enjoying a steady drop in suicide rates before enacting their law, as were all states. Connecticut's decline in suicides before the law was enacted fell at a slope of -0.45 whereas all non-red flag states were falling at a less aggressive -0.20. After passing their red flag law, Connecticut's suicide rate continued to fall, albeit at a slower pace of -0.07, while the rest of the nation ticked upward at 0.16. This means, all other things being equal (which they are not), that Connecticut's red flag law *might* be contributory to their continued decline of successful suicides.

But Indiana, the other state that passed a much more aggressive red flag law, saw their suicide rate rise after passage, though not quite as fast as the rest of the country. In theory, taking guns away from people showing suicidal tendencies should have worked in both states and worked to roughly the same degree, but they did not. Likewise, Indiana's firearm suicide rate was more than twice that of Connecticut when the laws were individually enacted.

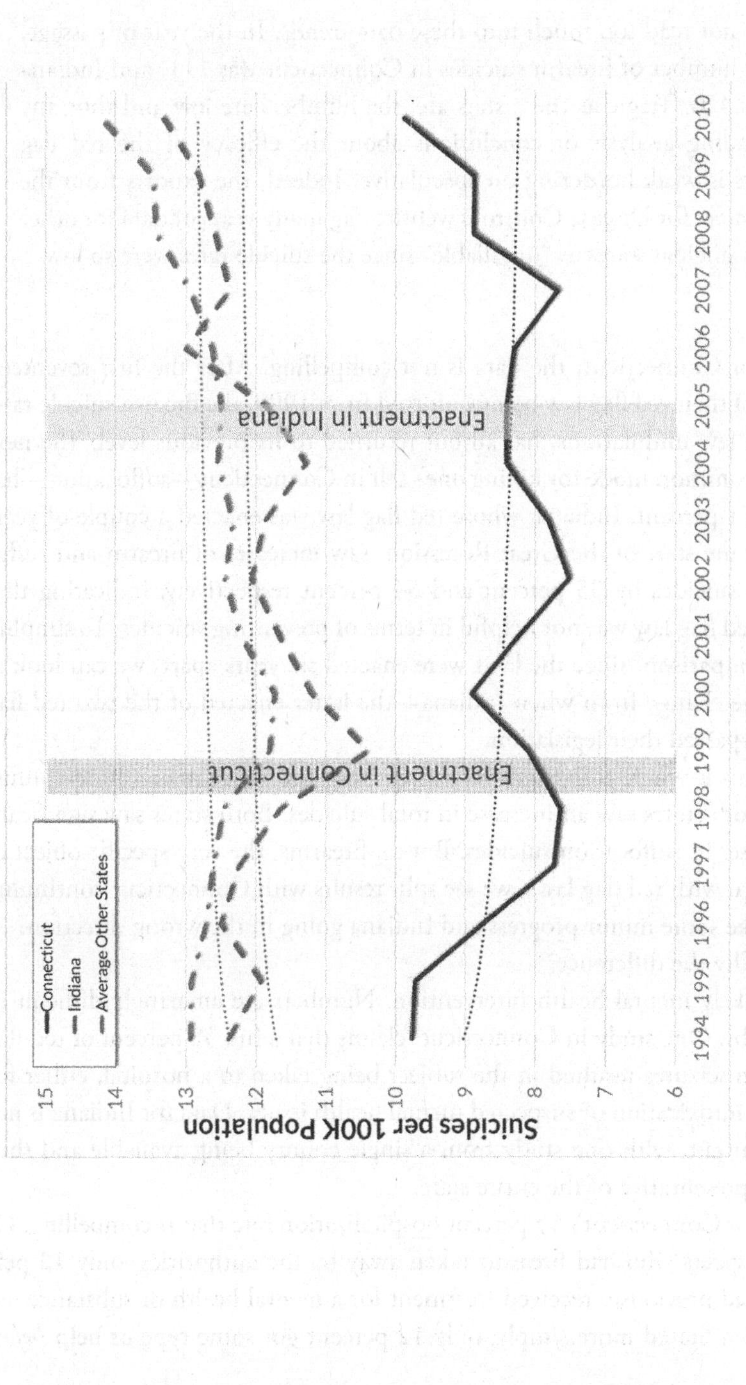

Suicides per 100K Population

Connecticut
Indiana
Average Other States

Enactment in Connecticut

Enactment in Indiana

6 7 8 9 10 11 12 13 14 15

1994 1995 1996 1997 1998 1999 2000 2001 2002 2003 2004 2005 2006 2007 2008 2009 2010

Centers for Disease Control, WISQARS database

A DATA QUALITY NOTE

Do not read too much into these data trends. In the year of passage, the number of firearm suicides in Connecticut was 111, and Indiana was 416. Tragic as these stats are, the numbers are low and thus any trending analysis or conclusions about the efficacy of the red flag laws is weak bordering on speculative. Indeed, the exports from the Centers for Disease Control's website flag many years of data for other less suicidal states as "unreliable" since the suicide rates were so low.

For Connecticut, the data is not compelling. After the first seventeen years of their red flag law being enforced from 1999, the firearm suicide rate, after a few undulations, has all but returned to its previous level. The next most common mode for killing one's self in Connecticut—suffocation—has risen 71 percent. Indiana, whose red flag law was enacted a couple of years before the start of the Great Recession, saw increases of firearm and suffocation suicides by 35 percent and 64 percent respectively, indicating that their red flag law was not helpful in terms of preventing suicides. To simplify the comparison, since the laws were enacted six years apart, we can look at just the change from when Indiana—the latter enacted of the two red flag laws—passed their legislation.

This is where things get very interesting and more than a little confusing. Both states saw an increase in total suicides. Both states saw significant increases in suffocation suicides. But on firearms, the very specific object of concern with red flag laws, we see split results with Connecticut continuing to make some minor progress and Indiana going in the wrong direction.

Why the difference?

Likely mental health intervention. Numbers are amazingly difficult to come by. One study in Connecticut[5] claims that a full 55 percent of red flag firearm seizures resulted in the subject being taken to a hospital, either for severe intoxication or suspected mental health issues. Data for Indiana is not so clear cut, with one study from a single county being available and thus not representative of the entire state.

It is Connecticut's 55 percent hospitalization rate that is compelling. Of the suspects who had firearms taken away by the authorities, only 12 percent had previously received treatment for a mental health or substance use disorder. Stated more simply, only 12 percent got some type of help *before*

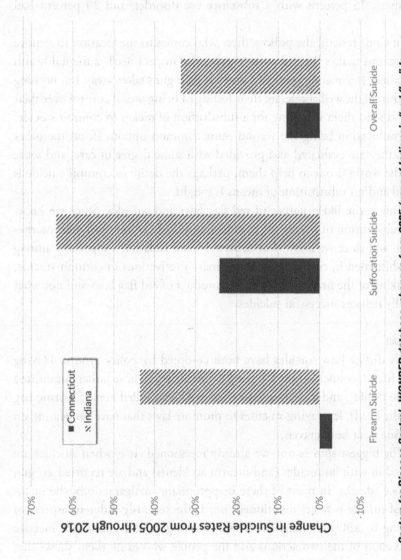

Centers for Disease Control, WONDER database, changes from 2005 (year of Indiana's "red flag" law enactment) through 2016

the firearm confiscation, and 55 percent got interventional help *afterwards*. Cops were getting people into the mental health treatment system who had previously been suffering in isolation. Of those who were eventually treated (some not released after evaluation), 45 percent were diagnosed with a mental illness, 26 percent with a substance use disorder, and 29 percent had both.

In Connecticut, the police officer who comes to the location to remove the firearms makes the call as to whether the suspect needs a mental health evaluation. If someone is suicidal and has their guns taken away, but nothing else, this might well accelerate their feeling of being out of control over their life and send them searching for a substitution of means to commit suicide, with suffocation being the second most common option. If, on the other hand, they are evaluated and provided with some degree of care, and sense that the world is out to help them, perhaps the desire to commit suicide is abated and no substitution of means is sought.

This is the likely nature of red flag laws and suicides. Since we know that substitution of means for committing suicide is universal and international, and since we know that depression and isolation—especially among old white men in rural areas—are primary motivations to commit suicide, the taking of the firearms may be a byproduct of red flag laws and not what actually reduces successful suicides.

The spin

I really dislike how suicides have been co-opted by policy groups. Having lost a friend to suicide (gun), having a good friend whose father committed suicide (knife), and a relative thrice removed who killed herself (plastic bag over the head), leveraging suicides to promote laws that have no bearing on the issue is, at best, craven.

The biggest spin is one we already mentioned. It is when suicides are lumped in with homicides (and firearm accidents) and are reported as "gun violence" deaths. In most of these inappropriate amalgamations, the inclusion of suicide is never mentioned, nor is the seriously different aspects of wanting to kill your neighbor versus wanting to kill yourself. Objective observation of the two actions and the people who cause them shows that they cannot be rationally coupled.

The other recurring bit of spin is that firearm availability is tied to suicides. What can be safely said, at least in America, is that the presence of a gun is more likely to cause a *gun* suicide but unlikely to prevent a *non-gun* suicide. In other words, the overall suicide rate does not change, just the mode in which it is accomplished.

Lastly, removing guns from someone with suicidal thoughts does not appear to statistically keep them from committing suicide. Again, the ready substitution of means allows for people with suicide ideation to complete the process. However, "red flag" laws that lead to treatment do appear to have a positive effect. The spin, however, is that it was the removal of the gun that was the cause that led to the effect. In the one state where we have clearer insight, gun removal was not the trigger.

By the numbers: guns and suicides

59%	US firearm deaths via suicide in 2016 (most recent CDC reporting year)
0.04	The correlation between per capita private gun ownership and suicide rates internationally (R^2)
32%, 20%, 71%	Twenty-first century increase in rates of all US suicides, firearm suicides, and handgun supply.

CHAPTER 3
Mass Public Shootings

We Are in The Midst of An Epidemic of
Mass Shootings.
—Headline on MSNBC's YouTube page

The rate of mass shootings per 100,000 population has gone DOWN by an
extraordinary degree.
—Email from a pro-gun activist

BOTH OF THE STATEMENTS ABOVE are wrong. Yet each shows how people can perceive the universe differently depending on which end of the telescope they look through.

The critical take-aways
- There is an original and enduring criminology definition for mass public shootings, but Congress screwed things up.
- The rate of mass public shootings was small and steady before the Columbine High School event, which then started an upward trend.
- Mass public shootings are a global occurrence, not just an American one.
- Mental health and changes in treatment are strongly correlated with mass public shootings.

- Mass shooters study one another and have discovered the venue is the most important element.

Definitions—pick the one you like or make up a new one

First, let us take a moment to once again condemn the American Congress for mucking things up.

Way back in the 1990s, criminologists devised a definition for what constitutes a "mass public shooting."[1] That definition specifies that a mass public shooting (MPS) occurs when four or more people are killed (not including the attacker), in one public location. Due to general acceptance of this definition in criminology circles, a large body of research was conducted and published based on that description. The accumulated studies started the world on a path toward understanding, perspective, and prevention.

Naturally, Congress had to put a stop to that.

In 2012, as part of a funding bill, Congress extracted a new definition for "mass public shooting" from their southern-most orifice, proclaiming with no academic basis that MPSs involved three or more killed "in a single incident" regardless of location. Breaking of the established definition encouraged various groups—most with agendas—to conjure up their own classification schemes as well, and to build their own databases of events, producing whatever fanciful conclusion they desired. In these databases I have seen:

- Shootings of as few as two people killed, one being the attacker
- Elderly couple murder/suicide
- Events that took place at multiple locations (e.g., kill a relative at home, then take out two co-workers at the office)
- One person shot and two stabbed to death
- And more . . .

This confusion, both accidental (Congress) and intentional (policy organizations), has only hurt the voting public. Fortunately, after dogged persistence on the part of criminologists and other number nuts, the media has slowly begun filtering proffered lists of "mass shootings" and often insists that the figures conform to the original and enduring definition.

Complicating matters a bit is that there exists another type of public mass murder with a different definition. "Active Shooter Events" (ASEs) are episodes where a person shoots at multiple people in public, often in several locations, and which might result in no deaths. In some instances, an ASE can also be an MPS, but the confusion over terminology has led many people to lump them all into one category. This, of course, reduces clarity over the sundry issues, which makes isolating rational policy impossible.

Throughout this chapter and this book, we will present data using the correct, original definition. This will annoy some policy groups and politicians for whom accuracy is a burden. Such annoyance is well earned.

The American trend

MPSs took a strange arc during the latter part of the twentieth century and into the twenty-first. There are a number of suspect causes, but chronologically speaking, there is a pre- and post-Columbine reality.

The year 1999 was a rough one. In the sixteen years before then (this span is chosen because common MPS databases only go back that far), America averaged less than two MPSs a year, and two years had no MPSs at all. As unfortunate as this rate of public carnage was, the number and severity of MPSs in the last quarter of the twentieth century was actually on the decline. So too were the average number of fatalities per incident.

Then came 1999. Five MPSs, more than double the previous annual average. One of the 1999 MPSs was the Columbine high school massacre, which changed the nature of all future MPSs.

America took an all too short breather after 1999, a year in which the United States had three times as many people killed in MPSs than average. Until 2005, the United States had only one MPS a year with a "nominal" number of fatalities. But starting in 2005, and escalating upward from there, the number of incidents and the number of people killed climbed.

Horrifying, yes. However, some *perspective* is necessary. In the worst year on record (2017), less than one hundred people died in MPSs. For that same year:

- Almost two hundred times that many people were murdered in total, regardless of means.
- Over four hundred times as many people died in motor vehicle deaths.
- More than six thousand times as many people died from cancer.

Given the low odds of dying in an MPS, it is curious as to why there is such fear of these events. Many explanations exist, but MPSs inspire dread for the same reason air disasters do—a complete lack of control over the probabilities.

Let's look at the list of alternate causes of death above to illustrate why people fear MPSs as they do.

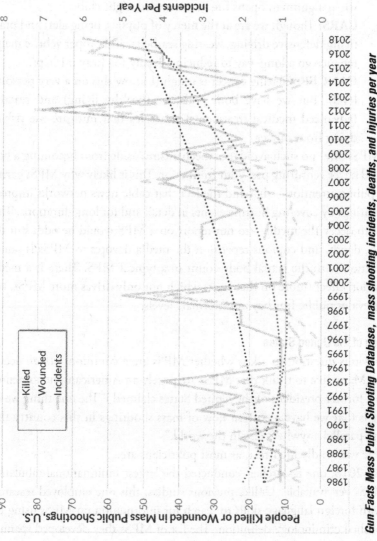

Gun Facts Mass Public Shooting Database, mass shooting incidents, deaths, and injuries per year

- **MURDER:** Most homicides occur in bad neighborhoods (which we know and avoid), during other criminal activities (in which most people are not involved), or by associating with bad actors (which most people don't). Such active situational avoidance keeps people from getting murdered, but we lack that level of control when a gunman opens fire in a crowded night club.
- **CARS:** Though we are at the mercy of physics, being alert and practicing defensive driving, wearing seatbelts, and proper vehicle maintenance go a long way to reducing deadly roadway mishaps.
- **CANCER:** Getting cancer is tough (I know this on a very personal level). But we have both proactive (healthy living) and reactive (advanced medical treatments) strategies that mitigate the risk of dying from cancer.

MPSs offer no such avoidance mechanisms, aside from becoming a hermit and never venturing past your front door. This is likely why MPSs garner such public attention—that and the fact that cable news networks improve their ratings by covering horrific events in detail and for long durations. That is not to decry the media—to not report on a MPS would be odd. But the length, depth, and copious repetition the media devotes to MPSs is out of proportion with the actual body count in a typical MPS. There is a media contagion effect (more on that later) which not only drives more MPSs, but also elevates public fear beyond "normal" levels.

Outside of the United States

An obvious question to ask is whether MPSs are a common *human* occurrence. Many like to think that MPSs are purely an American phenomenon. Even a former president of the United States claimed, "The one thing we do know is that we have a pattern now of mass shootings in this country that has no parallel anywhere else in the world."

He was wildly incorrect, as most politicians are.

In 2018, one researcher[2] conducted the largest multinational tabulation of MPSs yet available. Unlike previous studies, this one employed researchers with foreign language skills to search for information on MPSs using the established criminology definition. The list of MPSs they developed spanned fourteen years and calculated both the number of instances and the number of people killed on a per capita basis. Even given the robustness of this research, there are wide swaths of the planet where people are murdered en masse, primarily with guns, and the events are either unreported in the media, or in languages obscure enough to warrant not hiring yet another field researcher.

Provided with this database of global MPSs, if the American president was correct, then the United States would stand alone at the top of this list for the number of MPSs or the number killed in such tragedies.

America ranked fifty-eighth for incidents and sixty-second for deaths.

Granted, in the pantheon of violent nations, there were some dangerous places ahead of the United States on this list—Iraq, Columbia, and Rwanda. But in terms of the number of instances on a per population basis, Finland was fairly high at twenty-third, the overtly spiritual Nepal was twenty-fifth, modern Eastern European countries of Russia and Yugoslavia were forty-third and fifty-third respectively, and even Norway bested the "wild west" at forty-seventh. And Switzerland, though slightly below America in terms of the number of MPS incidents per capita (sixtieth), was deadlier (forty-fifth in terms of deaths, compared to America's rank).

Important to the discussion is that MPSs are a human issue, not a national one. People of fragile mental states, terrorist leanings, and outsized grudges will commit mass murder given enough stress. But humans face a multitude of different stressors. What causes a person to shoot up a school in Newtown, Connecticut is far different than the motive of a man who shoots up a labor camp in Jammu, India (and both events produced the same number of deaths).

One common argument is that we cannot compare First and Third World MPSs because the cultures and social stressors are vastly different. Aside from the already established observation that MPS are a global and human symptom, there is some validity to the argument that comparing two or more similar bodies of people should provide a fairer contrast. To whom, for example, should America be compared?

This is a trick question, as it begs the yet deeper question of what factors are relevant. Some political operatives have claimed that socioeconomic equivalency is a rational basis for comparison. I have significant reservations about this criterion; but the factors most commonly included in such comparisons are the educational attainment level of the residents in each country and the per capita gross domestic product (GDP), a rough measure of wealth. This is a viable "acid test" given that education is a proxy for overall socialization, and that per capita GDP is an indicator of industrialization and technical sophistication.

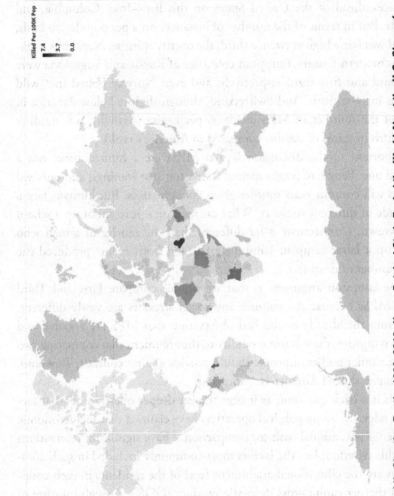

Killed Per 100K Pop
7.4
3.7
0.0

Mass Public Shooting Deaths 1998–2012, How a Botched Study Fooled the World About the U.S. Share of Mass Public Shootings, Lott, 2018

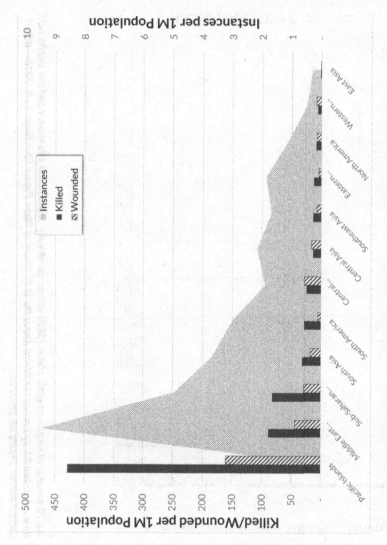

Mass Public Shootings by Region 1998–2012, How a Botched Study Fooled the World About the U.S. Share of Mass Public Shootings, Lott, 2018.

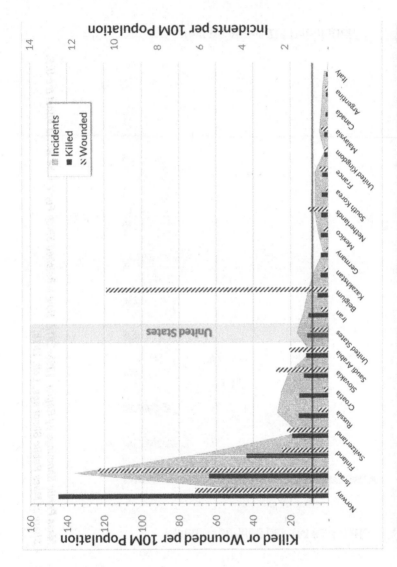

Top 25 percent of socioeconomic status (SES) scores combining educational attainment and per capita GDP, How a Botched Study Fooled the World About the U.S. Share of Mass Public Shootings, Lott, 2018—minus radical outlier events all countries

The socioeconomic score (SES) is a usable measurement to compare nations.[3] In 2010, the United States ranked second—one step behind Norway—on the SES index. This presents an odd problem for making comparisons to the United States since nearly every other country has a lower score. But if the theory that a high socioeconomic status is associated with a low rate of MPSs holds true—along with the explanation that America has an unusual MPS problem due to the availability of guns—then the top scoring socioeconomic nations should have low MPS rates except for America.

This chart shows countries in the top 25 percent of SES scores. Right away we see that the United States ranks ninth in the twenty-two most advanced nations in which any MPSs occurred. Not number one, but nearly at the midpoint of all comparable countries.

There are some oddities in the data that require a bit of consideration. First, Norway endured one major event in 2011, but for their relatively small population (1.5 percent that of the United States) this event had a very high body count (sixty-seven dead, more than the infamous "bump stock" MPS at a country music concert in Las Vegas). Israel is a hotbed of ethnic and religious conflict, so its high rate of MPS events and deaths is understandable. But after those two outliers, countries such as Finland, Switzerland, Germany, Belgium (held by some people as models of Western-nation gun control), and Russia (an autocratic state with associated arms restrictions) are in the same statistical region as the United States. The non-outlier countries with higher MPS death rates than the United States—Finland, Switzerland, Russia—averaged 2.4 times as many MPS deaths per capita than America.

Since our global MPS file covers fourteen years, there is the possibility of missing trends when we amalgamate over a decade of data. Trends provide important perspective, especially as various countries tighten or loosen gun availability, or as social dynamics change (such as the recent immigrant influx into Western Europe).

MPSs are on the rise globally and in the United States, even on a per capita basis. Outside of the United States, the number of incidents is rising twice as fast, and the number of people wounded in MPSs is escalating four times more rapidly. However, in the United States, the number of people killed in MPSs is rising at more than twice the rate as the rest of the world, even when we exclude the 2012 outlier year. The slower rate of growth in MPSs, combined with high rate of growth in MPS deaths, means American mass public shooters are obtaining higher aggregate body counts.

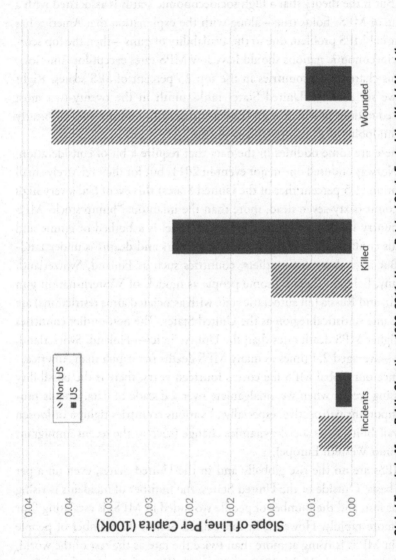

Global Trends in Mass Public Shootings 1998–2011, How a Botched Study Fooled the World About the U.S. Share of Mass Public Shootings, Lott, 2018—minus radical outlier events all countries; Excluding outlier year of 2001 for non-US due to two extreme mass murders with over 200 dead in each

Do keep in mind this represents a rate of growth, not total carnage. Before the Columbine massacre, the United States averaged 7.6 MPS deaths per incident, and afterwards 9.5, an increase of about 24 percent. Contrast the countries of Angola and Nigeria, which each had MPS events where more than two hundred people were killed.

Availability

America has always had guns. Plenty of guns. On a per capita basis, private ownership of firearms in the United States has—from the beginning—always been large compared to other nations. And according to firearm commerce reports by the federal government, the handgun supply in the United States nearly doubled from 1973 through the year 2000.

One theory offered by innumerable policy groups is that the more guns a country has, the more MPSs they will suffer. On a global basis—if the gun availability rates reported by the Small Arms Survey in 2007[4] are any indication—the hypothesis is inaccurate, bordering on inept. Indeed, using a worldwide perspective, the United States slides downward below the halfway point in terms of deaths from MPSs per gun in public circulation.

But this perspective can be deceiving. Foremost, nations with extremely low private gun availability (Uganda was on the bottom of the list with approximately one gun for every hundred people) will show very high death and wounding rates when the number of guns is the divisor. Indeed, you have to go a third of the way down the list of nations that have experienced MPSs before you encounter a large, populated, advanced-economy nation (Russia). This observation has not been lost on a few politicos who blindly claim—without the burden of statistical substantiation—that the United States has more MPSs than other "advanced" nations.

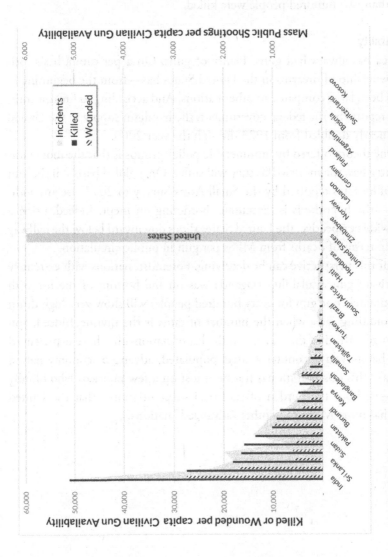

Mass Public Shootings per Civilian Gun Ownership Rates; Shooting info, How a Botched Study Fooled the World About the U.S. Share of Mass Public Shootings, Lott, 2018; Gun ownership data, Small Arms Survey 2007

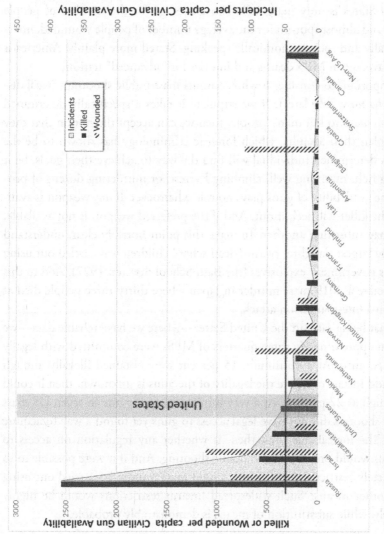

Mass Public Shootings per Civilian Gun Ownership Rates; Shooting info, How a Botched Study Fooled the World About the U.S. Share of Mass Public Shootings, Lott, 2018; Gun ownership data, Small Arms Survey 2007

This assertion is intellectually bereft. Using the socioeconomic index we employed before and looking only at the top 25 percent of nations that had any MPSs, we witness the United States creeping up the chart, from somewhere south of the midpoint to the fourth position. But when we average all non-US countries, we see that on a per capita gun availability basis, the United States is only marginally above average for the number of people killed, and almost spot-on for the average number of people wounded, internationally and socioeconomically speaking. Stated more plainly, America is about average in MPS deaths and injuries for "advanced" nations.

Important to consider is who commits mass public shootings (we'll discuss *who* now, *why* later). If we stipulate it takes a specifically determined mind to *want* to kill many people, then we can accept the notion that they likely plan their assaults, which forensic criminology has shown to be the case. A determined individual will find the way to achieve their goals, be it getting rich, marrying well, climbing Everest, or murdering dozens of people. The availability of guns plays no role whatsoever. If *any* weapon is available, the killer will seek it out. And if the preferred weapon is not available, they may substitute another. To make this point horribly clear, understand that the largest slaughter of American school children was carried out using surplus government explosives (the Bath School disaster, 1927). Add to this perspective a 2019 mass murder in Japan where thirty-three people died at work in a one-man arson attack.

That being said, in the United States—where we have reliable data—we see that approximately three-quarters of MPSs were committed with legally obtained guns. At a minimum, 15 percent were obtained illegally, though if we add instances where the legality of the guns is unknown, then it could be as high as 22 percent. At a very minimum, nearly one in seven US mass public shooters did not have legal access to guns yet found a way to acquire them. The logical question, then, is whether any regulation on access to firearms would prevent a mass public shooting. And if it were possible to so completely restrict access to guns, would mass murder be carried out using some other means? Such widespread firearm restrictions would be highly unlikely, while substitution of means is demonstrably probable.

A worthwhile recap

Before wading into other aspects of MPSs, it is worth our while to summarize what we know thus far:

- In terms of the likelihood of dying, your odds of being killed in a mass public shooting are astoundingly tiny. But it is scary because you have no way of mitigating the risk—to victims, they are random events.

- MPSs occur across the globe. It is *not* just an American problem.
- Such events happen in well-heeled countries, and the United States is not far above the average.
- The number of MPSs and the number of people wounded are growing much faster around the world than in the United States, but the number of people killed in American MPSs is advancing more quickly than elsewhere (though this is a bit of a statistical fluke).
- The availability of guns is not a determinate variable.

Why are mass public shootings in the United States becoming more lethal?
One confounding issue is the American lethality of MPSs. While the United States lags behind the rest of the world in the per capita growth of MPS events, we seem to produce shooters who are more successful in their killing, though the pre- and post-Columbine averages for deaths in MPSs is a short jump from 7.6 to 9.5 victims per MPS event. While the United States ranks halfway down the list of ninety-one countries for which we have records of MPSs, America's rate of deaths in MPSs is rising faster than everyone else.

Why?

Agenda-driven policy groups have lobbed a lot of notions into the public forum, most with no statistical backing or even common sense. Let's have a look at a few of these, and then let's also discuss one that I believe is a key part of the equation.

Weapon type
Foremost, understand that "assault weapon" is a legislative term, not a gun classification. Thus, the definition of "assault weapon" varies between federal, state, and local governments.

This legislative mishmash is maddening. In some legislation one type of firearm (the TEC-9) is a mere handgun. Elsewhere, it is an assault weapon. In yet another definition, it is both, depending on what capacity magazine is used in it. Likewise, in one piece of legislation a MINI-14 rifle is *not* an assault weapon; but its sibling, the Mini-14 Tactical, *is* an assault weapon, despite the fact that both rifles use the same ammunition, the same internal hardware (receiver, trigger, etc.), and can use identical magazines of any capacity—in other words, they are two identically functioning rifles.

Before we explore "assault weapons" in MPSs—as best as the topic can be explored—let's first focus on the basic types of guns and their use in MPSs. The results are likely not what you expect.

Firearm Type	Instances
Handgun	49%
Rifle	20%
Shotgun	13%
Handgun and Rifle	7%
Handgun and Shotgun	6%
All Three	4%

Using our MPS database,[5] which has all conforming events between 1997 and 2018, we see that handguns remain the most popular gun choice of mass shooters. Handguns were used in half of mass shootings and in combination with either or both rifles and shotguns for 13 percent. This majority handgun use is far afield from the public perception of MPSs and "assault weapons," which depressingly speaks to the success of some less than reputable policy groups.

The common visual presentation of "assault weapons" is rifles (AR-15, AK-47, etc.). However, not all rifles are "assault weapons." What this means is that less than 20 percent of MPS shooters who used a rifle used what is commonly perceived of as an "assault weapon." From the shooter's point of view, this is quite understandable. Rifles of any variety are difficult to conceal due to their long barrels and stocks. Even "assault weapons" with folding stocks are a bit long. A standard AR-15 is about forty inches (986mm) long and a compact AR-15 (folding stock and legal but short barrel) is still over twenty-four inches (609mm). An off-the-shelf Glock model 20 is a mere eight inches (205mm), making it much easier to conceal. It requires some degree of surprise to walk into an event with the intent of murdering many people. Because of this, most mass shooters lean toward handguns, not rifles or equally long shotguns, despite the potentially higher lethality of both of those alternatives. This paradigm, by the way, is also why the garden variety street thug and gang banger uses a handgun—concealability provides tactical advantages.

The Gun Facts research team pored through MPS databases to document where the weapon used conformed to the 1994 Federal Assault Weapons Ban, the one that expired in 2004. We determined that about 14 percent of the firearms used in MPSs would have been illegal for sale under the federal ban. Shortly after the Gun Facts project published those findings, another organization calculated the rate to be 13 percent, providing independent verification.

Nor is any one type of gun being used radically more frequently than in the past, with the exception of handguns, which in the years following the 1999 Columbine massacre have risen in use by mass shooters slightly (a slope of 0.17, for statistics fans). Rifle and shotgun use, as a percentage of total MPSs in any year, have not risen at all.

But things are changing. In the decade after the federal assault weapon ban expired, only one MPS involved such a firearm. But in the most recent years we have seen them used once or twice every year since 2015. Firearm manufacturers were expecting the ban to expire. Hence, the market demand for previously banned rifles was instantly satisfied once the ban expired. Yet it took ten years before such firearms started being used, with regularity, in MPSs. The "why" behind the recent uptick is of intellectual interest, though as you will see it is not explanatory in a ban/no-ban analysis.

Given all of the above, it appears that the type of gun that is available or used has had no measurable bearing on the number of people killed in MPSs. American MPS lethality is coming from a different source.

Magazine capacity

Much has been made of the number of bullets a gun can fire without reloading. For semi-automatic guns (not revolvers, derringers, and single-shot weapons), this boils down to "magazine capacity." Magazines—often incorrectly called "clips"—are containers into which rounds of ammunition are inserted, and the magazine is then inserted into the gun. If a shooter carries multiple magazines into an MPS, then his or her reload time is minimized due to the larger capacity magazines holding more ammo. But it takes very little practice to reload a semiautomatic gun in under two seconds,[6] making the killing efficiency of larger capacity magazines statistically suspect.

Semiautomatic firearms come from the factory with variable magazine capacities. The model 1911, the sidearm carried by American military members for many decades, has a magazine capacity of seven rounds. The Ruger LCP, reported to be the favorite handgun of 2017, holds six rounds. The Glock 19, also on the short list of very popular handguns, has a standard fifteen-round capacity. The Springfield XD(M) holds nineteen. These from-the-factory magazine capacities show that the vague notion of "standard capacity" is oxymoronic. Even the Glock handgun line ranges in capacities from six to seventeen rounds.

I advise ignoring ill-informed misclassifications by policy groups who claim that the larger the capacity magazine, the more lethal the MPS. They assert that the less a shooter has to reload, the more people they will kill. This is the basis for legislation to ban "high capacity magazines." However, the definition for "high capacity magazine" is much like the definition for "assault weapon" in that it is very flexible and changes from place to place, politician to politician.

DATA SANITY CHECK

The only database that tracks the magazine capacities used in MPSs is incomplete. Nearly 40 percent of all MPS are labeled "unknown" in the column for magazine capacity above certain legislative thresholds. This limitation is important given that there was a total of sixty-six MPSs in this database, covering a span of twenty years. Hence, the information below should be considered fragile.

Magazine capacity, statistically speaking, is associated with a higher body count. But there are some devilish details which need exposing, mainly due to a handful of very exceptional events.

Magazine Capacity	Average Deaths per Incident	% of Incidents between 1999–2018
10 or less	8	47%
10+	10	53%
15+	13	45%

From a purely aggregate perspective, there is a significant jump in the average number of deaths per MPS when magazine capacity climbs into either of the common legislative ranges of ten-plus and fifteen-plus rounds. But this is a bit skewed by shooters who can only be classified "exceptional" (for my fellow number crunchers, the adjusted R^2 for ten-plus and fifteen-plus round magazine capacities and the number of people killed in MPSs are 0.43 and 0.37 respectively, both with very high p values).

Our first clue is that the span of the average number of deaths in MPSs was not that large. Small capacity magazines contributed to an average of eight deaths per event, and magazines with fifteen or more rounds averaged thirteen deaths. But this is for *all* events aggregated.

If shooters using large capacity magazines had some other common trait, such as "cattle pen" scenario planning, then magazine capacity might play a major role. After all, if there are very few potential victims, there will be few deaths regardless of magazine capacity (the 2019 SunTrust shooting in Sebring, Florida is a case in point, as there were only a few people in the bank, and only five deaths). Is it possible that the higher death rate for MPSs using larger capacity magazines is driven by something other than the magazine capacity itself?

The relative lack of additional deaths per incident raised our suspicions about the skewing of data for "high capacity" magazines. A brief scan of just the MPSs where magazines of fifteen or more rounds were used exposed two elements: 1) most of these events were no more deadly than when lower capacity magazines were used (remember, there is an average of eight deaths in MPSs where magazines of less than ten rounds are used); and 2) a small number of very high body count events—twenty or more killed—created the incorrect impression that magazine capacity alone was the culprit. In other words, were five exceptional MPSs not on the list, the average number of people killed in each event would rival that of events where smaller capacity magazines were used.

Note that the five instances on the right side of the chart constitute 15 percent of the events but almost 50 percent of the deaths. These are the super killers, the mass shooters who achieved very high fatality rates through careful planning. A garden variety researcher would look at this chart and immediately ponder the skewing. Larger capacity magazines do not help to explain the low death rates on the left side of the chart—the 85 percent of events that account for the other half of deaths in events where larger capacity magazines

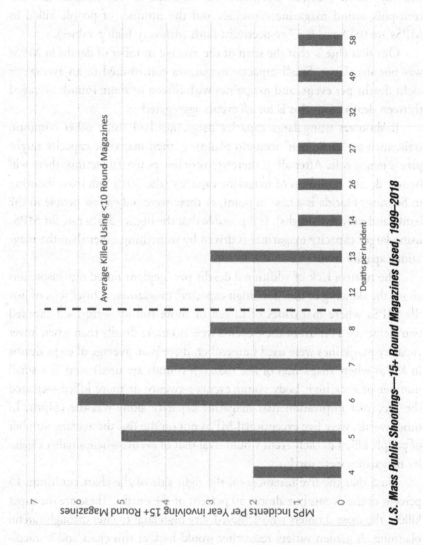

U.S. Mass Public Shootings—15+ Round Magazines Used, 1999–2018

were used. Nor does it explain events like the Parkland, Florida high school shooting where seventeen kids were killed by a gunman who had only ten-round magazines. But some of the right-side distortion is explained by events such as the Las Vegas country music concert shooting, where the gunman had exotic hundred-round magazines (fifty-eight dead), the Florida night club incident where the shooter targeted a crowded indoor event and used "jungle style" magazine pairs—when two thirty-round magazines are taped together, one upside down, so the shooter can spin the combination over to reload instead of feeling around for a second magazine—(forty-nine dead), or the college classroom shooting where the gunman blocked and even chained exit paths while using stock fifteen-round magazines (thirty-two dead).

In short, larger capacity magazines may be contributory to some high-end MPSs, but they are not a common factor for *all* such events.

Cattle pen scenarios

"I had a vision . . . of a very public place, only one way in and one way out. Preferably a bar/club on a busy night." Fortunately, this mass shooter, a rare female one, never got to carry out her plan after being arrested in 2019. But she had latched onto an expanding phenomenon among mass shooters.

I started conceptualizing and discussing "cattle pen" scenarios in 2007. My choice of terms belies my childhood working on a ranch and might be off-putting to some readers. But having seen what happens when you force as many Angus as possible into a small space before sending them off to slaughter . . . well, the metaphor was inescapable.

In April 2007, a court-certified madman entered Norris Hall at Virginia Tech University. He chained the doors shut, went up to the second floor, then dashed from classroom to classroom, firing from the doorway of each, which was the only path of escape for students. Twelve minutes after it began, thirty-two people were dead.

What caught my attention was that the shooter only used a handgun and only used magazines of the capacity for which the gun was designed. At that time, no mass shooter had ever killed that many people in an American MPS. The next closest was when a gunman killed twenty-four people in a Texas cafeteria, also using just handguns and their standard magazines. Like the Virginia Tech classrooms, the layout of Luby's Cafeteria offered few paths to escape, especially after the shooter had driven his pickup truck through the front entrance.

I defined MPS cattle pen scenarios as having two or more of the following attributes:

- Many people in "crowded" area (required)
- Limited exits or exit capacity (this and/or the next item)
- Few or no places to take cover (this and/or the previous item)

Any one of these factors increases the likelihood of a larger number of people being killed. All three combined almost guarantees it. Why are these contributing factors?

- **Many people in "crowded" area:** The ability to track and shoot moving targets is rare. It takes training and practice to achieve kills when there is a lot of air in between people actively fleeing (for example, the Tucson political rally event where six people were killed was in an outdoor setting where everyone could scramble). Shooting into a mob of tightly packed people assures someone will catch a bullet.
- **Limited exits or exit capacity:** Even if an area is not tightly packed, the inability to escape allows the shooter ample time to fire, calmly and slowly reload, and shoot again.
- **Few or no places to take cover:** As with fleeing the scene, being able to hide behind a barrier offers some means of avoiding a shooter.

Both the Las Vegas country music shooting and the Virginia Tech massacre provide good illustrations. In each, there were a lot of people in confined spaces. The Las Vegas event was an extreme example, as there were about twenty-two thousand people crammed into a venue sized to hold about twenty-two thousand people (to move, everyone in your immediate vicinity had to inhale). Virginia Tech classrooms appear to have had one main exit, though hurling oneself out a second-story window was an option in at least one of the classrooms that came under fire. Lastly, neither of these locations offered significant barricades for shelter. In short, students and music fans were herded into pens.

Some other examples of MPS cattle pens include:

- Texas church: twenty-six dead
- Florida night club: forty-nine dead
- California social services center: fourteen dead
- Colorado movie theater on opening night: twelve dead

- New York civil association with doors barred: thirteen dead
- Oklahoma post office work room: fifteen dead

And this is not an exhaustive list of MPS cattle pen scenarios.

"Gun-free" zones

It is a given that criminals do not obey laws. It is the very definition of the word "criminal."

This makes the underlying notion of "gun-free zones" a bit peculiar. Postponing for a moment a review of the effects that gun-free zones (GFZs) have on MPSs, it is good to ask aloud, "Would a criminal or a madman obey a gun-free zone sign?"

The answer is pretty obvious. From criminologist interviews of incarcerated felons, we know that they carry their guns *everywhere*, except perhaps into courthouses and parole offices (though I suspect a few have done so in the latter locations). This basic question about GFZs—would a criminal or a madman obey a gun-free zone sign—was posed to politicians when they debated the Gun-Free School Zones Act of 1990 and the Gun-Free Schools Act of 1994. We should note that these laws did not stop at schoolyard boundaries. Given the political angst of the era, as America was reeling from nearly three decades of increasing violent crime rates, similar laws were passed at state levels to cover college campuses, businesses, houses of worship, and more.

It did not appear to have the intended effect. Sticking with the legislation's original intent—to keep guns out of schools—and using MPSs as a weak proxy, we see that in terms of student deaths from MPSs in schools and colleges, the opposite occurred.

The parallel question is whether gun-free zones—including those outside of school settings—deter or facilitate MPSs. It may be counterintuitive to think that this matters, but it might. As will be seen in other chapters, criminals and even lunatics will avoid assaults if they think the person or the populace can harm them in return. Given the massive, multidecade rise in people with permits to carry guns in public (sneaking up on eighteen million at the end of 2018, or about forty-two times as many as there are police officers in the United States), the probability of a gunman encountering return fire has grown exponentially. The "deterrence effect," documented in criminology literature,[7] may be at play for MPSs.

That is, except possibly in gun-free zones. As our analysis of the statistically tiny number of school MPSs shows, gun-free zone legislation has

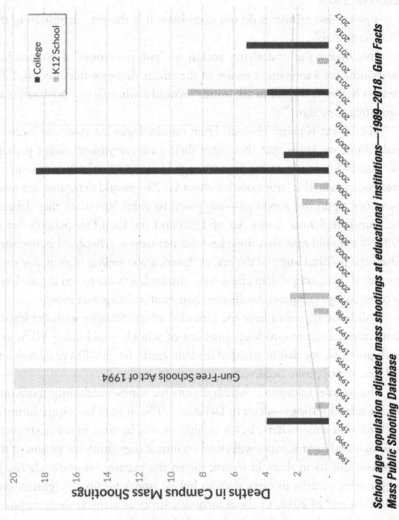

School age population adjusted mass shootings at educational institutions—1989–2018, Gun Facts Mass Public Shooting Database

not slowed the growth of such events. But what about all MPSs? This is a reasonable question, because laws making certain private locations gun-free zones—shopping malls, churches, workplaces—were enacted nearly in lock-step with the public-school legislation.

Gun-free zone	Percentage
Yes	88%
No	12%

For all years from 1988, in one MPS database that notes if the event occurred in a gun-free zone, nearly 90 percent of MPSs took place in such locations. Part of this derives from the expansive number of locations where carrying firearms was banned, either by legislation or by the property owners. But the nearly nine-to-one difference is so large that shooter location choice may well be a factor. In other words, are mass shooters more inclined to attack gun-free zones, or at least, disinclined to attack less regulated spaces? If shooters are indifferent to choosing GFZs over other locations, then we would likely see a fairly static ratio between the two types of locations over time. In other words, after the initial early 1990s push for GFZs, the number of such zones would not be increasing enough to skew the ratio based just on the probability of any location being a GFZ. Shooters may choose the location based on personal factors (their workplace, their school, etc.), but might not if those places were not GFZs.

But that does not appear to be the case. Measured in either the raw number of incidents, or the number of people killed, the rate of increase in MPSs outside of GFZs is practically zero, while the increase in incidents and deaths for GFZs rises steadily.

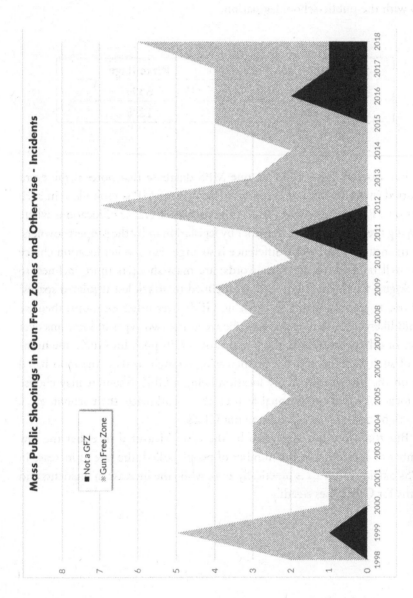

Mass Public Shootings in Gun Free Zones and Otherwise - Incidents

■ Not a GFZ
░ Gun Free Zone

Gun Facts Mass Public Shooting Database

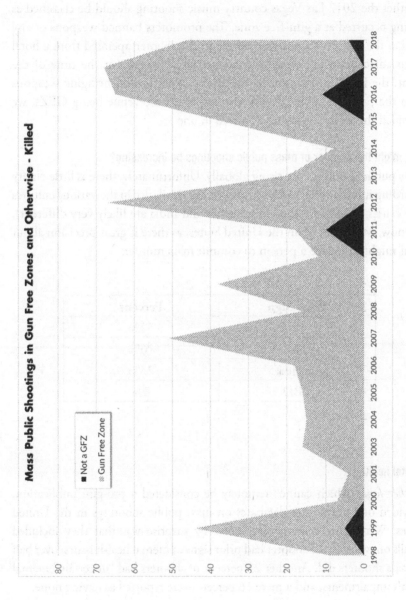

Mass Public Shootings in Gun Free Zones and Otherwise - Killed

■ Not a GFZ
⧱ Gun Free Zone

Gun Facts Mass Public Shooting Database

Two aspects about these charts are worth noting. First, years in which no MPSs occurred were omitted for the sake of a more accurate perspective on the rate of rise, or lack thereof. Second, there is controversy concerning whether the 2017 Las Vegas country music shooting should be classified as having occurred at a gun-free zone. The promoters banned weapons of any kind at the concert (a gun-free zone) but the shooter operated from a hotel room adjacent to the outdoor music venue. However, at the time of the event, the hotel in question had a strict prohibition on bringing weapons onto the premises. Due to both the hotel and the venue being GFZs, we classified this event as having occurred in one.

Why might the number of mass public shootings be increasing?

Mass public shootings are rising globally. Unfortunately, there is little clarity regarding international causes, and even less similarity in the various cultures (the causes of MPSs in the Unites States and India are likely very different). For now, we will focus on the United States, as there is great precision about what might influence a person to commit mass murder.

Prior Sign	Percent
Yes	52%
No	16%
Unclear	23%
TBD	8%

Mental health

Mother Jones, which cannot remotely be considered a pro-gun publication, provided one of the first databases on mass public shootings in the United States. What caught many researchers by surprise was that they included details on whether the shooter had prior signs of mental health issues; over half of mass shooters did. Another 23 percent of shooters had "uncertain" mental health impairments, and a mere 16 percent were reported as having none.

Though the public would always declare the shooter a madman, this was one of the earliest indicators that mental health was likely a contributing factor to MPSs. At least 52 percent, and maybe as high as 84 percent, of mass shooters had slipped a gear. The question is not whether mental health is a contributing factor—this is established. What is an open question is whether it is contributory to the increase in American MPSs.

This question is a bit tricky. There has been a population-adjusted upward swing in MPSs after the Columbine massacre. But has there been either an upward swing in people with mental health conditions, a lack of treatment for mental health patients, or an external influence that might push a mentally fragile person over the edge into committing mass murder?

It appears that two of the three might be true.

	Yes	No
Prior Signs	65%	35%
Seeing Professional	42%	58%

Knowing the percentage of the population that has mental health problems is impossible to determine with any accuracy. Many people live with chronic mental impairments in quiet. These people do not seek treatment and thus do not appear on any tabulation. Indeed, the American Psychological Association notes that upwards of 25 percent of primary care patients suffer from depression, but that their doctors identify less than a third of them. This means approximately 8 percent of the population—about twenty-seven million Americans—have untreated depression. And depression is but one of the mental health issues that might lead someone to commit an MPS. And from the Gun Facts MPS database, we see a mismatch between mass shooters who had prior signs of mental health issues and those who had previously been seen by a mental health professional.

As bad as that news is, it gets worse.

Deinstitutionalization

Starting in the 1980s, there has been a global movement in the psychiatric field toward *deinstitutionalization*. Before then, people demonstrating unusual behaviors, especially if their behaviors might be considered endangering to the patient or the public, were put into institutions. These facilities ranged from private sanitariums (think *Rain Man*) to horrid county facilities (think *One Flew Over the Cuckoo's Nest*).

But a combination of factors led to reducing psychiatric beds in institutions. There were budget reasons (politicians saw it as a way to divert spending elsewhere), a theory in the psychiatric field that patients did better if they remained engaged in regular society, and an array of new medications that if *properly* administered might allow patients to function normally in the real world.

Because of these factors, about 30 percent of psychiatric beds disappeared. As the number of beds decreased, the number of MPSs increased. This is no proof of causation, but it is an interesting datum to incorporate into our overall perspective on the intersection of mental health and mass shootings. If people who once would have been institutionalized are not, they are now largely unsupervised and in public. The shooter at Virginia Tech was put before a judge on a mental competency evaluation and let go not long before he killed thirty-two people in under twelve minutes.

The question is whether this is really a problem. As you can imagine, hard numbers are difficult to come by whenever "health" is involved. Medical privacy laws prevent public disclosure of the names of people temporarily detained for behavioral episodes (typically a seventy-two-hour hold) and thus prevent cross-referencing with public arrest records. Likewise, the divide between state and county mental health agencies and the court systems creates silos of interest and authority, and thus few people have explored this area in a way to satisfy criminologists.

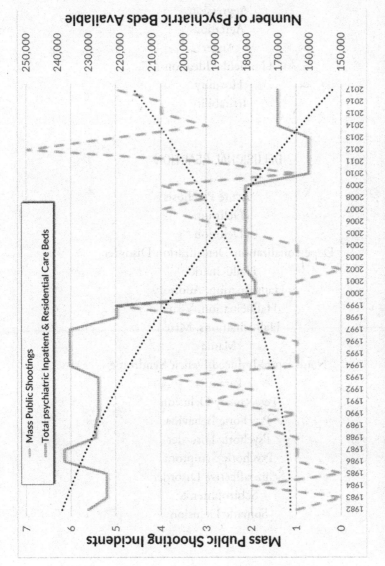

Psychiatric beds, National Association of State Mental Health Program Directors; Mass public shootings, Gun Facts Mass Public Shooting Database

VIOLENT REACTION

Activation Syndrome
Aggression
Agitation
Anger
Homicidal Ideation
Hostility
Irritability

DELUSIONAL REACTION

Acute Psychosis
Delirium
Delusion
Depersonalization/Derealization Disorder
Hallucination
Hallucination, Auditory
Hallucination, Visual
Hallucinations, Mixed
Mania
Neuroleptic-Induced Deficit Syndrome
Paranoia
Persecutory Delusion
Psychotic Behavior
Psychotic Disorder
Psychotic Symptom
Schizoaffective Disorder
Schizophrenia
Somatic Delusion

Medications

Part of the justification for deinstitutionalization was the availability of new classes of psychotropic medications. Psychotropics are drugs that affect a person's mental state. These include anti-depressants, anti-psychotics, and mood stabilizers.

One of our first jolts about the possibility of the intersection of mental health, medications, and mass shootings came with the Columbine massacre. It was reported that one of the shooters was not only taking a widely prescribed anti-depressant, but in one of their "basement tapes" stated he planned a cold-turkey withdrawal from the medication since doing so could amplify a sense of rage and thus make carrying out the massacre more reliable (this is why doctors tell you to "taper off" such medications).

It was a disturbing claim. This teenager was aware of an allegedly common side effect of a medication withdrawal that was associated with violent behavior. It would be easy to dismiss this as an aberration—a one-off case of a determined killer seeking whatever advantages he could find for his own personal killing field event.

But it is not quite that simple.

Many symptoms are associated with many medications both during their normal use and in withdrawal. The United States Food and Drug Administration (FDA) reports a laundry list of twenty-five possible psychological reactions. Some might be mild, such as a slight increase in irritability. Others are deadly warning signs, such as homicidal ideation, the formation in the mind of the notion of committing murder. Aggregated, there are two broad categories of psychological reactions to medications, or withdrawal from them, that may relate to MPSs—straight-up violent reactions or reactions that disconnect the patient from reality and thus make mass murder, and the horrific effects deriving from mass murder, seem rational.

As noted above, deinstitutionalization was facilitated, in part, by the availability of new classes of psychotropic medications. Many mark 1986 as the advent of the modern psychiatric medication revolution, with the introduction of a particular type of anti-depressant called selective serotonin reuptake inhibiters (SSRIs). This was the class of medication from which the Columbine shooter was withdrawing.

But are adverse reactions to psychotropic medications an important consideration as far as MPSs are concerned? With medical privacy laws preventing detailed investigation by all interested parties, it is impossible to tell. But the FDA tells us that adverse psychological reactions to these medications might line up really well with the rate of mass shootings.

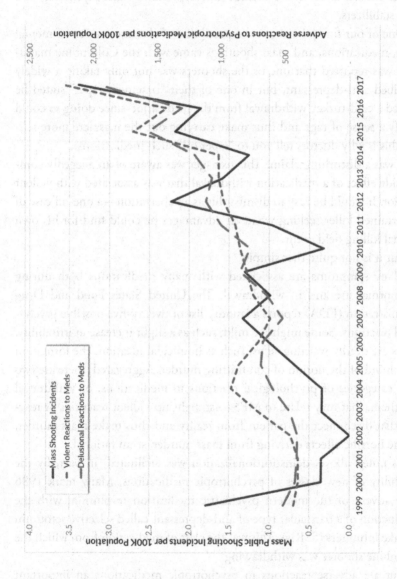

Medication Reactions from FDA Adverse Events Reporting System; Mass shootings, Mother Jones Mass Shooting Database, uses 3+ dead criteria

One FDA website allows anyone to extract the number of reported adverse reactions to any drug. We need to put a significant qualifier around the word *reported* for two reasons. First, there is incomplete reporting. Some in the field conclude that maybe 10 percent of adverse reactions are actually reported.[8] We also have to contend with the possibility that as the psychiatric profession becomes more aware of the FDA reporting processes, more reports are being filed even if there is not an increase in the actual rate of adverse reactions. But as the portion of the population taking these medications rises, the number of actual cases of adverse reactions rises as well.

What is striking is the covariance. My team of researchers employed an FDA website and tallied the reported adverse reactions to the top thirty-five psychotropic medications. Adjusting for both the adverse reactions—both violent and delusional—and for the number of mass public shootings per growth in the US population, we see in the post-Columbine world an amazingly tight correlation—an R^2 above 0.7, for the statistics junkies. In other words, it is quite possible that deinstitutionalization and/or adverse reactions to psychotropic drugs are contributory to the increase in MPSs.

Recall that one reason for deinstitutionalization—the reduction in confining the mentally fragile—was the availability of these new classes of medications, from anti-depressants to mood stabilizers to anti-psychotics. The fewer beds, the less hands-on, daily care for patients. The fewer beds, the more psychotropic drugs that are used. The more psychotropic drugs, the more MPSs.

One element herein is reliability. In the Parkland, Florida high school massacre, we saw an on-again, off-again patient who was on the autism spectrum. Interestingly, autism is the primary mental impairment associated with serial killers and mass murders.[9] Released reports from the Florida Department of Children and Families showed that the shooter was prescribed medications and was allegedly taking them at some point. One thing we know about people with various mental health conditions is that they are not the most reliable souls. Reports abound concerning people not taking their medications regularly, or even discontinuing their meds cold-turkey for a variety of reasons (one of the more common complaints from patients is that they don't like the general feeling they have while medicated and thus stop taking them). The modern process of self-maintenance via drugs while outside of institutions is an obvious problem point.

Media contagion effect

Don't blame me for the phrase "media contagion." My first exposure to the term came from a 2016 paper delivered at a meeting of the American Psychological Association.[10] Given how often mental health issues were prevalent in mass shooters, it is little wonder that people in the psychology field jumped headfirst into this rather deep pool of study (Google Scholar returns 6,200 items for the search phrase *psychology "mass shootings"*).

"Media contagion" describes the effect that mass media may have on inculcating the next shooter. In this context, "media" is rather broad. It includes traditional media (newspapers, radio, television, etc.) and digital (i.e., everything on the internet). What came to the attention of researchers studying mass public shootings was that new shooters routinely studied previous shooters. The Sandy Hook Elementary School assassin maintained a spreadsheet of four hundred mass murderers. In it, he detailed their massacres, the weapons they used, and other tidbits that appeared to satisfy his general interest in large-scale slaughter.

The media aids in this fatal research behavior. Given the timeline of commercialization of the internet, the ability to either spread information about mass shooters, or to research previous MPSs, has grown exponentially. For perspective's sake, understand that in 1997—just two years before the Columbine massacre—a mere 36 percent of American households had internet access of *any* kind. By 2015 that number was 87 percent. The Sandy Hook killer, who shot up an elementary school in 2012, had ample resources to infuse his imagination.

That the Columbine massacre occurred in 1999 is pivotal. The event received massive traditional media coverage, and news networks were fully ramped up on their early internet presence (the MSNBC website was launched in 1996). Alone, this was likely enough to help spread information about Columbine. What made it worth looking into by future mass murderers was the scope of bloodshed. According to one psychology researcher,[11] no juvenile had *ever* committed a multiple victim homicide in a North American school before 1975, and the first one was in Canada, not the United States. Before Columbine, the smattering of such events typically involved only two deaths. But with thirteen dead and twenty-one injured, Columbine provided a vivid, gory, and emotionally compelling redefinition of the previously unheard-of school shooting.

One organization that tracks just school shootings[12] reverse-mapped these events and explored what prior MPSs the newer killers researched. All digital roads led to Columbine.

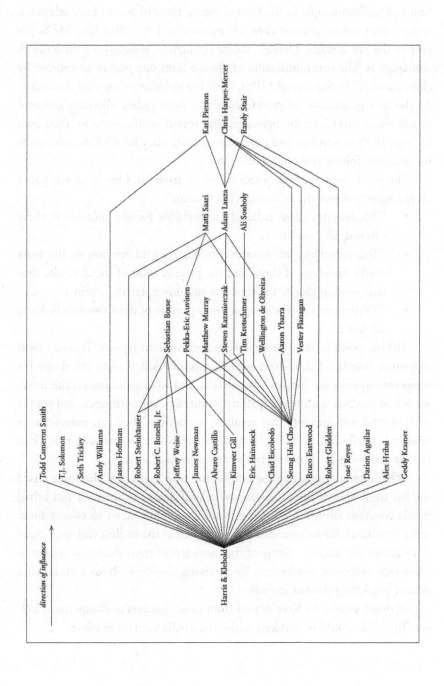

Media alone is an incomplete explanation. After all, there are over three hundred million people in the United States, most of whom have television and internet access, and yet there are on average fewer than four MPSs per year in the last decade. Hence, "media contagion" is nearly a misnomer. A contagion is "the communication of disease from one person to another by close contact." In the case of MPSs, there is a *voluntary* close digital contact. As the first generation of post-Columbine mass public shooters gathered details about this Colorado massacre, they found justifications for their own killings. In their writings and public statements, they have left breadcrumbs for others to follow and to amplify upon.

The psychology profession sees definitive patterns. One academic paper on the subject draws the following conclusions:[13]

- "'Media contagion' is largely responsible for the increase in these often-deadly outbursts."
- "The prevalence of these crimes has risen in relation to the mass media coverage of them and the proliferation of social media sites that tend to glorify the shooters and downplay the victims."
- "A cross-cutting trait among many profiles of mass shooters is desire for fame."

The last point is the most troubling, due to recent reports. Two common and often interlaced threads in post-Columbine killers were the desire for vengeance against an "unjust" population and to acquire fame. The intersection of the two is quite compelling to outcasts, misanthropes, and people with mental impairments that result in ostracism. They can perceive that wholesale retribution will earn them notoriety, which in turn will make their former surviving tormentors view them in fear and awe.

What is troubling is that the body count now matters. Columbine raised the bar from an average of about two school deaths to thirteen and raised media coverage from a brief mention on the nightly news to twenty-four/seven broadcasts for an extended period, as well as the endless collateral mentions across the internet. Some of the more recent mass shooters—either in pre-attack videos or confessions by surviving shooters—have mentioned a goal of breaking previous records.

In other words, we have moved from mass shooters to competition killers. This shift would be unlikely without a media contagion effect.

Do gun control laws help?

In regard to mass public shootings, we face a host of bedeviling issues when exploring whether any law might make a dent. For recapping purposes, here are some of the issues that we have already covered:

Infrequency: MPSs happen infrequently enough that obtaining robust statistical information on how laws may or may not change the frequency or lethality of such events is difficult. The main exception is that the time-series trends surrounding "gun-free zones" and mental health issues show concerning correlations.

Handguns: With the Supreme Court confirming handgun ownership is a fundamental right in the United States and given that handguns are the overwhelming firearm of choice in MPSs, impairing legal acquisition to other types of firearms would have a statistically small effect. Given "substitution of means," odds are that the smaller number of mass public shooters using rifles and shotguns would merely switch to handguns, or worse yet, bombs.

Legal/illegal acquisition: Even if the supply of one or another firearm type could be lowered, it might not make much of a difference. Using the "strength" of gun control law as defined (however willy-nilly) by a gun control advocacy group,[14] we see near zero (an R^2 of 0.007) correlation between gun control laws and whether MPS guns were legally or illegally obtained. The same analysis could be done on an international comparison basis, were details about firearm acquisition for all those events globally available.

This brings forth a rather uncomfortable question for many. If controlling access to firearms and their accessories does not materially affect the frequency or lethality of MPSs, are guns the actual problem? I'll play devil's advocate for a moment by hypothesizing that the actual disease is not mass shootings, but mass murder, and that guns are merely a tool of relative convenience. In recent postwar Middle East and Far East countries, we see improvised bombs as a recurring means for mass murder. In these regions, munitions are abundant, and the internet allows for easy communication of terrorist "how to" guides for bomb making. In this example, we have people intent on committing mass homicide and who also have access to guns, yet they took advantage of other resources to commit the acts.

From a purely statistical standpoint, handguns and mental illness are the dominant factors, with gun-free zones having a slightly higher than fifty/fifty correlation with MPS incidents and deaths. With handgun ownership constitutionally protected and thus not open for restrictions, that leaves improving mental health care and detection as the primary solution point, and a rethinking of the notion of gun-free zones as another.

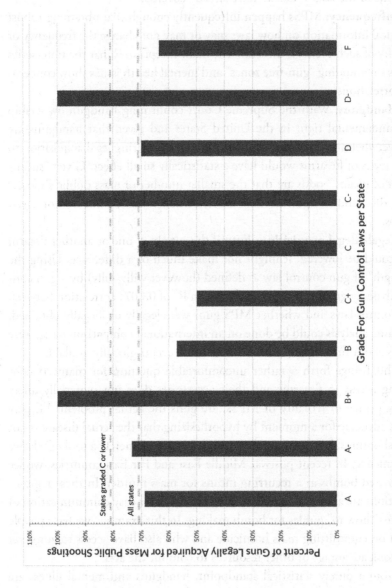

State grades, Giffords Law Center to Prevent Gun Violence—*Gun Law Scorecard; Acquisition, Gun Facts Mass Public Shooting Database*

By the numbers: mass public shootings

3.3	Increase (slope of the line) in non-US MPSs from 1998 through 2012
0.2	Increase (slope of the line) in US MPSs from 1998 through 2012
0.06	Increase (slope of the line) in the number killed in US MPSs 1982 through fall of 2019
0.5%	Fraction of all US homicides from MPSs
1.9, 3.3	Average annual MPSs in the last 18 years of the twentieth century and first 18 years of the twenty-first
7.8, 9.7	Average annual MPS deaths in the last 18 years of the twentieth century and first 18 years of the twenty-first
89%	MPSs that occurred in "gun-free zones"
65%, 42%	Shooters who had prior histories of mental health issues and those who were seeing mental health professionals before the attack
85%	Guns used that were obtained legally

CHAPTER 4
Defensive Gun Use

Gun owners only kill a couple of hundred criminals a year.

Gun owners use guns for self-defense two million times a year.

BOTH CLAIMS ARE CORRECT, WHICH shows both the nature of self-defense gun use and how basic data can be used to misrepresent the situation. Welcome to the other side of the gun coin, which we'll be flipping furiously in this chapter.

The critical take-aways
- Guns are used frequently to prevent crimes, real and perceived— more frequently than for crimes.
- Shooting guns in self-defense is rare compared to using them for defense without shooting.
- Shooting and killing an attacker is statistically rare.
- The net effect on suppressing violent crime via defensive gun use is appreciable.

What is a DGU?
Self-defense, be it personal, defense of family, or protection of property, is the primary reason people own guns. According to a Pew Research Center survey—which mirrors other surveys on the subject—67 percent of Americans who own guns do so for self-defense.[1] Compare this with a much lower

38 percent who own them for hunting, 30 percent who are into shooting sports, and a mere 13 percent who are collectors. Protection from criminal activities are the top concern of the people in the roughly 40 percent of households that own guns.

Concern of victimization drives this 67 percent of American gun owners. Many criminologists have dug into gun sales data, localized crime data, and like Pew, surveyed gun and non-gun owners. They have noticed a correlation between gun sales and violent crime. This correlation has led one group of researchers to claim that more guns sold leads to more gun crime. Other researchers, using survey data melded with crime and gun sales data, conclude that the *perception* of violent crime leads to more gun sales—if a person thinks crime is bad, especially where they live, they are more apt to buy a gun. The latter perspective appears to be correct, and as one team of criminologists summarized: "Crime affects gun ownership, in addition to any effects that gun ownership may have on crime."[2]

The amusing side effect of this is that the *perception* of the risk of being victimized may not be accurate. From late 1969 through 1993, violent crime in America climbed steeply, more than doubling. In response, the number of handguns in America went up nearly 70 percent, based on historical estimates of gun stockpiles supplemented with BATF firearm commerce reports. From its peak in 1993 through 2017, the violent crime rate in America fell to nearly the same level it was in 1970. But during that period the handgun supply doubled. Back in 1994, a large study showed that 74 percent of handgun owners kept them for self-defense, so perhaps the 7 percent reduction is a minor recognition by the public about changing crime patterns.

Why are handgun sales rising when violent crime is declining? There isn't a single explanation, but the surveys at Pew Research noted that since 2008, 57 percent of Americans—well, at least those registered to vote—think crime has gotten worse. I won't waste valuable paper to explore the various reasons why, but shock-rocker Marilyn Manson likely hit the nail squarely when he opined: "Times have not become more violent. They have just become more televised."

People buy guns primarily for self-defense. The question is: are they actually defending themselves? If not, then the legal acquisition of guns eventually leads to a few of those guns leaking into the underground markets, which is the primary source for street crime and gang guns. If that were the case, then it might be a net social negative. On the flip side of this coin, if guns are used often to prevent the crimes that people perceive are an active endangerment, private gun ownership might be a net social positive.

Our first problem, as illustrated with the two quotes that opened this chapter, is defining what in Hades a defensive gun use (DGU) is. As with the difference between an assault *rifle* and an assault *weapon*, the definition helps one or another group shape—or misshape—public perception.

In the broadest sense of the phrase, a DGU is when a gun is used in *any* manner as an act of defense. Ignoring for the moment a generalized deterrence effect, which we'll discuss later, the common modes of DGUs, in descending order of frequency, include:

- Telling a perpetrator that you have a gun
- Demonstrating that you have a gun (brandishing, chambering a round behind a closed door)
- Pointing a gun at the perpetrator
- Firing a warning shot
- Firing to wound
- Firing to kill
- Successfully killing the perpetrator (the first quote at the top of this chapter)

This list might seem simple enough, but when it comes to measuring DGUs we encounter our first problem, namely that many instances in the first four or five modes listed above are not always reported to police, and thus do not enter the hard statistics the FBI handily gathers. In order to get a more realistic grasp on whether DGUs are important to policy, the only viable tool is to survey people. Per the Bureau of Justice Statistics,[3] about a third of victimizations where the assailant had a gun were reported to police. Crimes of a petty nature, but which included a DGU, were likely reported even less frequently. Because of this, raw numbers about DGUs, even if the government succinctly collected them, would be wildly under-reported.

So, criminologists lean on surveys of the populace, and that comes with more than a few headaches.

One problem is delayed perception. How a victim remembers an event that occurred last year can be very different than the actual details. It gets even worse if the researcher, seeking more respondents, allow for recalled events going back several years. God love 'em, but people tend to fill in the blanks when memory for specifics weakens. They may recall using a gun when they didn't, not report using a gun when they did, and maybe not even get the year of the crime correct.

Surveys of DGUs can also capture some not-quite-legal activities. Surveys of this type are normally conducted anonymously (the respondent is not identified) via random digit telephone dialing. There are an unknowable number of responses from people who may be engaged in illegal activities (e.g., drugs) and yet truthfully report about shooting at an attacker (e.g., a rival drug dealer). Paranoid people in this same group might not mention a DGU for fear that the surveyor is actually a detective. The good news is that street toughs tend not to be survey takers, so the degree of their survey pollution is likely low.

There may also be episodes where the eventual DGU was in response to an escalating situation created by the defender. In other words, if you picked a fight with someone who then savagely attacked you, and you pulled a gun, was that really a DGU? Technically, yes, though the moral parameters are flexible. Though the person who shot may have been legal and morally justified in their defense, they may have instigated the confrontation itself.

Finally, the survey questions asked about DGUs can affect responses. Take the following questions as an example: (a) have you used a gun in self-defense, (b) have you used a gun to defend yourself and/or your property, (c) have you fired a gun in self-defense? As you can likely guess, the three questions, all designed to assess DGUs, would produce different results. To their credit, researchers over time have clarified their question structure and we have a more-or-less normalized set of surveys from which to make some initial conclusions.

The survey data

Various criminologists, polling companies, and news organizations have performed DGU surveys, which were dutifully gathered and correlated in one book, *Targeting Gun*, by respected criminologist Gary Kleck.[4] I recommend this book for those quirky academic types who you avoid at cocktail parties. It is a deeply dense tome with more statistical detail than most people with engineering degrees can tolerate.

On the low end of correctly executed surveys, there are over six hundred thousand DGUs each year in the United States. On the high end, the estimate tops three million. The average for all of the correctly conducted surveys is around two million times a year. The most cited study, from the same criminologist who gathered all the results into one heap, claims 2.5 million DGUs per year.

There is one sadly lonely orphan of a study that claims that there are a mere sixty-five thousand DGUs per year, or about 8 percent of the next highest survey. As you might guess, this is the survey that some policy organizations like to cite because it diminishes the rate of DGUs and thus discounts their possible social benefit.

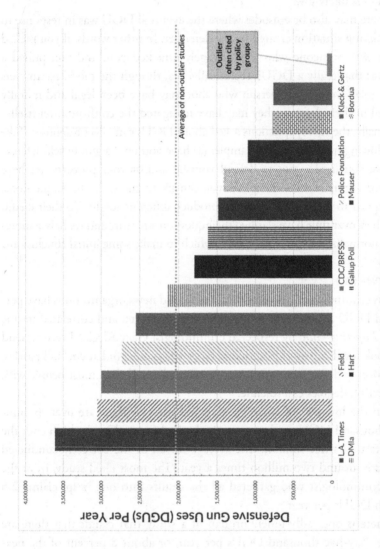

Surveys of defensive gun uses; Targeting Guns; Gary Kleck

TOO MANY PROBLEMS WITH NCVS

The National Crime Victimization Survey (NCVS) is the butt-ugly stepchild of DGU studies. One criminologist went as far as to say "the NCVS estimate is radically wrong," which in the common and polite world of academic parlance is a "fighting words" statement.

The problems that make this survey an outlier are many, and as such it should be cited by nobody. Some of the peculiarities that makes the NCVS inappropriate for exploring DGUs include:

- The survey is not anonymous, which is a major problem in getting unedited responses.
- To amplify this error, the respondents know that the survey is being conducted by a Federal agency—and sponsored by the Department of Justice—and as such may be reluctant to fully disclose details.
- A generalized screening question about victimization prevents many people from responding.
- The self-defense question asked does not inquire about the use of guns. That information has to be voluntarily coughed up by the victim.

There are more NCVS survey defects I could bore you with, but this short list alone is justification for explaining and thus ignoring this outlier.

But are the other surveys worth a damn? They are, but we have to take some limitations of surveying into account. Most of the more cited surveys were large enough to be nationally representative, but the results for subsets of overall DGUs—say the number of warning shots fired—were small enough to have isolated statistical fragility. That being said, the numbers remain stable between the surveys even when we eliminate every survey that would not achieve a high level of statistical validity using America's population in 2017 (for the statistics junkies, a confidence level of 99 percent and a confidence interval of ±5 percent).

But let's make things simple and (to the dismay of data purists) a little amalgamated. We'll use the average of the remaining viable surveys that together average out to two million DGUs per year in the United State. The

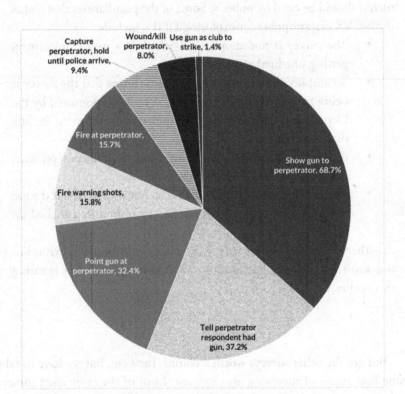

Guns in America; Police Foundation; 1996

one survey published by the Police Foundation, aside from having a "larger than most" sample size, also provides the best presented list of the various types of DGUs. Together, for non-animal and non-military/police DGUs, we see this following:

	Combined Instances	Percent of All Instances
Not "used" (brandish, inform)	115.3%	63.8%
Use without firing at perpetrator	33.8%	18.7%
Fire without intent to hit	15.8%	8.7%
Fire with intent to hit (wound or kill)	15.7%	8.7%

For the quick-minded reader, yes, the numbers add up to more than 100 percent. The reason is that victims often perform several DGU actions within a single event ("I have a gun . . . seriously, here it is . . . halt or I'll shoot . . . *Bang!*" Four separate actions). When we combine these many ways of performing a DGU into four main categories—not actually using the gun (showing, telling, capturing the perpetrators), using the gun without firing it (pointing the gun at the perpetrator or using it as a cudgel), firing the gun but not trying to wound or kill the perpetrator, or firing at the perp—we see that 83 percent of all DGUs occur without bullets flying. The next step is to note that 91 percent of DGUs are done without any attempt to actually shoot the perpetrator.

This is why the FBI reported that in 2017 there were only 299 justifiable firearm homicides (the number is likely larger since some cases need to be heard by a jury before a determination is made). The interesting contrast is that police only had 423 justifiable firearm homicides in the same year. Stated differently, civilians legally aced criminals at 82 percent the rate that cops do, and even the police were restrained in the number of people they capped.

The uncertainty principle

There is yet another and insanely unmeasurable kind of DGU, namely crimes not committed because the perpetrator was not willing to take the chance that the victim was armed.

Put yourself in the shoes of a criminal, which will be easy for any politicians reading this book. Imagine two houses you want to burglarize. One has a Prius in the driveway with a "Coexist" bumper sticker. You know the one. The other has a Ford pickup truck with "Support Your Local Police" sticker. You might think that there is a higher chance of the pickup-truck house having an armed resident in it than the Prius home.

Would this make you choose the former to rob? If so, you think like a crook.

Criminologists have an odd habit or two. One is that they occasionally break *into* prison to conduct inmate surveys. In some of the more elaborate polls of future parolees, criminologists select inmates who will lose nothing by discussing their crimes in detail. It is through these incarcerated felon surveys and interviews that criminologists have learned much about criminal behavior, including what they know and think about guns—where they get them, what they do with them, and how they get rid of them.

And how scared they are of them.

One paper,[5] albeit a little long in the tooth, was a landmark in this field and subsequent research has not invalidated it. An entire section of the study was devoted to what criminals thought when "confronting armed victims." Of the incarcerated felons surveyed, at most 10 percent "strongly disagreed" with questions concerning whether it was dumb to deal with armed victims. And the statement that these prisoners were mildly opposed to was, "Most criminals are more worried about meeting an armed victim than they are about running into the police." The average response to all questions about armed victims was 65 percent agreement with the idea that the possibility or certainty of a victim being armed was something criminals disliked and thought about often. In other words, about two-thirds of thugs think twice if their victim *might* have a gun.

This is telling because nearly 40 percent of the surveyed inmates had at some time or another decided to not commit a crime because they either knew or just *believed* that the victim was armed. Of these inmates, 69 percent knew another criminal who had been shot, shot at, wounded, captured, or killed by a victim with a gun. Clearly, the possibility of an armed victim weighs heavily on the minds of criminals.

There is one proof point about DGUs—though this has quirks—that requires pondering. Not all states allow people to carry guns in public, and even in the states where it is wide-open, not everyone carries. Measuring gun availability and DGUs for ATM muggings, thus, would not be an accurate

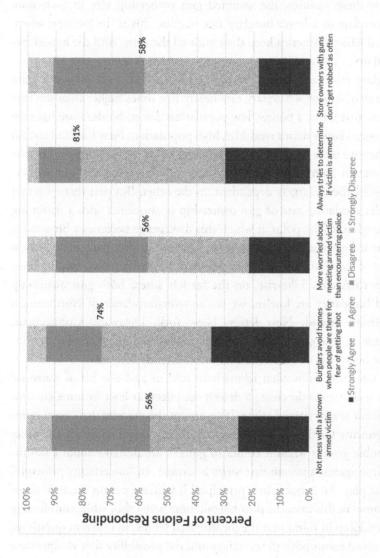

The Armed Criminal in America, A Survey of Incarcerated Felons; James Wright, Peter Rossi; 1985

datapoint. But every state does allow a person to keep a gun in their home (though some make this as difficult and expensive as possible). Given that about 73 percent of DGUs occur either in the home or nearby,[6] this is a better proxy to measure whether DGUs deter crime.

Given these realities, the assumed gun ownership rate in each state should correlate to a lower burglary rate because this is the location where Mister and Missus America keep their guns all the time. And the hypothesis does hold up . . . to a point.

Burglary rates, as you can see, are highly volatile, with the worst state (New Mexico) having a burglary rate nearly five times higher than the best state (New York). But a poorer, low population desert, border state has very different social issues than a wealthier, high population, New England coastal state. When we use a trendline that compensates for fluctuations, we see that below a certain point of low burglary rates, and covariant low gun ownership rates, neither is largely dependent on the other. But past that—up to a point—the escalating rate of gun ownership is associated with a flattening rate of burglaries. The point at which this divergence becomes a bit weak is where the burglary curve starts to slope downward. Past that point there is a mixture of moderate and very-low population density states, ranging from Kentucky to Alaska. Likewise, on the far left where both gun ownership rates and burglaries are lowish, we see an overabundance of Northeastern states (Rhode Island, New Jersey, New York, Delaware, Connecticut, Massachusetts, Maryland, New Hampshire, and Maine) where the icy winters make burglaries and other crimes inconsistently frequent.

The takeaway from what felons have told us and one bit of statistical evidence is that guns do create a deterrence effect, at least in some circumstances or for some types of crime. If we accept the premise that career criminals—ignoring for the moment terrorists, lunatics, and hotheads, the other three trouble groups when it comes to guns —are hesitant about committing a crime against a person that *might* be armed, an "uncertainty principle" is likely at play. An "uncertainty principle" is where a person is uncertain of the outcome; in this case, the possible outcome being shot while committing a burglary. Keep in mind that the incarcerated felons, in different questions, were surveyed about both the certainty and the possibility that victims were armed, and in all cases the majority opinion was that it concerned them. They demonstrated the "uncertainty principle" in survey responses.

The uncertainty of whether or not a victim is armed separates criminals into at least two classes, one of which will continue the crime unabated (the fearless criminals) and those who, if they have any doubt at all, will move along to another victim (the rational criminal). About 26 percent of

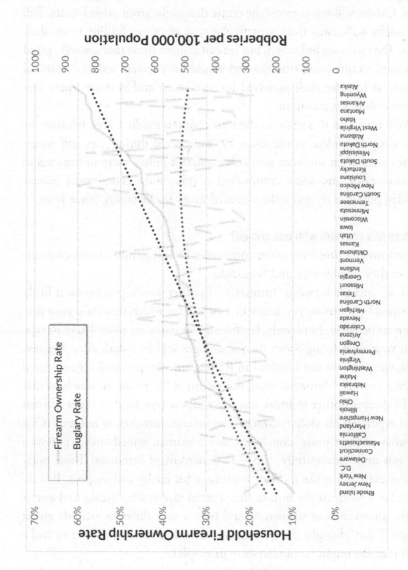

FBI, Crime in the United States, 2017

the felons *strongly* agreed with the dangers of confronting an armed person, and another 39 percent agreed but were somewhat less troubled. We have a range of 26–65 percent of felons who would at least think twice before committing their crime. Some will still commit the crime, but against another victim. Others will not commit the crime that night given other factors. Still more might walk away from a particular type of crime, finding it too dangerous. The ratios are unknown, but we can assume those that *strongly* agreed that armed victims were troublesome would have overall reduced criminal activities, at least for their preferred form of crime and in states where firearm ownership was common.

We'll touch on this again in the next chapter, Public Carry, because the radical drop in violent crime since 1993 occurred during a period where America went from nineteen states that allowed public carry of firearms to forty-two states, and some criminologists (plus some economists) believe expanded public carry was at least contributory to the falling crime rates.

How does this compare with gun crimes?

We run into two problems when comparing DGUs against crimes committed, and they involve rape and homicides.

Most rapes are between "intimates." In other words, you are most likely to be raped by someone you know in a setting for which they have your permission to be there. Husbands, boyfriends, or dates are more likely to rape you in your own living room than a stranger will in a dark alley. Because of this, weapons are not involved in 85 percent of rapes, and a gun is used in only 3 percent.[7] Strong-arming the victim is the norm, so much so that the FBI doesn't bother to break out the weapon type used in rapes in their annual reporting on violent crimes. The inverse, however, is not true. One somewhat antique study[8] concluded that a woman armed with a gun or a knife was only "successfully" raped in 3 percent of instances. These polar opposite extremes make a direct contrast a bit tricky and suspect. But do take in for a moment the notion that a serial rapist, who breaks-and-enters into the apartments of women, would have a very different attitude about a victim if they thought the woman was armed (deterrence effect) or had a hunch that she might be (uncertainty principle).

Measuring the degree of DGUs that prevent homicides is hampered by the fact that we cannot know which assaults that were repelled were intended to be homicides. If someone is aggressively breaking down your door before a warning shot scares them off, were they there to commit a hot home invasion, rape, or murder? We simply do not know and even if the victim was certain in their own mind, it is not absolute knowledge. Some victim surveys suggest that of the average two million DGUs every year, about four hundred thousand prevented serious injury or death,[9] but that is too vague to know how many DGUs stopped how many intended homicides.

However, robberies and aggravated assaults are much clearer and there are some robust comparisons to be made.

The tall bars on the far right (chart on next page) of both clusters are the estimated DGUs for each category of crime based on the number of DGUs per year, and a breakdown of DGUs provided by the same pair of criminologists who devised the four hundred thousand number. The shorter bars on the left of each cluster are the number of times guns were used to commit the same type of crime. In other words, the chart compares the use of guns to commit robberies and assaults against the times guns were used to stop the same types of crime. I'll save you some eye squinting and mental math. For both robberies and aggravated assaults, guns are used more or less four times as often to prevent the crime than to commit it.

This then begs the question: does the radical variation of international firearm ownership affect the aggregate defense against crime by country? In other words, from nation to nation, does the highly variable rate of private gun ownership cause certain types of crime to be higher or lower? From the data above, it is clear than Americans—in the nation with the highest per capita private gun ownership—use guns significantly more often to prevent crimes than to commit them. In theory, lower gun ownership rates might lead to more crimes under the hypothesis that a lack of potentially fatal resistance provides criminals less reluctance to commit those crimes.

Since we just looked at assaults and burglaries in America, and thus have a foundation for comparison, let's start there. According to the United Nations Office on Drugs and Crime and looking only at countries that top the socio-economic index (so we are roughly comparing to America) and for which the Small Arms Survey has estimates on gun ownership rates, we see two things. First, the covariance between gun ownership and getting assaulted is weak, scoring a mere 0.01 on a scale of zero to one. But this makes sense because, as we noted before, assaults are typically spontaneous acts and the victim has to defend with whatever skills and ad hoc weapons they may have access to in whatever environment they are in. Second, we see that as per capita gun ownership rates fall, the odds of getting assaulted rises, slowly but resolutely. The hypothesis at play is that you are more likely to get punched in the nose in countries where the attacker knows you probably don't have a gun.

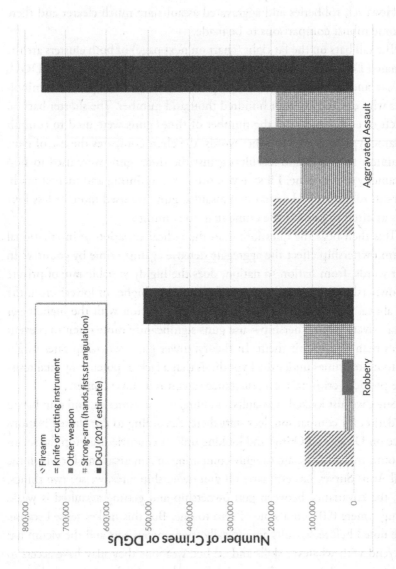

Crime, FBI, Crime in the United States, 2017; DGU breakdown, Armed resistance to crime: the prevalence and nature of self-defense with a gun; Gary Kleck, Marc Gertz; 1995

The story for burglaries is a bit different. Burglary rates rise as gun ownership rates fall, but only up to a point. However, it is interesting to note that the nation with the highest gun ownership rate (the Unites States, on the far left of the chart) has a slightly lower burglary rate than the nation with the lowest burglary rate (the Netherlands) in this chart. The difference in the Netherland's burglary rate compared to the United States is +6 percent and their gun ownership rate is -97 percent.

The astute reader—that would be you—likely noticed that we did not contrast robbery rates. The reason is that the definitions of that crime used by the United Nations and the FBI are so different that the United Nations reports US robbery rates to be only 3 percent of what the American government claims, whereas their measurements of assaults and burglaries are very similar. For now, we'll have to assume . . . nothing. We could assume that the trends are similar for robberies as they are for assaults and burglaries. But that would lack accuracy, and would be misleading.

The spin

There is a lot of spinning in the political ether when it comes to defensive gun uses.

The most common spin is the low-balling of DGU estimates. You saw above that there is a large collection of DGU surveys from criminologists, media companies, and polling outfits. That they all cluster around two million DGUs per year gives us some degree of comfort that this is likely accurate. One lone measurement, compliments of the National Crime Victimization Survey (NCVS) reports a wildly lower rate. The problems here are doubled. First, the methodology of NCVS is so out-of-the-norm that working criminologists say they the DGU measurements therein are ridiculous. Second, certain ideologues cite this data and ignore the other dozen studies. If someone is telling you that DGUs are rare, ask them if they are citing NCVS data, and if they are doing so, try to educate them or find yourself a more intelligent dinner companion.

On the other side, there is still the antisocial use of guns. Though for some categories of crime DGUs outpace gun crimes by four-to-one, the fact is that criminals use guns. A radical disposition to either the DGU, false lack of DGU, or blindness to criminal gun use is myopic.

Factions that campaign for gun control never discuss the deterrence effect or the uncertainty principle, despite felon surveys by criminologists showing that these are real and compelling elements. A good question to

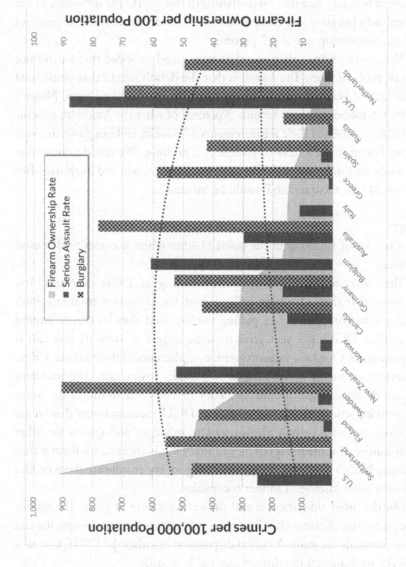

U.N. Office on Drugs and Crime, 2017

ask your soon-to-be-former dinner companion is what they know about the rate of alerting, brandishing, warning shots, and intentional wounding in self-defense. Odds are they will change the subject on you.

Worst of all, though, is when one faction notes, accurately, that guns are numerically rarely used to kill criminals. But numerically and statistically, they are used very frequently to prevent crimes without killing the criminal in question. This omission is, in itself, criminal.

By the numbers: defensive gun use

3,609,682; 2,002,922; 764,036	The high, average, and low estimates of annual DGUs
400,000	Estimated DGUs that prevent serious injury or death annually
299	Justifiable homicides
67%	Gun owners whose primary motivation to own is self-defense
83%	DGU where no shot is fired
65%	Felons who agree that a potentially armed victim is something to worry about
4.3, 3.9	Times guns are used to prevent robberies and assaults over when guns are used to commit those crimes

CHAPTER 5
Public Carry

I have a permit to carry, but really never do.

I always carry in public. Every day. Never had to use it though.

I stopped a liquor store robbery because I was carrying.

ALL TRUE STATEMENTS TOLD TO me by different folks over the years. People are different. Situations are different. But guns carried in public are nearly a national norm and are growing in terms of the number of people who can carry and shrinking in the requirements to do so. Understanding this rather historic political, legislative, and criminological experiment is important to understanding people, guns, and violence.

The critical take-aways
- There has been a massive expansion of public carry in the United States since 1988.
- This may have been contributory to the multi-decade drop in violent crime.
- There appears to be no statistical negatives in terms of crime to this change.

What is "public carry"?

As the name implies, "public carry" is the right or privilege (depending on your legal and constitutional opinions) to carry a gun in public places. But this immediately brings to the fore the questions of "what is *carry*" and "what is *public*"?

The question of the definition of "carry" is the easier of the two to answer. There are two forms of public carry: concealed or open. Concealed carry means that you carry your firearm in such a way that nobody sees it (e.g., under your jacket, in your purse, etc.) Open carry means you carry in such a way that people see you are armed (e.g., hip holster, rifle slung over your back, etc.). Laws vary from state to state about both forms of carry, but concealed carry is the norm. In some states you can carry concealed, but not open. In very few instances, you can carry open but not concealed. In some states you need a permit to carry concealed, but not open, and in others it is legal to carry open if you are in a rural area. California, being . . . well . . . California, managed to functionally outlaw both concealed and open carry, and found itself in court because of that since the right to "bear arms" has not been fully adjudicated.

Though conceptually simple, the variations from state to state make cross-sectional analysis complex. However, the norm for public carry—at least in forty-two states—is concealed. There are a number of reasons this is the typical legislative choice, but a primary reason is that some citizens have highly emotional reactions to guns and thus seeing a person who is not a police officer openly carrying a gun is frightening to them. Indeed, for a tiny minority, even seeing a gun on a cop's belt is traumatizing. As of this writing, nearly nineteen million people in the United States have permits to carry guns publicly, and another twenty-eight million adults live in states where they have dispensed with permits altogether.

Where things get a bit more complex is that states differ widely in how a person can legally carry, if it is at all legal in that state. Obtaining a concealed carry of weapon (CCW) license in one state is only a paperwork process. In another, it requires training and testing. In a smallish but growing number of states, they have eliminated the licensing process completely. In no state can a convicted felon, or at least a felon with a record of criminal violence, own, much less carry, a gun in public (I know more than a few readers just perked-up since they know from news reports that criminals with rap sheets are caught carrying guns all the time—but then again, breaking the law is part of a criminal's job description, and thus laws about carrying guns in public are routinely ignored).

To make this legislative pandemonium even less navigable, there are two types of states that grant CCWs. They are known as "shall issue," which is where you *will* be issued a CCW if you have no disqualifying criminal or mental health record and pass any other requirements (e.g., training), and the other is known as a "may issue" state in which the local authorities—the county sheriff or a city's chief of police—*may* (or may not) issue a CCW. Often in *may issue* states, the de facto process is to deny all applicants unless there is a special exception. It has been noted by some pro-gun activists that the exceedingly rare San Francisco Bay Area CCW can be had if one donates to a sheriff's election fund, you personally know a mayor, are famous, or a US senator (the San Francisco-based gun control activist Senator Dianne Feinstein had a concealed carry permit, adding irony to our review).

If you can stand any more craziness, some states do not require a permit to carry for their residents but offer permits for people from other states. In other words, if you want to carry in State-X but live in State-Y, State-X will provide you with a concealed carry permit. And between many states, but by no means on anything resembling a consistent basis, a carry permit from one state will be honored in other states. Entire books are published annually to inform CCW holders about when, where, and how they can carry and where their permits are honored or not.

MODE	COUNT
No permits required	15
Shall issue	27
May issue	9

As of Fall 2019, the major category breakdowns for the fifty states and the District of Columbia are both surprising and not. Most of the states that do not require any permit to carry a gun in public did until recently (one state, Vermont, never had a permit-to-carry policy in its entire history). A number of reasons for this exist, but to understand it better, we have to understand that thirty years ago only ten states allowed concealed carry at all.

The grand American experiment

In 1988, nine states had legislation that allowed people to carry guns in public places. The tenth state, Vermont, simply had never outlawed the practice from its founding (this is why no-permit carry is called "Vermont carry," though it is also called "constitutional carry," "no-permit carry," and "unrestricted carry"— in this book, we'll call it no-permit carry to avoid the stigma of ideological alignment). But by 2017, that number had climbed to forty-three once a court more or less ordered the District of Columbia (which for convenience's sake we are calling a "state") to start issuing carry permits.

That is a lot of change in a fairly short amount of time. It is perhaps the most comprehensive social and legislative experiment in modern American history. Before 1988, states had, over time, and especially in the 1970s and 1980s, passed many gun control measures. Public carry had various prohibitions going back to the 1700s. In numerous states, especially in the deep south and in California, there was a general prohibition against carrying guns in public, but a tacit understanding that such laws would only be enforced against troublemakers and minorities.

A CONSTITUTIONAL LAW SIDEBAR

As of 2019, there is a vigorous debate erupting among constitutional scholars about public carry. The Second Amendment to the US Constitution says that the "right of the people to *keep* and *bear* arms shall not be infringed." In various Supreme Court cases, this was certified as an individual right (*Dred Scot*, though not in dicta, 1856; *Cruikshank*, 1876; *Presser*, 1886; *Heller*, 2008).

The Heller case certified the right to *keep* guns, but the Supreme Court has not yet addressed what the right to *bear* arms means. Some scholars tenaciously hang onto the militia aspect of the Second Amendment and think that bearing arms is only allowed in service to militia duty. On the other side, many scholars jump right to the list of rights citizens have that were enumerated in the Dred Scott case, the earliest mention of said "gun rights," where the court proclaimed citizens had the right "to keep and carry arms wherever they went." It is worth remembering that a number of Supreme Court justices who ruled on the Dred Scott case were alive when the Second Amendment was ratified, supposedly had an unvarnished understanding of the right, and thus this is a substantial claim.

Florida was put into play in 1988. Actually, it was in 1987 that Florida changed their law to a "non-discretionary" permitting system for concealed carry of firearms in public. In other words, they changed from *may* issue to *shall* issue. The law was activated late in 1987, so many people simply say that Florida functionally switched to a shall-issue state in 1988.

I was a witness to it, living in Florida through that decade.

What made this a turning point in terms of public carry was that Florida was not a backwater state. Before 1988, the states that allowed for public carry included Indiana (five million residents), Maine (about one million), New Hampshire (about the same), North Carolina (6.3 million), North Dakota (0.7 million), Vermont (0.5 million), Washington (4.5 million), Wisconsin (4.7 million) and the thinly populated Wyoming (0.5 million).

Florida easily bested them all with over twelve million residents. Florida has many major metropolitan areas including Jacksonville, Miami, Tampa, and Walt Disney World's own Orlando, all with typical big city problems. Florida was also ethnically diverse with everyone from slave descendants to Cuban refugees to Seminole Indians. In other words, it was the first big test of what would happen if the public at large had the ability to carry guns in public.

It is important to note that this was during a period where the United States, and Florida more so than other states, was enduring a steep rise in violent crime. According to the FBI's Uniform Crime Reporting system, in the ten years preceding passage of a "shall issue" CCW process in Florida, violent crime had gone up 29 percent in the nation and 46 percent in Florida. When the change in the law was first proposed, talking points from the expected competing factions were equally predictable. Those in favor of the law cited the rising lawlessness in the Sunshine State and thought the ability to carry a gun in public was an equalizer. Those opposing the legislation predicted an escalation in the already rapidly growing violence rate.

Other states were watching, and for good reason. Neighboring Georgia had a ten-year violent crime rise of 31 percent. Pennsylvania's was also 31 percent. Oregon had gone up 18 percent. All three of these states enacted "shall issue" concealed carry in 1989, a year or more after Florida took the plunge. They waited to see what happened in the land of alligators and tourist traps, a swampy joint where tourists buy alligator shoes. After Florida switched to "shall-issue" concealed carry, these three states took the plunge themselves.

The results were provocative.

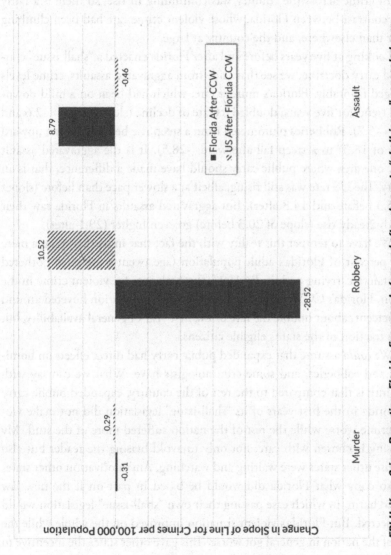

FBI Uniform Crime Reporting, Florida, five years before and after change to "shall-issue" concealed carry permitting. Compares slope-of-line before and after CCW enactment.

Nationally, violent crime continued to rise until 1993. So, the five-year gap from when Florida changed to a "shall-issue" public permitting system and when the rest of the nation peaked in terms of violence is rather instructive. The five years after the change to "shall issue" was in a period where violent crime across the country was continuing to rise, so there is a fairly clear contrast between Florida, whose violent crime rate had been climbing faster than elsewhere, and the country at large.

Looking at five years before and after Florida enacted a "shall-issue" concealed carry doctrine, we see that aside from aggravated assaults, crime levels changed favorably. Florida's murder rate, which had been on a mild downward trend for five years, doubled its rate of decline (slopes of pre = -2.6 and post = -5.7). Robberies plummeted from a steep rise beforehand (an upward slope of 18.3) to a steep fall afterward (-28.5). It is the aggravated assault rates, one area where public carry should have made a difference, that is an oddity. The US rate was still rising, albeit at a slower pace than before (slopes of 15.3 before and 14.8 after). But aggravated assaults in Florida saw their already steady rise (slope of 20.3 before) go even higher (29.1 after).

We have to temper this reality with the fact that in the first year, a mere 0.36 percent of Florida's adult population (age twenty-one plus) bothered to obtain a carrying permit. By 1993, the peak year for violent crime in the nation, Florida's CCW permit rate for the adult population hovered around 0.7 percent, about double the rate of the first year of general availability, but still a fraction of the state's eligible citizens.

We *could* assume that expanded public carry had direct effects on homicides and robberies, and some criminologists have. What we can say with certainty is that compared to the rest of the country, expanded public carry in Florida in the first years of its "shall-issue" legislation did not make violent crime worse while the rest of the nation suffered more of the stuff. My phrasing is chosen with care, not only to avoid biasing the reader but also because other states were waiting and watching. Any motivation other states had to copy what Florida did would be based in part on if the new law caused harm, in which case passing their own "shall-issue" legislation would be rejected. But Florida's violent situation improved on the whole while the fate of the nation in general got worse. This gave other states the incentive to give "shall-issue" concealed carry permitting a spin.

Between 1988 and 2019, America went from a maximum of 10 percent of the population living in "shall-issue" or "no-permit" states to 73 percent. During that period, the US population grew 19 percent and the national violent crime rate fell about 42 percent. This is *not* proof that expanded public carry reduces crime (it might) but it is reasonable proof that it does not make the problem worse. There has been no mass exchange of bullets between feuding factions that had public carry permits, though firefights are still popular in cities with demarked street gang turf.

But other things were in play. There was general economic prosperity after the Soviet Union collapsed and military spending was reduced. Some subsegments of the population that were subject to violence (committing and receiving) availed themselves more frequently of abortion services and reduced the young male population, the source of most violence.[1] Disco had died, to everyone's relief.

But there was a covariant and rather big change in reaction to the escalating violent crime situation. Many states passed "tough on crime" laws around that pivotal year of 1993. Some of these addressed habitual criminality and stuck repeat felons in prison for extended periods of time. It was well understood that recidivism rates among all classes of criminals was high, and that included violent crimes, including crimes committed with guns. What state legislatures were simultaneously doing, in chaotic patterns, were allowing more people to carry guns publicly while keeping criminals, violent and otherwise, in prison for longer stretches.

A quick aside about cities, gangs, and guns. Among those released from prison for a violent offense, about 11 percent of such felons are again arrested for yet another violent offense.[2] But remember our example from before, where a street gang member arrested for a murder charge in a major metro center is the lead suspect in two or more other murders. Thus, the intersection of guns, big cities, and street gangs continues to bend the curve when it comes to norms and numbers. But since "get tough on crime" laws are state wide, and assuming local prosecutors are doing their job, more thugs than before were off the streets and unavailable to continue their criminal acts.

The most popular of these 1990s era "get tough" laws are nominally called "three strikes." As the name implies, if you commit three of the more imprisonable crimes, the third one will get you serious time, often life without parole. These laws are not a new novelty. American habitual felon laws go all the way back to 1797. Five other states enacted them before Florida did, and the Sunshine State passed theirs in 1995, well after the demonstrated lowering of violent crime they enjoyed after passing "shall-issue" public carry. But between 1993—the year when violent crime was at its apex—and 1996, twenty-three other states also passed three-strike laws. As of 2012, thirty-two states had habitual felon statutes in place. This was not

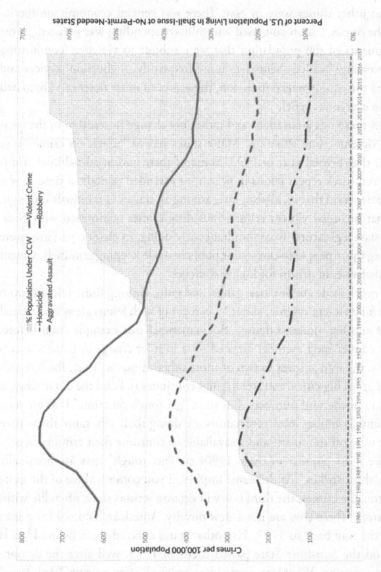

Crime, FBI Uniform Crime Reporting; Concealed carry permits, state reporting gathered by the Crime Prevention Research Center; annual population estimates, US Census Department

as fast and as thorough a roll-out of legislation as public-carry laws were, but it was a compelling factor in the overall American violent crime reduction.

But three-strike laws gather a lot of repeat felons, and not necessarily violent ones. Relying on the same Bureau of Justice Statistics reports mentioned previously, we see that an estimated 68 percent of released prisoners were arrested in the first three years after release, 79 percent within six years, and 83 percent within nine years. But of these recidivists, only 11 percent had previously been incarcerated for violent crimes and rearrested for the same degree of infraction in the first year after getting out of the slammer. However, roughly 7–10 percent of paroled prisoners previously incarcerated for property, drug, and public order crimes were arrested for acts of violence. One of the interesting side effects of three-strike laws is that they scoop up some number of people who will eventually become violent predators, and thus more likely to use a gun. However, we have no clarity into how many violent offenders in the making this might be.

Before we get back to the core topic of public carry, it is worth noting that another flavor of "get tough" laws were enacted in a few states, and these expressly addressed gun crimes. There are variations, but around 1993—that insanely violent year—California passed a law commonly called *10-20-Life*. Simply stated, if you use a gun in a crime, you get ten years in the pokey. Fire the gun during a crime, and it goes up to twenty years. Wound or kill someone and you might never get out.

Problematically, California also passed a three-strikes law around the same time. Thus, separating which affected violence is a bit of a fool's errand. But whereas many three-strike prisoners are not violent repeat offenders, and those doing hard time under a *10-20-Life* sentencing are, we can rationally assume that the latter was a significant factor in terms of homicide rates.

And it may well have been. In the year that *10-20-Life* was passed, California's homicide rate was a full 40 percent above the national average. Within a decade, California's rate fell to the national average, and this was during a period when the national homicide rate was dropping as well. California is not unique in having large metropolitan areas, but it has a few that also have very large and robust street gang populations. Los Angeles, of course, tops major metro areas in 1993 homicides with an approximate rate of thirty-one homicides per hundred thousand people, or more than triple the national average. Fresno follows at twenty-three, then San Francisco at eighteen. But then smaller cities chime in. Oakland was at forty-one, Long Beach at twenty-nine, Santa Anna at twenty-seven, and the capital Sacramento at twenty-two.

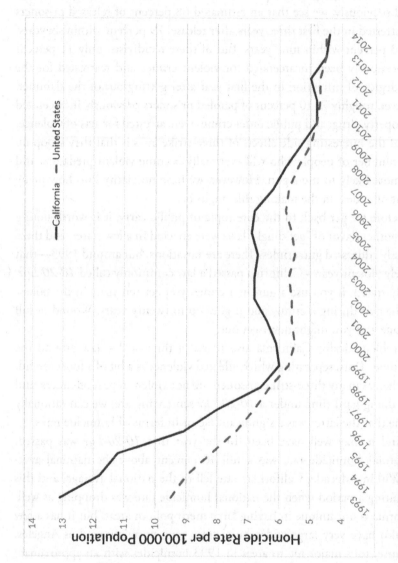

Homicide Rate per 100,000 Population

FBI Uniform Crime Reporting

— California   — United States

The point is that we cannot pin 100 percent of the crime drop across the nation on public carry. There was a broad and often deep reaction to the spiraling crime rate across the country. "Get tough" laws had an impact, and public carry also likely had an impact. At the very least, we can conclude that public carry did not increase violent crime because we can see how those with licenses to carry behave.

When a state switches from a regime of disallowing people to publicly carry (aside, of course, from the criminal class that is carrying regardless of the law) to a system of permitted or no-permit-required carry, a natural question is whether these newly anointed "pistol packers" are causing harm. If you lived in Florida, as I did, during the campaigning for and against enacting a "shall-issue" system for public carry, you would have heard the hypothesis repeatedly stated that public carry would lead to mass and spontaneous gun violence. Certain groups even created flyers to hand out at airports and near Walt Disney World to warn tourists about the soon-to-be-enacted law.

We already explored the broad numbers, seeing if people carrying in public created an aggregate rise or fall in violent crimes. But there is a more specific way of looking at this question. Some states report on the number of CCW permits that are revoked, and they occasionally provide the statistics for why the revocation occurred. Yet other states keep painstakingly detailed records of the crimes committed by CCW holders and the population at large.

Texas was the most paranoid of all 1990s-era states that enacted "shall-issue" public carry, which went against the state's public image and branding. From their start in 1996, Texas produced annual reports on what crimes CCW licensees are convicted. These crimes range from child neglect to terrorist threats and a lot of borderline comical offenses such as "tampering with a consumer product." You can grab all the annual reports from the Texas Department of Public Safety website. It does not much matter if you fetch an edition from the year after "shall-issue" public carry came into effect (1996) or the most recent (2018). One thing is immediately visible on their laundry list of 127 offenses: namely, that there are a lot of zeros in the report.

Texas had nearly 1.4 million active CCWs in 2018. Of that population, there were 163 criminal convictions of people with CCWs. Of all convictions in Texas for 2018, this distilled less than 0.4 percent of all crimes being committed by CCW holders. With nearly fourteen million people above the age of twenty-one and thus eligible for a CCW (ignoring the fraction ineligible due to felony convictions and such), nearly 10 percent of the Texas adult population had a CCW. Rearranging all this messy data, we see that at least for Texas:

- 10 percent of the population carries, or can because they have a permit
- 0.4 percent of crimes that can get your CCW canceled are committed by them

It is worth noting that many crimes that make revoking your Texas CCW permit are not violent crimes. In terms of frequency of offenses compared to the general population (and ignoring a single "one-off" offense for carrying while a permit had been suspended) the most statistically frequent crime compared to the general population was that of improper relationships between educators and students. When it comes to the most frequent crime committed by Texas CCW licensees, assaults resulting in bodily injury of a family member topped the list, but CCW holders constituted 0.2 percent of such crimes while being 10 percent of the adult population.

People should be inquisitively cynical. It may be that this broad set of felonies, violent and not in Texas, may not be representative of violence committed by CCW licensees outside of Texas, a point worth exploring.

When we reduce the list of Texas crimes the public safety department lists to violent crimes, we have just under seventy remaining. I purposely used a broad definition of "violent crime" and let in such offenses as "aggravated sexual assault of elderly or disabled person" and "unlawful restraint of a minor." I'll note in passing that no CCW licensees committed either of those crimes in Texas in 2018, and indeed committed exactly zero of forty-six other offenses on the violent crime list. Of all violent crimes in Texas, CCW holders averaged a rather tiny 0.6 percent of all convictions for a total of 148 crimes. And it is certainly worth documenting that Texas is not the saintliest state in America. In 2018, the Texas violent crime rate was 8 percent higher than the national average, though lower than nearby Oklahoma, Louisiana, and Arkansas. In other words, Texas is a meaner state than most others, but their CCW holders are less mean that the Texas population at large.

The other question that the inquisitive and cynical person might and should ask is if Texas is some sort of national outlier. I reported on Texas first simply because they have the most consistent and comprehensive data reporting available. It is positively obsessive/compulsive in nature and a welcome relief for researchers accustomed to raking through mountains of discombobulated data to assemble statistically reliable knowledge.

One such outfit that does this with regularity is the Crime Prevention Research Center. They routinely produce a report on public carry and annually update estimates of the total number of CCW licensees based on state-by-state reporting. They also summarize what can be known about the rate at which public carry licenses are revoked, which is an imperfect assessment of whether CCW licensees are troublemakers or not. In all states, a permit to carry can be taken away for committing a crime, and often the permit-pulling crime can be petty.

As wonderful as the Center's reporting is, there are two significant limitations. First, only sixteen states publicly report CCW revocation stats. Thankfully, many of the big states are on the list—Florida, Maryland, Washington, etc. So, despite only having sixteen of thirty-six states that issue permits (the other legal-carry states not requiring a license) as of the end of 2018, we have a clear enough view into how often CCW holders run afoul of the law.

The second limitation of this list is that it is not entirely clean. In some states, a CCW license can be revoked for merely moving within the state and not reporting the relocation to the licensing authority. Other states report a license as "revoked" if you move out of the state. A few moving violations can get your ticket yanked elsewhere, as can carrying while not having your permit on you. So, the number of "real crime" related concealed carry permit revocations in the Center's report are, if anything, over-stated. But this does not hamper the cynically inquisitive as this represents the absolute worst-case scenario.

On average, only 0.17 percent of public carry permits get revoked, which is roughly analogous with the 0.2 percent rate of Texas criminal convictions. Maryland had the highest revocation rate of 0.66 percent, and Maryland is considered a "may-issue" state, and thus pretty stingy in giving out public carry licenses, which would make even a small number of CCW revocations statistically large. On the low end, Texas took licenses from a tiny 0.01 percent of holder, beating out Oklahoma (0.02 percent) Washington State (0.04 percent), and Florida (0.07 percent).

Skipping permits altogether

I have to admit, when states started scrapping their public carry laws, I had mixed thoughts. Given how long I had been studying guns, control, and policy, this indecision was an odd sensation.

"No-permit" carry is both a new and an ancient phenomenon. As I noted before, Vermont never got interested in regulating the public carry of guns among people lacking criminal records and stuck to its position for nearly 230 years now. Much later, Alaska became the first state that had previously enacted "shall-issue" public carry (1994) and then dumped the permit system entirely (2003). This gambit caught the attention of Arizona, Arkansas, Kansas, Maine, and Wyoming, who did the same (2010, 2013, 2015, 2015, and 2011, respectively). Other states have done so even more recently (Idaho in 2016, Mississippi in 2016, Missouri in 2017, North Dakota in 2017, Oklahoma in 2019, South Dakota in 2019, and West Virginia in 2016).

There are more than a few difficulties in testing whether no-permit public carry affects crime or your chances of getting shot. Some of the limitations and complications include:

- Most "no-permit" states have not had this as law long enough to have a sufficient number of years of post-passage crime data to evaluate.

- Two of the six states that have had it long enough for testing also have very sparse populations, which makes any change in the raw *number* of crimes appear to be an outsized change in the *rate* of crimes.

- The six states are very different, from frozen Alaska (population density 1.3 people per square mile) to sun baked Arizona (population density 60.1).

- At the time of this analysis, crime data was only available through 2018, meaning two of the six states could only reveal three years of post-enactment info, and that is too short a period for robust trend analysis.

The wholesale effect of these issues is that it is too early to draw any *conclusions*. For now, we can at least expose some initial observations. Using a five year span before enactment, a three year span after enactment (given the hard-stop we face with 2018 being the last available year for crime data), looking only at the states that are not thinly populated, and comparing crime trends against the national average for the same years, all of the "no-permit" states followed national trends in crime, but often in exaggerated scales. Murders had a mild upward trend. Robberies still declined, but not as fast as before, while the nation as a whole was steady.

But aggravated assaults . . . there was a surprise. The hypothesis is that the utter uncertainty of if someone is armed or not in public might make hotheaded people less likely to throw a punch. Both the nation and the no-permit carry states got worse in terms of assaults, but the no-permit states (known to some as "free to carry" states) had a trend rate change—change in the slope-of-line numbers—that was nearly three times that of the country. Arkansas and Kansas had the largest swings, though it was Arizona and Kansas that had the biggest changes when compared to the nation as a whole.

Don't be tempted to read much into this. There is a small number of states, a short timeline for trend analysis, and a lot more states and data to review in the coming years.

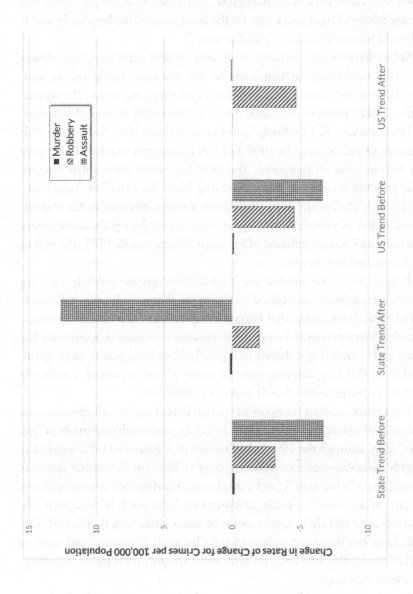

FBI Uniform Crime Reporting, changes in slope-of-line crime rates for high density no-permit states, five years before and three years after enactment of no-permit laws and three years after

Public non-carry

As I'm writing this, the news of a mass public shooting in a bar last night is on my computer monitor. Some people in a bar got into an argument, two fellows left, came back with handguns, and killed four people. Both had pending felony charges and a sign on the front door of the bar clearly said it disallowed weapons inside, a "gun-free zone."

When states began enacting "shall-issue" public carry laws, they almost universally prohibited carrying guns in schools, bars, sports arenas, and, depending on the state, college campuses and shopping malls. The reasons for the "place" restrictions varied, but it is interesting to note that federal legislation making K-12 schools "gun-free zones" was launched in step with expansion of public carry. In 1990 and 1994, Congress enacted laws to prohibit having guns on campuses. This may have been some small reaction to the growing number of states switching from "no carry" or "may-issue" doctrines to "shall-issue" laws. But it was more a reaction to the continued escalation of violent crime, and the start of student-perpetrator school shootings, which were unheard of in North America until 1975 (the first of which occurred in Canada).

Regardless of the motivation, prohibitions against publicly carrying guns in certain places flourished to the point that one disgruntled person created a Facebook meme that begged the question, "Why bother getting a concealed carry permit if I can't carry anywhere?" Given that America has swiftly and resoundingly shifted to a greatly liberalized public carry norm, all while prohibiting carrying guns in many places, a natural question is whether "gun-free zones" (GFZ) make any difference.

On a macro scale, it is impossible to tell. Foremost, we had simultaneous expansion of public carry, enactment of GFZs, and implementation of "get tough" laws, through the 1990s. Add to that that state-level GFZ legislation is highly variable—one state allowing carry in location X, another state not allowing carry in location X, and a third state allowing each county to allow/ban carry in location X. Finding statistical clarity is unlikely to happen. We could calculate and chart relative ratios between states with significantly different laws, but those comparisons would be small in number and weak in conclusiveness. But two areas do offer some insight; mass public shootings and school shootings.

I won't repeat much from the separate chapter on mass public shootings, aside from saying that GFZs appear to have done nothing to prevent these horrifying events, with 88 percent of mass shootings occurring in GFZs. But this observation has to be tempered by the reality that mass shooters are unaffected by laws in general, intent instead on completing their "missions." So said, their choice of location is likely guided primarily by vengeance (schools, workplaces, etc.), ideology (gay nightclubs), or opportunity (movie theaters and concerts).

K-12 schools, on the other hand, provide some better insight. Foremost, the various federal and state legislations made carrying a gun on a K-12 campus *verboten* unless you were a cop, including the campus-specific variety called "school resource officers." The hypothesis behind the federal and state "gun free school" legislation was that by prohibiting guns on campuses, the number of school shootings and the number of students killed would fall. It is highly unlikely that any parent with a CCW would accidentally shoot a kid while picking their own child up from school. It was a blanket prohibition, applying not just to CCW licensees but to the public at large, including students, gang members, teachers . . . everyone.

However, banning guns from campuses did not abate school shootings. Instead, they escalated. In the thirty years since gun-free school legislation launched, the student population—as a percent of the total population—has been declining, but the rate of both the frequency of, and fatalities from, school shootings has been rising. That this mirrors the situation we see for mass public shootings is of concerning interest. Other factors appear to be driving the interest in killing a bunch of people (mass public shootings), killing your classmates (school shootings), and the intersection of the two.

Some people suggest "gun-free zones" attract shooters. I don't think we can say this. Very few instances of surviving mass shooters, or those who left manifestos, said they specifically sought-out "gun-free zones." We might safely assume that some perpetrators chose a desired location for a shooting—their school, their office, etc.—and were comforted knowing they were not going to encounter return fire from armed citizens (e.g., a lack of a deterrence effect). This may be a natural filter, one where individuals who *want* to commit a shooting (mass, school, or otherwise) might hesitate if the location was *not* a "gun-free zone," and thus their aborted killing spree was not added to the list of mass shootings. Location avoidance and purposeful selection are different criteria, though they may have the same net effect.

Past this broad, national effect in school shootings, we see various states prohibiting people from publicly carrying firearms in other locations. Depending on the state, you might not be allowed to carry in a church, a bar, a restaurant, a state park, or on a college campus. These more microscopic topics are beyond the scope of this book or the patience of the average voter. When the Gun Facts project explored these laws in 2014, we did not

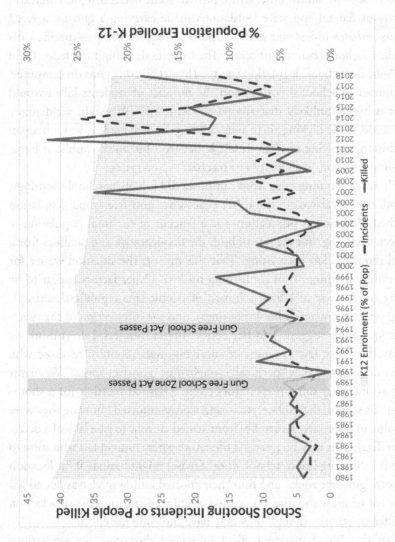

List of school shootings, Wikipedia; Student population, National Center for Education Statistics

find them lowering state-wide violent crime, which you would expect since these locations involve progressively smaller parts of the population and thus any effect would be a mere portion of the overall picture. That being said, we did find that states allowing public carry in college campuses fared better overall on murder and robbery. States where you could carry in church had lower firearm homicides rates. And oddly, states where one could carry in bars and restaurants had lower rates of rape. But in all this, we have to accept that the overall rate of people carrying concealed is a precursor to specific places to carry, and thus these little observations are to be taken with a full packet of salt.

Before moving on, though, let's explore this idea that it is a good idea to allow people to carry guns in bars. Some states are now permitting this, and the lack of bloodshed in those states, especially when compared to the story that opened this section—the one about the two killers who came back to a "gun-free zone" bar and killed four patrons—is of interest.

Booze makes for irresponsible behavior. Having spent a bit of my time in places ranging from dive bars to high-end cocktail lounges in five-star hotels, I can at least attest that alcohol does lower the average person's perception of what is a dumb thing to do. Hooch especially seems to add people onto the short list of acceptable sexual partners, with many dismaying mornings following.

The prohibition of guns in places that serve alcohol led to some rather odd situations. In most states enacting "guns-and-booze" restrictions, it was illegal to be in a bar with your concealed weapon (regardless of whether you were drinking or not) but it was legal to be in a restaurant that served cocktails. This led to situations where people dining out could not pee if they had to walk through the restaurant's bar to get to the restrooms. I have met one fellow who once had to leave the building, lock his gun in his car, hit the porcelain, go back to his car, retrieve his gun, and then order dessert. Interestingly, he was also a teetotaler.

Comical unintended consequences aside, some states began to wonder if this was really necessary. As we noted earlier, CCW licensees commit very few crimes. They also go through a bit of paperwork, often some pricey training, buy expensive holsters and car gun safes, and more. In short, state legislators began wondering if keeping your licensed-to-carry plumber from having a cold one with the boys before heading home after work was really problematic. Would the average armed bar patron cause problems, or even perhaps stop them (such as the news story that opened this section)?

Using our original study from 2014, we see a mildly negative correlation for all manner of violent crime (murder, robbery, assaults, and firearm homicides) in states where carrying guns in bars is allowed—except for rape, which went down by an even larger margin. By "negative correlation" I mean that when carrying in booze slinging establishments was allowed, crime rates went down. Between 16–21 percent of non-rape violent crimes were disassociated (negatively correlated) with carrying in bars, and rapes were negatively associated at a 46 percent rate. Keep in mind that this was for "bars and restaurants" since many states amalgamate the two in legislation, but the fundamental fact that violence tends to be lower in states where carrying guns into such businesses goes against the common legislative assumption that it is dumb.

The Wild West appears to have been tamed.

By the numbers: public carry

18,600,000	Americans with concealed carry permits
24,400,000	Adults living in states where no permit is required to carry
420%	Increase in the number of states allowing public carry since 1988

CHAPTER 6

Crime and Guns

Ten thousand people were murdered with guns last year.

My gun didn't kill anyone.

Fifty-four percent of US counties had no murders at all, much less gun murders.

THE FACT THAT ALL OF the above statements are true shows why the public's perception of the daily danger of guns is often out of whack. Indeed, I became involved with criminology and gun issues because what I saw on the nightly TV news was very different that what was happening in my city. The first fatal shooting I experienced in my hometown didn't occur until I was eighteen years old, and even then it was a cop who had to shoot a deranged, drug addled, knife-wielding woman.

When one dives into the deep muck of violent crimes and how they are committed, their perspective gets nearly as warped as their conversational talking point. On that latter element, if you do ever engage a working criminologist on his field of study, you will be instantly flabbergasted and a tad bit disquieted by how calmly they discuss murder, rape, beatings, assaults, elder abuse, pedophilia, and the entire spectrum of inhuman debasement, all while smiling that smile academics wear when gleefully imparting their knowledge to others. This explains why so few criminologists are invited to dinner parties—they make the other guests nauseous.

The critical take-aways

- Guns are the primary tool for homicides, and a minority tool for all other violent crime
- Repeat violent offenders (especially street gang members) make up a disproportionate number of homicides
- Homicides rates rise with city-wide population counts, but not with population density

The five bad actors

There are good people and bad. The former group we don't much care about. From a purely statistical standpoint, most people who own guns don't cause trouble at all, much less trouble with guns. As we noted in the chapter on Gun Availability, somewhere around fifty-one million American households have one or more guns, making them available to over a hundred million people. Yet there are not a hundred million shootings in a year. This means that subsegments of the population are responsible for gun violence.

There are five primary types of bad actors when it comes to guns. Accepting that each group has subgroups, this short classification list is useful in understanding the role guns play in violence, the motivations of those who misuse guns, how and why they acquire them, and what might be done to prevent future gun violence. The five groups are:

CRIMINALS: These are "career" thugs, mainly soloists, for who committing crime is a means of gain. This includes liquor store robbers, muggers, etc.

GANGS: Though active in crime for profit, gang members have defined group cultures (unlike the soloist criminal) that endorse and promote violence for non-profit purposes (e.g., disrespect, territorial boundaries, etc.).

TERRORISTS: People who seek to make political or societal change through fear.

LUNATICS: People with severe mental impairments that cause them to commit acts of violence due to an incomplete capacity for moral judgement. (As a clarification for this terminology, when the Gun Facts project stated codifying who shouldn't have guns, we set the standard in public discussion with criminals, lunatics, terrorists, and hotheads. It is a Gun Facts meme, part of our branding, and now part of the public dialogue. It may sound harsh to some ears, but given how vested we are in the term, I want to keep it in the nomenclature and thus we have continued to use it both here and for the Gun Facts project.)

HOTHEADS: People with anger control issues who, given the right set of circumstances, will misuse a gun.

What is instantly apparent is that these are very dissimilar people; all bad actors, but with distinctly different end goals. They also have distinctive modes for obtaining guns. For example, criminals and gang members are quite adroit at navigating underground sources and acquiring firearms "off the radar." Terrorists and hotheads most often acquire their guns legally. Lunatics—at least when we look into mass public shooting incidents—show a mixed sourcing between legal gun buys and stealing guns, typically from family members.

As we drill down through gun crimes, keep the five actors in mind as it helps inform you as to where the bulk of gunplay derives. Using gun trace data from the Bureau of Alcohol, Tobacco and Firearms (BATF) for 2017, and attempting to add this Five Bad Actor schema to their data, and assuming that most or all of the illegal possession of firearms entries were tied to the criminal classes (including gang members) we see upwards of 83 percent of traced crime guns being used for criminal *intent*.

From this same data we see that hotheads, who typically lack premeditated *intent* for their actions, at worst rack up 17 percent of gun homicides. America is relatively terrorist-activity free, so they only commit a fraction of a percentage of gun deaths. Since mental health–driven misuse of guns is not commonly classified in gun trace records, our only consistent indicator are mass public shootings, which would undercount the actual number of cases, though in 2017, three of the four mass public shooters had prior signs of mental health disorders.

The big perspective

As horrifying as the 14,123 murders in 2018 are, they represent only 11 percent as many rapes, 5 percent as many robberies, and 2 percent of assaults. What murders make up for in permeance of outcomes, they lack in relative frequency.

But when it comes to guns, they are the number one tool of choice for people aiming (pun not intended) to kill. This is not to dismiss the 1,515 knife homicides, 672 people beaten to death, or the 442 people bludgeoned with everything from hammers to golf clubs. But, 73 percent of American murders do come from flying bullets.

Compared to the rest of the world, or at least those that score high on socioeconomic indexes, America is a murderous place. In terms of total homicides, regardless of how Yanks go about it, they committed about 4.7 homicides for every hundred thousand people, and 3.4 gun homicides. This compares unfavorably to the average homicide rate of 1.3 for the top thirty-five non-US countries on the socioeconomic index.

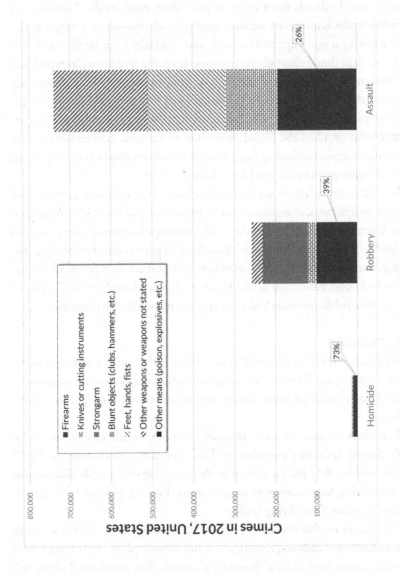

Firearms as a percentage of each crime category—FBI, Crime in the United States, 2017

Of course, compared to other highly developed countries, the United States has about six times as many street gang members per capita,[1] which is where guns and murders start to get sickeningly interesting, and where we begin to see the center of the storm.

These factors cause a question to become lodged in our collective prefrontal lobes, namely, "Are firearm homicides tied specifically to guns or to other factors?" This has been a topic deeply analyzed by criminologists and sociologists for decades. Even head shrinkers get in on the game. Though we covered this a bit in the chapter on Gun Availability, it is time to look at this from other angles.

First, as you can guess from the general numbers, there is a tight covariance between total homicides and gun homicides on a state-by-state basis. What is worth noting is that the firearm homicide rate is *disassociated* with the gun ownership rate in each state (R^2 of 0.01 where zero is no covariance and one is complete covariance). In other words, the per capita number of guns in any state has no bearing on the per capita number of gun murders.

But firearm ownership rates may have a bearing on what weapons are used in crimes other than murder. For example, there is no covariance between firearm ownership rates and robberies committed with firearms (and keep in mind robberies include events like ATM muggings and liquor store hold-ups) though the rate of robberies falls as gun ownership rates rise (the hypothesis being that robbery become a less attractive career choice when victims are more likely to open fire). There is a significant uptick in the use of knives and pure muscle ("strongarm") for robberies (an R^2 of 0.25 and 0.29 for knives and strongarm robberies, with those rates rising as the rate of gun ownership falls). The theory here, of course, is that in less armed states, criminals either don't have to rely on guns to commit their crimes, or, knowing that their victims are unarmed, chose to use simpler, more direct means. Robbing without a gun also eliminates the problem of the local district attorney adding gun charges for the judge to consider when a thug's trial comes up on the docket.

Interestingly, the same cannot be said for assaults. Across the board, the type of weapon used in an aggravated assault has a meager covariance between 0.01 and 0.05, which basically means there is no covariance at all. Whereas the crime of robbery tends to be premeditated, and thus a concern over the victim being armed is a forethought, when it comes to losing your cool and wanting to assault someone, the perpetrator simply uses whatever weapon is at hand, even if it is just their hands.

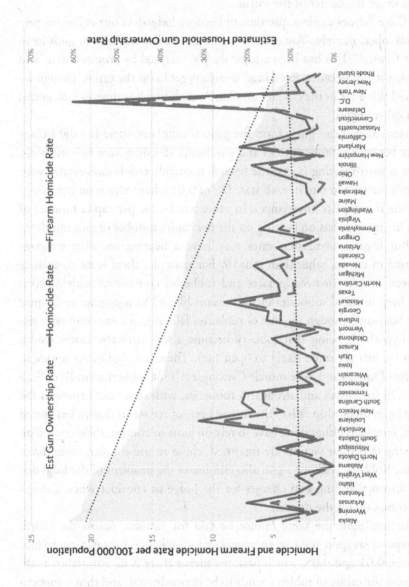

Homicide data, FBI Crime in the United States 2018; Gun ownership rate, average of Behavioral Risk Factor Surveillance System (BRFSS) and YouGov survey

Let's summarize this unaligned set of realities:

MURDER: If you are in the killing business, you use a gun (and if you are in a street gang, you typically have one with you).

ROBBERY: You use other weapons if you live in a state with fewer guns, but even in states with guns, you are slightly less likely than elsewhere to use a gun.

ASSAULTS: This spontaneous crime relies on the weapon at hand.

Given all these nasty observations, a good place to dive deeper into crimes and guns is with homicides, since these events are permanent and where guns, as a percentage of the crime category, are most often used.

Who, where, why?

"Who is using guns to kill?" is an obvious question. If you are a typical suburban homeowner with a revolver in your nightstand, odds are you have not committed a homicide or ever will. If, on the other hand, you are a member in good standing of the Chicago branch of the Latin Kings street gang, odds are you have iced one or more people, possibly since breakfast. Knowing the who, where, and why of firearm homicides quickly deepens our understanding of the topic.

After we get a little sidetracked, that is.

What we are worried about is how *likely* it is a person might be to get shot on purpose. The basic metric is the homicide *rate*, which is commonly expressed as the number of murders per hundred thousand people in a given region. The problem is not all given regions are the same. For example, the top two metropolitan statistical areas (MSAs) for homicides have populations of 90,789 and 35,185 people, and these regions have population densities (the number of people per square mile) of 847 and 1,063 respectively. Contrast this with the locale having the third highest homicide *rate*—it has 2,112,005 people, a population density of 10,690, and it is in a US territory offshore, not a state or on the mainland. Because of this, you have to dig one layer deeper to avoid arriving at an invalid conclusion.

It is easy enough to contain our exploration to US states, but the population and population density metrics could throw off a less detailed analysis. Simply put, when there are few people around, a small *number* of homicides creates a large *rate* of homicides (if your town has five hundred people and had one murder last year, then your murder rate is an off-the-charts two hundred per hundred thousand population statistical base, or about thirty-seven times the national average). Those first two entries mentioned above—Pine Bluff, Arkansas and Fairbanks, Alaska, with populations of 90,789 and 35,185—had homicide rates of twenty-eight and thirty murders per every hundred thousand people, and neither location had that many people at all. Detroit, Michigan has a homicide rate that is nearly half that of the two thinly populated MSAs but has a population at least nineteen times bigger. This is why Pine Bluffs had twenty-seven murders and the Detroit MSA had 339.

To make matters a little more complicated, a "metropolitan statistical area" is not always what it seems. For example, the FBI reports homicide stats for the "Atlanta-Sandy Springs-Roswell, Georgia" MSA. In that rather broad swath of land, the population density is 624 people in every square mile. But anyone who has driven on I-75 or I-85 during rush hour feels the intense compression of the city of Atlanta's 3,574 people per square mile.

The best way to look at this is in some major chunks. By breaking up metropolitan regions, as reported by the FBI, into quintiles (five clusters) based on homicide rates, and looking at both the average population and the average population density, we see that the population density does not track with homicide rates (the number of murders per capita) but does, up to a point, track with overall population. This makes intuitive sense given that the more people a criminal or hothead encounters on a daily basis, the more likely it is they will pull a trigger.

But even this obscures details. Since a metropolitan statistical area can, and often does, include core cities, neighboring suburbs and largely vacant county lands, we don't see where the gun violence accumulates. For example, the MSA that includes Chicago (a town largely associated with crime, even outside of City Hall) is named "Chicago-Joliet-Naperville, IL-IN-WI Metro Area." Naperville is about an hour outside of town and Joliet is about the same. You would have to spend forty minutes driving interstate highways to travel from the farm-land adjacent Joliet (population 148,000) to Chicago (population 2,700,000) and reach the notorious Chicago South Side, where a lot of gun play ensues.

Spending time with MSAs instead of actual cities and towns is a little necessary and leads to my only rant in this book.

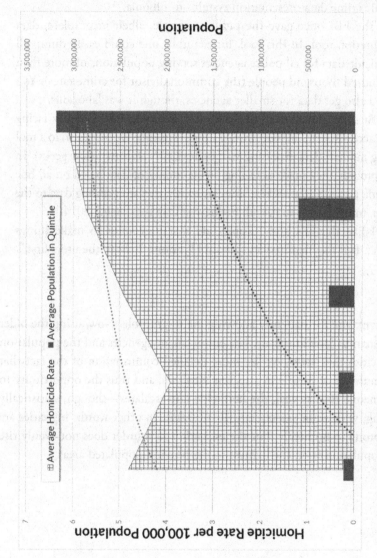

FBI, Crime in the United States, 2017 (the 2018 tables were not linked at the FBI web site at the time this book was compiled)

THE SORRY STATE OF FBI DATA AVAILABILITY

My former career as an IT guru, mainframe, database administrator, and all-around data geek leads me to ask if the FBI outsourced their public crime data presentation systems to Elbonia.

The FBI once gave the public a simple, albeit incomplete, data exploration tool. In this tool, for example, one could easily dump all homicide data for all police agencies serving populations of more than a hundred thousand people (the common divisor for crime rates). You could also get data for smaller agencies, though it was laborious.

At some point, the FBI decided to modernize the publicly facing data access system, moving from a simple but effective web form to a tool using modern data exporting standards (JSON, for my fellow geeks). In the process, they made accessing broad chunks of data based on ad hoc criteria virtually impossible. Simultaneously, they quit adding data to the older, more useable tool, with the newest data there being 2014.

I like the FBI and I appreciate that they want to make things newer. But they ignored an age-old IT axiom, "talk to the users first."

Thank you for patiently allowing me to grumble. Now, using the older FBI system to look at specific law enforcement agencies and the population of the cities they serve, we see more detailed confirmation of the fact that as the number of people in a region increases, and thus the opportunity to kill someone rises as well, the homicide rate escalates—though, statistically speaking, with weak association (R^2 of 0.04). In other words, big cities are more prone to homicide, but the escalation in murder does not evenly rise with population from the lightest to the heaviest populated areas.

	Percent of Murders	% of US Population
Top 20 by Population	39%	35%
Top 20 by Homicide Rate	13%	10%

SOURCE: FBI Uniform Crime Statistics 2014

One more way to explore this is to look at the top-side magnitude of the situation. When we sort the list of cities by population or the number of homicides, we see that the largest of the cities have a murder rate higher than the national average, and closely aligned to the same percentage shift for cities with high homicide rates. Graphically, the population-driven nature of murder manifests itself as you would expect, with the rate of homicides rising with city-by-city population counts.

A tiny recap is in order at this juncture. We see that gun crime is linked more to homicides than other violent crimes. It is also linked to big cities. We also see big cities have almost 42 percent of the nation's gang members, with smaller cities holding another 27 percent. This means that metropolitan areas have nearly 70 percent of the street gang problem.[2] So, we definitely know the "where" in our set of crime-and-gun questions. You are likely already guessing about the "who," which will lead us toward the "why."

One missing info-nugget is the repeat frequency of gun crimes. In other words, if a mugger put a gun in your back at the ATM yesterday, how many other times did he do this in the course of the year? For decades cops and criminologists have noted that most crime is repeat crime—that once someone commits a crime, especially if they get away with it, they do it again . . . and again . . . and again. You likely recall my mentioning that in one metropolitan city a homicide suspect was also the lead suspect in two *or more* other homicides. Let's assume, just for a moment, that this holds true for all cities and towns (this is not statistically proven, but it at least gives us something to ponder). If so, the 10,265 firearm homicides in 2018 could have been committed by as few as 3,400 individuals. If we are focused on inner-city street gangs, most of these repeat killers are well-known to the police, and this has not been unnoticed by criminologists and a few forward-thinking political leaders. Many modern gang intervention

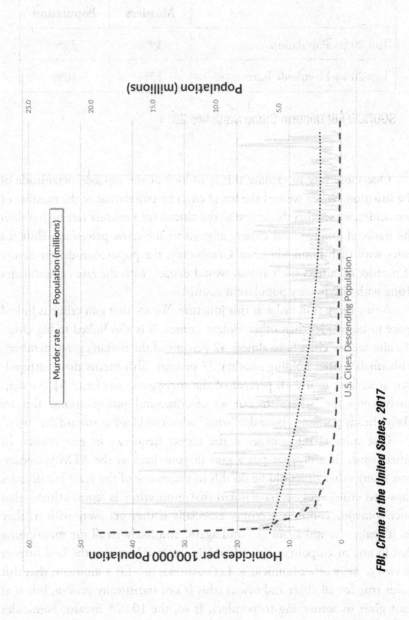

FBI, *Crime in the United States, 2017*

programs involve the police and courts being keenly focused on a handful of bad boys with the intent of reducing both net repeat violence by these criminals, as well as group cultural norms about violence (i.e., if you take down a gang member known for repeat homicides, other gang members get the message).

Let's follow this lead to see how many previously violent people (including murderers) are caught and jailed for even more violent crimes. About 64 percent of violent offenders released from jail are rearrested within a year and a half. Of those who were incarcerated for violent crimes, 11 percent were arrested again for another violent crime in the first year after release. About 2 percent of all recidivism arrests were for homicides, and in the most recent year, 1.4 percent of all violent crimes were murders.[3] And though confined to California juvenile offenders, one tally[4] concluded that someone who had killed before was 1,467 percent more likely to be currently adjudicated for another homicide, which is really large when compared to prior–current recidivism status for robbery (294 percent) or aggravated assault (200 percent).

But these are the people who get caught. Some criminals manage to commit repeat crimes and never encounter a cop or a judge. Others get killed in the rough streets where they reside before the authorities catch up with them. On the low end of the range, using the 11 percent violence recidivism rate, there can be as few as 1,500 people conducting most of the big city kills, and on the high end, using our three-for-one suspect rate, it is 3,400. Of course, the actual number is higher, but we have evidence from multiple vectors that repeat offenders in cities may be small in number but large in total lifetime mayhem, including murders and gun murders.

Continuing the triangulation, we know that homicides cluster in cities and among repeat offenders. Repeat offenders fall into three basic categories—gang members, street criminals, and habitual thugs. This last group is the least trackable as they may display a range of violent behaviors, from wife beating to barroom brawling. Their violence is also not a natural byproduct of their daily activity, whereas "violence as a tool" is the common thread for muggers and gangbangers alike.

Gangs are a bit more interesting because of the subcultures they enforce. Your run-of-the-mill liquor store stick-up artist is a soloist and uses the mere threat of violence, sometimes at gun point, primarily for his financial gain. Street gang members commit violence as part of a lifestyle, a creed, a club. This is reflected in their recidivism rates. In terms of the violent crime recidivism rates for gang members versus non-gang members, gangstas go back to jail anywhere from about twice[5] to as often as eleven times more often[6] (and these are very different studies of very different populations using very different approaches). Street gangs, which are much more prevalent in cities as opposed to suburbs (where you may find an occasional convenience store hold-up) and rural areas, are also repeat customers in courts and prisons on violent crime charges.

This is not to let robbers get away with it, though. When it comes to the sheer number of people, cities with bigger populations have a better correlation for robbery than with murder. However, guns are used less often for robberies (39 percent of the time) than they are for homicides (73 percent), and typically without the trigger being pulled (e.g., "Give me the money and nobody gets hurt"). More robberies but fewer guns used in them, nationally speaking. What this means, in a somewhat indirect way, is that gang-centric gun homicides spike because (a) they are the tool of choice for murder ,(b) the gang members are in effect career criminals who repeat their acts over and over again, and (c) murder is a perfectly legitimate activity between gangs.

Recapping once again: The leading clusters for gun violence are cities and street gangs, with an assist from robbery specialists in the same towns. Which means we should revisit one of the true statements made at the very beginning of this chapter, namely, "54 percent of US counties had no murders at all, much less gun murders."

The FBI gathers crime data down to township levels, and if you have the time and patience, you can acquire, reformat, cross-load, and analyze crime data down to the county level. There are over three thousand counties, sixty-four parishes, nineteen boroughs, ten census areas, and forty-one independent cities in the United States. Some counties have confounding mixtures of cities, towns, and rural regions. Others are basically one big city (hello Los Angeles, San Francisco, and Duval!). Yet many counties are backwater stretches where livestock easily outnumbers humans by an order of magnitude.

We take the "54 percent of counties had no murders" with a bit-o-wisdom, namely that some counties have few opportunities to commit homicide. What is unsaid in that simple soundbite is that even in counties where homicides do occur, the number of homicides are low and so is the population, which results in high homicide *rates*. This creates some misleading "homicide heat maps" where much of the rural Southeastern United States looks bloody, but actually isn't. For perspective's sake, in the year 2014, Los Angeles County topped the charts with 526 murders, but San Diego—with its unforgivably nice weather—had only seventy-four homicides. San Diego has 31 percent of L.A. County's population but only 14 percent of the killings. Yet both cities operate under the same California gun laws.

To make this a bit more vivid, here are all the counties in America coded by their percentage of murders nationwide. The hot spots include the typical suspects—L.A., Chicago, Detroit, Houston, Philadelphia, Miami, and Baltimore by themselves accounted for nearly 17 percent of all homicides. All of them are known for street gang activity.

Criminal motivations

A thug is, by dictionary definition, "a cruel or vicious ruffian, robber, or murderer." That the word derives from Hindi ("thag," which literally means rogue, cheat) shows that America is not alone in enduring thuggery.

One amusing little tidbit of insight is that the primary reason criminals carry guns in public is for self-defense, be it from their victims or from other criminals. In one rather thorough, albeit older, survey of incarcerated felons,[7] almost 63 percent reported that self-defense was either a very or somewhat important criteria for being armed. Less than 51 percent said the gun was necessary for committing their intended crimes. This agrees with a number of studies of street gang members, where between 37–85 percent of gang members carry guns for protection.[8]

Herein, we see that guns for self-defense during criminal activities are generally more important than using guns to actually commit crimes. This is amplified in the older study where 72 percent of felons confided that they used a gun so that they wouldn't have to "hurt their victims." Stated a little less delicately, pointing a gun at someone kept the criminal from having to beat them up, cut them, or in some other way injure them. How nice.

The largely unanswerable question is: What is the ratio between using guns to commit a specific crime versus how often criminals use guns as an act of defense? Law-and-order types might scoff at the distinction since both are criminal uses of guns, but it does play into the difference between career criminals (e.g., robbers) and street gang members. But we can get a quick idea about this divide from some high-level numbers.

In 2001, the National Gang Threat Assessment, a product of the FBI, estimated that there were in excess of 1.4 million gang members roaming through cities and towns. With the National Gang Crime Research Center reporting[9] that at least 72 percent of gang members do carry guns in public (and we will assume that they did not bother to obtain a permit beforehand), we see in any given year that at least one million gang members are packing

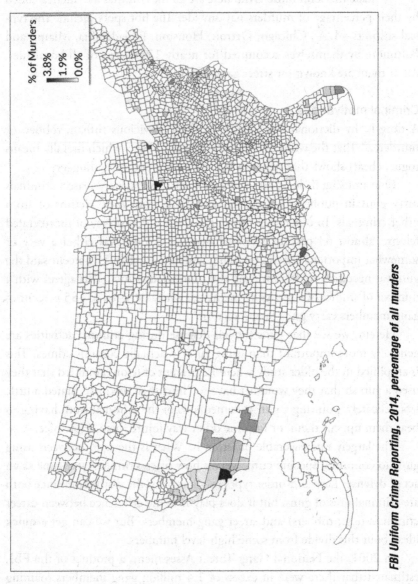

% of Murders
3.8%
1.9%
0.0%

FBI Uniform Crime Reporting, 2014, percentage of all murders

heat. Contrast this million-plus armed gang members with fewer than a hundred thousand firearm robberies in the most recent reporting year, an order of magnitude difference. Though there were not a million gang shootings last year, the sheer firepower in the hands of gang members and their willingness to actually shoot people over any social infraction, compared to 72 percent of robbery specialists who have stated they use to guns to keep from having to injure their victims shows how guns and violence among the criminal classes emerges. It also shows that in term of pure firepower and the will to use it, gangs rule.

Terrorists' motivations

The motivations of terrorists are nearly singular. The overarching goal of terror is to instill fear in the general population with the endgame of changing society. As such, there tends to be no small-scale terrorism—large numbers invoke terror, small numbers do not.

On this topic we get a bit off into the weeds because guns themselves are not necessarily of interest to terrorists. In fact, the two largest terrorist attacks in the United States—one foreign and one domestic, resulting in 2,977 and 168 deaths respectively—didn't involve guns at all (9/11 and the Oklahoma City bombing, in case you were ready to Google those numbers). This is not to say guns are not used to generate terror in the populace, but they are infrequent, and the comparative body count is low.

Mass public shootings (MPSs) are the most reliable indicator and one we have databases to reference. From 1982 through the fall of 2019, intentional terrorism accounted for maybe 3 percent of MPSs, and that is classifying some events like the Pulse Nightclub massacre as such (the perpetrator of this attack had a rather complex set of motivations, but he also claimed in a 9-1-1 call that his acts were in retaliation for US military operations). Even given this possibly high range inclusion, we see a total of sixty-eight people killed using guns in terrorist activities over a thirty-seven-year period, or less than two people per year when we average out the spikes. And that is spread across only three events, one of which occurred on military bases and the attacker had a long history of mental health and alcohol abuse problems.

We saw that among criminals, self-defense was a bigger issue than the actual commission of a crime. Among terrorists, many of whom intend to die during their attack, the motivation is inverted. The primary reason for acquiring a gun is to commit the crime of terror, and its use in self-defense would only be to either get away from the police or to take out as many cops as possible in the attempt.

Hothead motivations

Of all the five bad actors, hotheads are the toughest to assess. This is due to a number of disassociated factors.

First, hotheads do what they do typically without premeditation. Their crimes tend to be spontaneous. As such, their use of firearms is a matter of convenience—they happened to have a gun on them or nearby. Nearly 40 percent of robberies (largely planned events) involved a gun and only 26 percent of assaults (largely unplanned events) did. This gets even muddier because some unknowable number of firearm assaults may actually be gang related but are not classified as such due to non-specific circumstances.

Because of this, it might be inappropriate to assign any motivation to acquire or carry a gun for hothead crimes. Whereas 26 percent of assaults involved a gun, 25 percent involved body parts—hands, fists, and feet (and for the record, 17 percent involved knives and the rest involved other weapons or were not classified in reporting).

Lunatic motivations

"Lunatic" is unfortunate phrasing on my part. My acquaintances in the mental health field dislike the term and are quite vocal in their discontent toward me. For our more criminological purposes, however, it is a commonly popular term that the Guns Facts project has been using for years to encapsulate all manifestations of dissociative mental illness that might cause someone to acquire a gun and use it against another person (and we have already covered using a gun on one's self in chapter 2 which, of course, often has a mental health ignition).

When it comes to "why" they shoot and thus acquire guns, we can picture a rather long array of motivations paired with certain mental conditions. On one end, you have people who are "socially functional," but harbor great and perhaps psychotic resentments. According to one "review of literature" academic paper on mass and serial killers,[10] the most common mental impairment of the attacker is being on the autism spectrum and the second was being subjected to severe psychosocial stressors, such as bullying, ostracization, and other abuses. In these cases, revenge for maltreatment is a common motivation. The Parkland High School shooter is a case study—he is autistic and had encountered serious social stresses. The same can be said for the Sandy Hook assassin.

On the other end of the range are people who are rather detached from reality. There have been more than a few mass public shootings carried out by people who were overtly psychotic. The movie theater massacre in Aurora,

Colorado—where the attacker dressed as the Joker and shot-up the audience during a showing of *The Dark Knight*—is an example. At Virginia Tech, the shooter had recently been before a judge who was trying to determine if the future mass murderer needed to be involuntarily committed for his mental health issues. In these cases, there is no clear motivation because even the attacker is incapable of lucidly comprehending their actions.

Taken together, we see virtually no commonality for the motivations to acquire and misuse guns among the five bad actors, aside from some similarities between the gang and career criminal varietals. Even within those two groups, a distinction between their primary purposes for using a gun is different. One underexplored area is the mental health of street gang members. Tantalizing though a bit scattered across the field, we see some studies showing a high level of mental health conditions among gang members. One study[11] claims that 44 percent of the members had moderate psychopathy. Nearly all, by operational definition, are sociopaths.

Where in the hell are the crime guns coming from?

Studying how these five groups get their guns has caused many migraines among criminologists.

As I showed in the chapter on Gun Availability, the Bureau of Justice Statistics has some broad data about where crime guns come from. But high-level data doesn't tell us about the individual clusters, and as their motives and social status indicate, the path to acquiring guns is very different in each group as well. No single legislative approach covers all the bases, and because the modus operandi for getting guns for the first two groups—gang members and working criminals—avoids detection by leveraging underground markets, the bulk of the problem cannot be addressed with supply-side controls.

Though the Bureau of Justice Statistics reports are informative, they do not break down gun acquisition by these five groups. Instead, sundry criminologists have investigated individual groups of bad actors and a few have looked into how crime guns, later misused, were acquired. In each group, you will find a mixture of legal and illegal acquisition. Sadly, these studies tend to be highly localized (one city, one county) and thus are not nationally representative. But it is a start. Some generalizations drawn from these studies give us a little direction:

CRIMINALS AND GANGS: The rate of bad actors in these two groups that have prior felony convictions is quite high, hence the high recidivism rates. Prior felonies prohibit legally acquiring guns. With the National

Instant Criminal Background Check System (NICS) in place since the late 1990s, retail sources have largely dried-up except through "strawman" sales. Recalling the significant concentration of gun misuse in larger cities among gang members, this helps explain the minimum 40 percent of crime guns that come from underground sources, and these guns are both readily available and bypass all background checks. One study in Chicago[12] discovered that at least 6 percent of crime guns were obtained the same day the criminal went looking for firepower, and more than half got their guns in under two months. In short, most of the individuals in this group of bad actors simply access local networks where secondhand and occasionally stolen guns can be had.

TERRORISTS: So few terrorist acts occur that this is a bit misleading. With mass public shootings being our only solid indicator, and with only three terror related incidents occurring since 1982, the findings are uncompelling. That being said, those three events—Pulse Nightclub, San Bernardino Regional Center, and Chattanooga Military Centers—were all conducted using legally acquired guns. A fourth incident—the Fort Hood shooting, which the government declined to classify as a terrorist event but for which the shooter had been monitored for such possibilities—was also done with legally acquired guns.

LUNATICS: There are a number of barriers to knowing about people with mental illnesses and their guns. First is the definition of "mentally ill." Keep in mind it was not very long ago (1973) that the Diagnostic and Statistical Manual of Mental Disorders classified homosexuality as a mental illness. Second, sane people who legally acquired a gun can lose their minds later on, which complicates things, especially using mental health histories in background check records. Third, some people misusing a gun may be mentally ill and undiagnosed, thus misclassified. And the bar is pretty high, at least at the federal level, for disallowing someone to buy a gun for mental health reasons ("adjudicated as a mental defective" or "committed to any mental institution"). Even then, the data is not uniformly codified and academic surveys that calculate gun acquisition among the mentally ill show little. From the Gun Facts Mass Public Shooting database, the detailed data is so small as to be statistically unreliable. That being said, 80 percent of mass public shooters in our database that had shown signs of mental illness before they went on a rampage acquired their guns legally (most of the rest were stolen, typically from family members). However, there is no available tally of whether these individuals were sane at the time they bought their guns.

HOTHEADS: As with the mentally ill, it is nearly impossible to find unanimity about gun acquisition. A person who misuses a gun in a fit of anger might include a common street thug who is always armed (illegal acquisition), a person who finds their spouse cheating on them (could be legal or illegal), a road rage incident (either), or a bar argument (either). Simply put, the modes of hothead eruptions and the types of people who lose their cool and have access to a gun is so multifaceted as to defy serious analysis. If we look at mass public shootings at venues where a common element is the spontaneity of the shooting (bars, restaurant, workplaces) we again see roughly 80 percent legal acquisition rates on a very small set of data (sixteen instances). But this is meaningless. According to the FBI's roster of homicides listed by circumstances, events that had impulsive causes (romantic triangles, brawls, arguments) accounted for 51 percent of those committed with firearms (and 62 percent of all homicides regardless of weapon type). With 4,761 such events in 2017, with so many associated with other bad behaviors (narcotics and alcohol), and with the lion's share being from undefined arguments (which may be between gang members or other people disbarred from legal gun ownership), the 80 percent figure is at very best weak guidance.

The spin

Pointing a gun at someone, aside from acts of self-defense, is a crime. More so if you pull the trigger. Intentional use of a gun in a crime—which occurs at least three hundred thousand times a year—is a significantly larger problem than gun deaths by suicides (22,938) and accidents (495). Some policy groups never discuss crime, shy away from mentioning gang violence, or they focus on only statistical corner cases (i.e., mass public shooting deaths, which in 2018, a busy year for such horrors, had six such events but were only 0.7 percent of all firearm homicides).

But not all gun crime is isolated to gangs and career criminals, though most of it is. One political faction may correctly relay data on the scope of inner-city gang violence with guns, while another faction will tell about how often guns are misused in domestic violence. Neither side shows the complete spectrum. This is not only because it is to the disadvantage of their arguments, but also fewer voters are like you and willing to read through the confounding details.

The biggest spin is simply ignoring daily crime committed by people for whom criminality is a lifestyle. For example's sake, in 2017—the last year in which FBI crime tables were properly linked on the FBI's web site—659 husbands and wives killed one another by any means, a subset of that being by firearm. The relationship between the murderer and victim was completely unknown for 7,557 more (body lying in an alley scenario), 1,469 were perfect strangers, and 2,999 were "acquaintances," many of whom were "criminal acquaintances." If an advocate is not discussing day-in and day-out street crime, then they have sinister reasons.

Worse yet may be the unintentional amplification of fear. Crime continues, but it is way, way down. Murder rates, where guns figure in about 73 percent of the time, had 9.5 stiffs for every hundred thousand people in 1993, and "only" 5.0 in 2018, practically half the rate. Robberies (guns used in 39 percent of instances) dropped from 272 in 1991 down to 86.2, a three times reduction. Even aggravated assaults (gun use 26 percent of the time) have declined from an all time high of 441 to the modern low of 246. Any faction hyping violent crime—to either push for or against gun control—is stoking fear in an era when things are relatively peaceful . . . providing you don't live in poor neighborhoods in large cities. If you do, duck.

The big question, and hence the battleground for spin masters, is how to keep the Five Bad Actors from getting guns (most don't care if good actors have peashooters or AR-15s). What we know from the data is that the bulk of gun violence occurs within larger cities and within poor neighborhoods and is closely associated with street gangs (for 2018, blacks aged seventeen to twenty-nine, active gang activity years, constituted 63 percent of all homicide victims in that age range, 25 percent of all murders, and yet they composed only 2.8 percent of America's population). We also know that the bulk of crime guns come from underground sources. Hence, the foremost segment of gun violence to address occurs within the tough streets of America's cities and illegal gun markets. Most of the spin about guns never mentions this.

The key question to ask when you suspect you are being spun is "what is the big picture?" Since crimes involving guns are highly variable in magnitude, motivation, and the sourcing of guns, knowing the sizes of each cluster is essential to having perspective.

By the numbers: crime and guns

302,617	Murders, robberies, and assault involving a gun in 2018
73%, 39%, 26%	Murder, robberies, and assault where guns were used
4.8, 6.2	Murder rates for the lowest and highest quintiles by population
1,000,000	Number of armed gang members in America on any given day
0.7%	Percentage of homicides caused by mass public shootings in a busy year

CHAPTER 7

Gun Accidents

A child accidentally shot another child in Chicago today …

Nearly nobody is accidentally killed with a gun.

THE BIKERS HAD BEEN DRINKING most of the day at a backyard party. One was showing off his gun when a fellow one-percenter dared him to shoot a beer can off his head. The volunteer put his back against a tree, his beer on his head, and the fellow with the gun successfully shot the can. Amazed, the volunteer said, "Bet you can't do it again."

You can guess what happened next. But would you guess the second shot was classified as a fatal firearm *accident*?

Anything moving at a high velocity is deadly. Bullets, cars, flu viruses, asteroids. The question is if any are inherently more dangerous than others when used carelessly. After all, if nobody did stupid things with cars or guns, then we would not need that many insurance policies. But people are not always smart and cautious, and so it might be a cause for concern of even legislation if they routinely acted foolishly. If they do not, then there would be little reason to panic.

The critical take-aways

- Firearm accident rates have been falling for several decades
- They account for about 1.3 percent of firearm deaths, though 20 percent of firearm woundings
- Firearms rank near the bottom of the list of causes of accidental deaths

It's getting better all the time . . . but why?

America has seen a mass decline in fatal firearm accidents since the early 1980s. There has also been a less dramatic decline in non-fatal firearm wounding, though the most recent data upsets the progress.

Though the Centers for Disease Control (CDC) make long-term data on fatalities readily available, they only present injury data going back to 2001. This reporting nightmare is going to get worse since the CDC notes on the WISQARS (Web-based Injury Statistics Query and Reporting System) web site that they "will no longer show unstable nonfatal national estimates" after the summer of 2019. That is important since so many data points about firearm injury and death, depending on which part of the population you explore, are small enough to face elimination from CDC reporting.

Before 2016, non-fatal firearm accidents were dropping at a rate faster than the deadly kind. However, for the full thirty-six-year reporting period, fatal firearm accidents dropped at a rate twice as fast as the most recent decade. Stated more simply, both fatal and non-fatal gun accidents dropped

Cause	Times More Than Guns
Poisoning	118
Motor Vehicle Traffic	78
Fall	70
Suffocation	13
Unspecified Injury	13
Drowning	8

Table continued on next page.

Cause	Times More Than Guns
Fire/Flame	6
Natural/Environmental	3
Other specified, classifiable Injury	3
Other land transport	3
Other specified, not elsewhere classified	3
Other Pedestrian	2
Other transport	2
Struck by or against	2
Machinery	1
Firearm	1

Centers for Disease Control WONDER database

far and steadily for the eighties, nineties, and aughts, and now they are leveling out.

In the most recent reporting year, a total of 486 people died when a gun went off unexpectedly. It is worth putting this number into context. Humans are rather prolific when it comes to death-by-stupidity. Though accidental firearm deaths are not at the rock bottom of the list of deadly mishaps—cyclist run-ins, cutting and piercing, burned by hot objects, and overexertion score lower—they are really rare. For every one person you read about dying due to accidental gun fire, eight times as many accidentally drown, seventy times as many fall to their deaths, and an astounding 118 times as many manage to swallow something poisonous that was not meant to be swallowed.

Yet this is a bit of an incomplete story. As our deceased biker friend demonstrated, not every "accident" is really an accident. The average

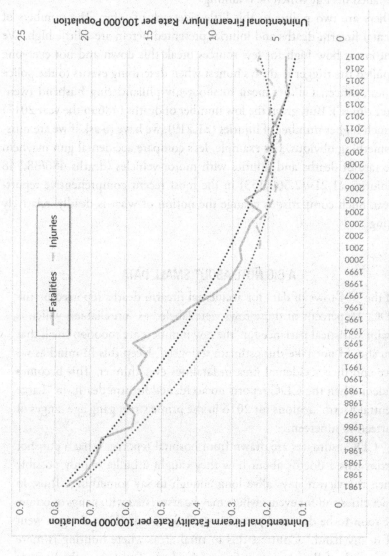

Centers for Disease Control WONDER and WISQARS databases

American, for whatever reason, imagines a gun accident as one where the gun fires unexpectedly, which is quite different than when Biker-Tom shoots Biker-Bill in the forehead instead of in the Budweiser label, and also different from when a hunter does not see another hunter downrange past the white-tailed deer at which he is aiming.

There are two points to this little sidetrack of mine. The numbers of accidental firearm deaths and injuries presented herein are a little high. We cannot know how high for few sources break this down and not everyone who pulled the trigger is always honest when describing events to the police ("Honest, officer, I didn't mean to shoot my philandering husband twenty-three times"). But, given the low number of deaths (486 in the year 2017) but much higher number of injuries (21,219), we have to ask if we are missing something obvious. For example, let's compare accidental gun mayhem to the rate of deaths and injuries with motor-vehicles (deaths 486/38,748 and injuries 21,219/2,500,353) in the most recent comprehensive reporting year. Such comparisons change the notion of what is deadly, relatively speaking.

A BIG NOTE ABOUT SMALL DATA

Of the 314 rows of data for accidental firearm deaths reported by the CDC, 16 percent of those rows were labeled as "unreliable," which is quaint statistical parlance for "the raw numbers are soooooo small that you should not take this estimate seriously." Keep this in mind as we slice and dice accidental firearm fatalities ever thinner. This becomes evident when the CDC reports no accidental firearm deaths in "Large Central Metro" regions for 2016 in the prime street gang age ranges of thirteen to nineteen.

CDC estimates are drawn from hospital reports. What a gunshot victim tells a doctor about how they caught a bullet is only possible when the victim stays alive long enough to say something. Thus, in inner cities and for events which may be associated with gangs or crime, the soon-to-be deceased person is unlikely to say, "Doc, the gun went off in my hand." Contrast this to rural areas where hunting is more active and a fellow hunter (often a friend of a family member) brings the gunshot victim to the hospital and describes what happened.

Race (1999–2016)	Rate per 100K Pop (2016)	Rate of Change (slope) 1999–2016	Reported Household Gun Ownership Rates (Pew, 2017)
White	0.36	-0.01	49%
Hispanic	0.35	-0.01	21%
Black	0.58	-0.02	32%
Sex			
Male	0.91	-0.03	
Female	0.00	0.00	
Age			
10–14			
15–19		0.02	
20–24	0.50	-0.06	
25–34	0.60	-0.03	
35–44		-0.01	
45–54	0.95	0.00	
55–64	0.60	-0.03	
65–74		0.05	

Table continued on next page.

Race (1999–2016)	Rate per 100K Pop (2016)	Rate of Change (slope) 1999–2016	Reported Household Gun Ownership Rates (Pew, 2017)
Urbanicity			
Large Central Metro	0.60	-0.30	19%
Large Fringe Metro	0.00	-0.13	28%
Medium Metro	0.90	-0.25	19%
Small Metro	0.00	-0.15	19%
Micropolitan (Nonmetro)	1.80	-0.34	28%
NonCore (Nonmetro)	2.00	-0.45	46%

The current state and long-term trends are interesting enough, but I am compelled to note that women score a big, fat zero in the CDC's reporting of accidental firearm deaths. We know women participate less frequently in dangerous gunplay activities, be it in inner-city street gangs or back country hunting. Their relative inactivity with guns in general likely keeps them from catching fatal slugs.

So, skipping past the ladies, we see some glaring facts. First, accidental gun deaths are falling for whites and Hispanics, but the rate for blacks is falling twice as fast. We see the rate falling fastest for people in their early twenties and rising fastest for old guys. And even though the accidental gun death rate is largest for non-metropolitan areas—rural and small-town America—that is where accidental gun deaths are declining most steeply.

Some folks have assumed declining participation in hunting sports explains the rural decline in accidental gun deaths, but hunting is an incomplete picture. According to one rather large-scale review[1] of nearly two million emergency room visits for firearm injuries between 1993 and 2008, only 1.95 percent of those injuries were from hunting. Another study[2] of just children under the age of fourteen still tallied 14 percent of their accidental gun injuries as "hunting or sports" related. Thus, longer-term declines in accidental shootings are only weakly associated with the hunting caste.

The fastest rates of decline by urbanicity are those places with the highest accidental gun death rates, which makes perfect sense given that places where such events are rare don't have far to fall (e.g., if accidental gun deaths were near zero in one place, it could not drop much further). From 1999 through 2016, the number of "Hunting License, Tags, Permits & Stamps" as reported by the US Fish and Wildlife Services has hardly fallen at all, sagging from 12 percent of the US population to 11 percent. And in this, there is serious overlap as this includes "Non-Resident" licenses, which avid hunters buy in states they visit, effectively doubling-up some of the total license count. The rate of hunting—if the number of hunting licenses are a reliable proxy—has not diminished in proportion to the decline in gun accident deaths. Other factors must be involved.

Cause of accidents
Drunken biker misadventures aside, there are three primary ways in which guns cause accidental death and injury:

DESIGN AND MANUFACTURING: The gun has a design flaw and was manufactured in such a way that it fires when the person wielding the gun did not intend it to.

RECKLESSNESS: People ignore basic firearm safety rules.

STUPIDITY: Using a gun in a way that actively invites disaster.

Design and manufacturing

A COMMON LEGISLATIVE MISCONCEPTION

Starting late last century, certain activists noted that the US firearms industry wasn't all that big—about 2 percent the size of the US automobile industry in terms of revenues. So, they decided to attempt litigating smaller gun makers to death and as a byproduct, force larger companies to accept new restrictions on making and selling guns.

In reaction, other activists and the gun industry helped enact the Protection of Lawful Commerce in Arms Act (PLCAA). The law negated using the courts to sue gun makers due to harm "resulting from the misuse of their products by others." Stated differently, if someone shoots you, you cannot sue Smith & Wesson.

The bill specifically allows you to sue Smith & Wesson, or any other gun makers, if the product they sell has a design and manufacturing defect. The law also allows for other common litigation including breach of contract issues, criminal acts carried out by the maker, knowingly violating laws concerning sale and marketing, and more. This little historical recap is important because, though rare, certain design or manufacturing defects could allow a gun to discharge when the user did not intend for it to do so, leading to an accidental gun death or injury.

Guns can inadvertently fire. Though infrequent and ever decreasing as firearm design and manufacturing technology improves, some guns—mainly older ones with relatively primitive mechanisms—can still go off inadvertently. Forgive a little technical talk, but some gun design background info may be necessary for any reader who has never fired a gun. Gunnies can skip ahead a few paragraphs.

In all modern guns, there is a small rod called a firing pin. This metal object is slammed into an ignitor on the cartridge called a primer (I'm skipping over "rimfire" rounds for the sake of simplicity) and once ignited, the gunpowder in the cartridge ignites and forces the bullet down the gun's barrel.

In modern gun designs, aside from extreme circumstances, the firing pin cannot make contact with the primer without the trigger being pulled. If you push on the firing pin of any modern gun, it will feel "spongy" but not require a great deal of force to make it slide toward the primer. It takes a fairly fast, forceful, and unrelenting blow (delivered by a different part of the gun called the "hammer") to spike the firing pin into the primer with sufficient force to ignite. Thus the "spongy" feeling spring is designed to be sensitive to velocity. Think of yourself as a firing pin and being hit by either a VW going a hundred miles per hour or a freight train going one mile per hour. The former will slam you (ignite via the firing pin) and the latter will not.

This gets us to the first and primary mode when a design defect might cause an accidental firearm death or injury—and it explains in part why firearm accident rates are dropping as older guns exit the market and newer designs replace them. If a gun is dropped from a sufficient height and at a specific angle, and if the spring restraining the firing pin is weak enough, the gun could theoretically discharge without the trigger being pulled. But we don't have to ponder the theoretical possibilities of this because this has been tested many times over many decades.

One of the older studies I found goes all the way back to 1987, and the copy I have is positively quaint for its typewriter-produced text (any kids reading this book should Google "typewriter" and know that your parents lived in dark and primitive times). The National Institute of Justice publication[3] tested twenty different pistols of that era by dropping them on "a solid slab of concrete from a height of 39.4 inches (1 meter)." They repeated the test seven times, from seven different angles, for every gun on the list.

Nineteen of the twenty showed no indication of the primer being touched by the firing pin, and the one that was "rejected" failed one of the seven drops.

Now, twenty guns from nine makers in a test conducted in the late 1980s is not completely convincing, but it is a start to understanding that in terms of accidental gun deaths, the likely number is bordering zero. California, in the current century, created a roster of "approved" handguns that had to pass a similar drop test. At its peak there were over 1,400 handguns on the list, and many gun makers simply didn't bother submitting older models for testing since it only affected gun sales in California and thus it was unprofitable to go through the rigamarole. All 1,400 of these guns passed the drop test (it is worth noting that California's list of safe guns is shrinking because certification lasts for only five years, and California later added new requirements which no gun maker can effectively meet (namely, microstamping of used cartridges) —thus, attrition has brought the list down below eight hundred).

Aside from drop tests, it is also theoretically possible that other design defects could make a gun go *bang* when you don't want it to, but even in these modes some degree of human involvement is required. For example, there is a gizmo on many guns called a "manual safety." This is a small lever on the side of the gun, which when put in one position, prevents the gun from being fired even if you pull the trigger (these safeties have existed for at least 120 years). Another common mechanism is "grip safety" which prevents a gun from firing, even if you pull the trigger, unless you are grasping the pistol grip. The US Military's Model 1911 (so named for the year of its final design, though work started on the basic concept in the 1890s) has a grip safety. Going even further, some makers prevent the gun's hammer from resting on the firing pin if there is a round in the chamber (a common carry practice for some people, including many police officers).

I cover these details because, from a design standpoint as it relates to accidental discharges, guns have been getting safer and safer. The obvious question then is, "How many of the 486 allegedly accidental gun deaths were caused by defective design or manufacturing?" Despite being the smallest issue with regard to guns, a sanity check is appropriate to assure that gun makers are not wantonly endangering the public through sloppy design, engineering, or craftmanship. One true measure is to look at the number of lawsuits filed against gun makers for endangering defective designs. Another would be how often firearms are recalled when the makers discover defects.

Which gets us to the odd subject of the Consumer Product Safety Commission.

Back in 1972, when Ralph Nader was relevant, the American federal government founded the Consumer Product Safety Commission (CPSC). According to the CPSC website, Congress directed the Commission to "protect the public against unreasonable risks of injuries and deaths associated with consumer products." But guns were specifically removed from the scope of their oversight. The reasons are varied, but it came down to the obvious and the political.

On the practical side, nobody argues that guns are not dangerous, not even companies who make guns. In fact, being dangerous is the intent of guns, be it the endangerment of white-tailed deer or people breaking and entering into your home. This created a bit of a conflict of purposes, namely the regulation of a purposefully dangerous device by an organization mandated to make devices safer. One might as well create the Department of TNT Explosive Force Reduction. It all rather defeats the purpose.

The other problem was purely political. Gun control was becoming a hot topic in the early 1970s and some folks feared the CSPC could be hijacked in order to regulate the firearm industry into non-existence, somewhat as the Centers for Disease Control was accused of doing in the 1990s. CPSC commissioners are appointed by the US president, and presidents range from NRA members to avid gun control enthusiasts. In theory, a president could staff the CPSC's leadership ranks with anti-gun regulators, and by doing so strangle the gun-making industry through endless regulations, fines, litigation, and all the other weapons of commerce destruction the government routinely wields. This was the other reasoning behind taking guns out of the purview of the CPSC.

Which leads to the CPSC's amusingly odd web page that lists recalls of several gun safes but no guns (well, a few air rifles, but those are not "firearms" per se, as they use no gunpowder).

For our purposes then, we turn to a gun control advocacy group[4] and a web page they maintain with recall notices from gun makers. As you might expect, the presented list was shy on detail, instead linking out to (often dead) web pages. But it was easy enough for Gun Facts researchers to rip through the list and classify how many of the sixty recalls were threatening unsuspecting people.

There were some comical entries. For example, one of the recalls this advocacy group felt was important to include involved the manufacturer failing to stamp on the side of the gun what caliber of bullet it used. I have no doubt someone in this world of ours is dimwitted enough to attempt forcing a large bullet into a small pistol, but these absurdities result in bafflement, not bloodshed. In another case listed on this group's web page, if the shooter used ammunition on the powerful end of the scale (what some gunnies call "hot loads"), the gun's safety might accidentally slip into the *safe* position, making it impossible to pull the trigger. Annoying, yes. Dangerous, not really.

Before going further, two things are worth noting. Nearly all of the recalls listed on that web page were voluntarily made by the gun makers and/or the problem was identified by the gun maker during routine testing. Though it is impossible to tally them all (because not every recall notice provided the details) many specified that no consumer reports of problems were given. Stated a bit differently, there were nearly no instances of mobs of bleeding gun owners storming the offices of gun makers demanding their money back. This is confirmed by the fact that of the fifty-seven recalls over the last nineteen years, only 12 percent had ever generated litigation for defects. As we know, lawyers will litigate anything where a payday is involved, regardless of how speculative the case, and will brag about it as part of the shakedown process.

Despite there being no mass carnage or herds of free-range ambulance chasers, almost 25 percent of the recalls involved situations where a round *could* be fired without the user having their finger on the trigger. I say "could" mainly because the gun makers said that, the wording likely being legalistic evasive language. Most of these instances, though, included more detailed explanations that in effect said, "this *could* happen under these sets of circumstances that have not actually occurred." About an equal number of recalls were for guns that *could* discharge if dropped from high places (no reports for guns being dropped from low places) which includes anything above the point where humans normally use guns (above shoulder height).

Of the fifty-seven recalls, 26 percent *might* be from a defect in design or manufacturing (my shortened math is due to the fact that some defects could cause the gun to discharge either if the trigger was not pulled but some other function was occurring—such as the slide was closing—or the gun was dropped). But pair this seemingly large number with the 144,511,868 new guns added to the American inventory so far this century (well, at least through 2016, that being the last year that the Bureau of Alcohol, Tobacco and Firearms report *Firearms in Commerce* was published).

In the face of ever-falling rates of accidental gun deaths and the very low rate of defective product litigation concerning firearms, quality of design and manufacturing is a fraction of a fraction of the overall issue of guns and people getting shot.

Recklessness and stupidity

After exploring the demonstrably small number of accidental shootings due to defective design, we have to look at human, not mechanical failings. It is tempting to discuss firearm recklessness separately from firearm stupidity, but there is such an overlap between the two it is often impossible to segregate them. Take our intoxicated biker friends who opened this chapter. The one with the gun was reckless for shooting in the direction of his pal. The one who got shot was stupid when he said, "Bet you can't do it again."

As with cars and power tools, there are a multitude of ways in which guns can be dangerously misused. The modes fall into two major groups; active misuse and passive misuse. An *active* misuse is when someone "of age" is manipulating a gun in such a way as it fires either (a) when they do not want it to, or (b) in a direction that it should not. A *passive* misuse is when a gun owner leaves it unattended in such a way that the gun is either (a) subject to disruptions that causes it to fire (e.g., dropped from a high place onto a hard surface), or (b) is acquired by a person unqualified to handle it, a child for instance.

Active accidental firearm deaths and wounding are likely the most prominent given the multiplier effect of stupidity, and the distinct association with general bad decision making. Many academic papers (too many to list) have documented an association between alcoholism and firearm misuse. The Centers for Disease Control provided a high-level perspective when they concluded that nearly 35 percent of homicide and suicide victims tested positive for alcohol,[5] a factoid illustrated by our intoxicated biker drama. The same can be said for sundry stupidities of drug use, criminal activity, and endangerment with automobiles. In one rather comprehensive study[6] within a single state where all gunshot wounding is reported to the police, accidental shooters, when compared to the general population, were much more likely to have previously been arrested, been violent, busted for intoxication, driven recklessly, accumulated traffic tickets, or had lost their drivers licenses.

Phrased more succinctly, people who are reckless doing A, B, and/or C are much more prone to being reckless with a gun.

Frustratingly, hard numbers are not easy to come by. In cases of *active* recklessness with a gun, we have multiple arenas in which truthful or accurate reporting makes everything suspect. Using some very old data from an insurance company that investigated gun accident claims, one criminologist[7] tallied some of these "accidents." Maybe 14 percent occurred while cleaning a loaded gun. Another 5 percent while the victim was playing Russian roulette. About 17 percent were actually failed suicide attempts but reported as accidents to avoid embarrassment or intervention. Triangulating a few reports concluded that 12 percent of cases occurred when people were "scuffling for possession" or "playing with" a gun, though an equal number were claimed to be such but were actually homicides.

Hard to find a bright bulb in this chandelier.

It is unimportant to determine which are acts of stupidity or recklessness, since the latter is a subset of the former. What is important is that the nature of gun accidents is tremendously skewed due to people being dumb. The ways in which they are exercising their right to be stupid may well serve to help them. As we saw in the chapter on suicides, abusing drugs or alcohol is tied to a higher risk of suicides. In this chapter drugs and booze are associated with a higher risk of gun accidents. And the same can be said for a criminal lifestyle. The predisposition to self-endangering activities, such as hanging out with drunken bikers wielding guns, is the primary indicator of the likelihood of a gun going off perhaps unintentionally, but with the stupid person's active participation.

It is *passive* recklessness that breaks our hearts.

In society, and as an element of law, there are people we will collectively name "incompetent actors." This cluster includes everyone whose brains are insufficient to make informed and rational judgements. That this list includes both mental defectives and teenage boys is comically unsurprising, and that the law prevents incompetent actors from exercising the full breadth of rights—voting, contracting, buying a gun—is also expected.

Guns and ammo left in places where incompetent actors can find them is a small part of the already small number of accidental gun mishaps. Though the incompetent actor "user" may have purposefully pulled the trigger on the gun, they did so not understanding the ramifications. This includes when a deranged and seriously mentally ill teenager stole a relative's guns and shot up his high school. It also includes when a teenager intentionally swipes a parental firearm and launches a bullet into his buddy while horsing around. And, it also happens when a toddler finds a gun his gang-banger older brother left tucked between the mattresses of their shared bedroom.

The mentally ill and the foolish teenager are relatively unimportant here due to simplicity and complexity. For the former, the problem isn't guns or even unmonitored access to them. It is quite directly the mental illness and the associated incapacity to know that what they are doing is immoral, illegal and insane. Yes, anyone living with a seriously mentally ill person should keep firearms safe, but one does not always know the mental health of visitors, or even a masked but deepening crisis in the head of a loved one. As for teenagers, we know from the sundry street gang studies that the prime ages for recruitment are in the inductee's teenage years, a phase of incomplete competency. It is because of this that a great degree of "accidental" gun injuries occur among teens associated with gangs. And in that we find yet muddier waters since many reported "accidents" are not accidents at all.

So, let's look at kids. Real kids. Little ones who have not yet reached puberty.

To provide perspective, in the most recent reporting year, the Centers for Disease Control estimate a total of seventy-four children (ages zero to fourteen) died from gun accidents. Seventy-four is emotionally seventy-four too many, but statistically it is a very small subset of the estimated 4,114 (1.8 percent) accidental child deaths that same year and an even smaller fraction of the 37,848 (0.2 percent) firearm deaths from all circumstances. And even this number is likely overstated given some harsh realities about unfit parents who murder children, then in a panic claim a gun accidentally discharged. We know this to be true because about 60 percent of homicides of children are at the hands of their parents,[8] who then have a vested interest in having an alibi, and thus the number of actual "accidental" gun deaths falls by some undeterminable set.

Most studies in this subsegment of unintentional gun injuries is very statistically weak. Seventy four annual accidental child gun deaths equates to less than two children per state per year. Drawing statistical validity from such small samples is mathematically impossible. To make matters even less reliable, most of the academic studies concerning children and guns are done in very small geographic areas, or a subsection of an already small number. However, these academic studies routinely look at a larger population, namely all gun injuries, which includes more than just deaths.

How many more? I wish recent data was more direct. The Centers for Disease Control gladly dump the number of non-fatal gun accidents by age and shows that people between the ages of twenty-five and twenty-nine have the highest number of such woundings. But for children the CDC suppresses the data because the numbers are too low to be statistically valid. In fact, they display data for only three of the eighteen age groups, indicating that even adults are not getting accidentally shot very often.

One of the more comprehensive studies[9] gives some insights, but insights to be taken with a sack or two of salt. Based on data from an annual sample of about a hundred hand-selected hospitals—less than 2 percent of the hospitals in the United States—we can at least approximate when and how kids are "accidentally" shot. They report that of non-fatal "accidental" shootings, 80 percent were where the child was "shot by themselves or by a friend, a relative, or another person known to them." In other words, not by a stranger. This makes intuitive sense as the child needs to be in the proximity of a gun that is being used recklessly, and that is more likely to happen in the home than at the corner playground.

Additionally, we see less than 25 percent of these unfortunate events occurring with children under age ten. There is common speculation that pre-adolescent curiosity of adult things leads some kids to find guns in the home and thus imitate what they have seen on TV. It is also rather unsurprising that the rate of such misadventure is three to four times higher for boys than girls. Though the totality of kids + guns + accidents is small, the lion's share of it comes from kids getting guns in their home environment.

From here, things get increasingly statistically sketchy. Several hours of poring through Google Scholar shows that when it comes to children, for sake of argument using the CDC's cutoff age of fourteen, there were very few academic papers available, at least for the US population (and given vast cultural differences concerning children and human life, introducing foreign studies into this chapter would not help). But there were scores of papers that included "children" up to age nineteen or twenty-four, the next two CDC age bracket boundaries. Since we know quite a bit about teenage involvement in street gangs, these papers do not help illuminate the causes of the accidental deaths of children.

The spin

When wading through the cesspool of ideological spin by various policy organizations and politicians, fewer and fewer are discussing firearm accidents. The data about long-term trends has caught up to them and so the topic has become an uncompelling issue in and of itself, much less as a tool for invoking fear and votes.

Yet when certain policy proposals are discussed, some unsavory data is provided. Here is what you need to know when absorbing information from outfits with agendas.

AGE: Many peer-reviewed papers have been authored about gun accidents and children. However, nearly all of these papers classify "children" ranging in age up to nineteen and twenty-four years old. The behaviors of actual children—your darling little babies—and teenagers—your surly and argumentative spawns—are radically different. How they conduct themselves in general, and around guns, is also very different.

LOCALITY: Likewise, these papers rarely look at the nexus to street crime. The prime recruitment age for new gang members is the teenage years, and gun accidents for Large Central Metro and Medium Metro areas track well with gang participation rates.

SMALL NUMBERS: Some academics attempt to tie various legislative proposals (safe storage or general gun law strictness) to gun safety. But the number of accidental gun deaths is so small as to be labeled "unreliable" by the Centers for Disease Control. Quality statistical analysis is not possible for accidental gun deaths, though it may be possible for gun injuries.

By the numbers: firearm accidents

1.3%, 20.4%	Accidental firearm deaths and woundings as a percentage of total firearm deaths and woundings
16	Where accidental firearm deaths ranked on the CDC's top-twenty list of accidental death causes
80%	How far accidental firearm death rates have dropped from 1981 through 2017
74	Maximum number of children "accidentally" killed by firearms in the latest reporting year

CHAPTER 8

Guns in the United States, United Kingdom, and Australia

The UK has strict gun control and a lot less gun murders.

The UK had lower homicide rates even when you could buy machine guns there.

IT IS UNFAIR TO COMPARE any two nations. Frankly, the stark differences in culture, history, degrees of deference to authority, and modes of criminality are just too volatile for most appraisals.

But this has not stopped some people from trying.

Most commonly, at least in the twenty-first century, such comparisons have been made between the United States and either the United Kingdom or Australia, depending on what political points were trying to be scored. Comparing a commoner in London to an uptown urbanite in Chicago would be as useful as contrasting Martians and Venusians. Take this one step further and look for similarities between the Peckham Boys (London street gang) with the Gangster Disciples (Chicago) and the exaggeration grows much larger.

Contrasting the United States with Australia might be a slightly more relevant process, but it is still worlds apart (pun intended). Two commonalities of heritage between Yanks and Aussies provides for some minor similarities, most notably being the rejected byproducts of Mother England. Many of the people who colonized America were running from the law and we all know about Australia's penal colony kickstart. There is an ancient joke about a Scotsman being interviewed for a work visa by an Australian bureaucrat. When asked if the Scot had even been convicted of a crime, the Scotsman replied, "Is it still a requirement for entry?"

Another point of US and Aussie similarities is that both nations are sub-divided, with a great deal of authority residing in the US states and Australian states. One major difference as it relates to guns and law is that in the United States, the government at all levels is generally prohibited from preventing people from owning guns via the US Constitution's Second Amendment. In Oz, the federal government has no powers to regulate guns, but the several states do. That latter reality has led to a fair bit of misunderstanding about the mechanics of Australian gun control history and effectiveness, given that the authority equation is inverted down under. In the United States, dis-tributed authority to the states combined with an enumerated public right at the national level has led to an endless series of state-level gun laws and a seemingly endless array of lawsuits against those laws. In short, significant confusion about guns reigns about both nations.

The history of US and UK gun laws

One important aspect of UK guns and crime is that most of the hard data that can and should be used omits Ireland and Scotland. Ireland, well, has had its troubles. They have endured significant issues in terms of violence, the illegal importation of weapons, and sectarian bloodshed. Scotland, as the joke I retold above demonstrates, has a degree of independence and inde-pendent thinking from the rest of the United Kingdom. Since part of my bloodline is Scottish (Henry family that came over after the '45) I appreciate their drive to be not-so-British.

This is why most crime statistics you get from the United Kingdom specifically say, "England and Wales," being the last fully operating cogs of the British Empire. They are also uniformly under every stricture of UK gun control and not alarmingly affected by civil wars and cranky attitudes about independence. For our purposes, "England and Wales" will be used inter-changeably with "United Kingdom" throughout this chapter.

Year	US	UK
1903		Perfunctory License for Pistols
1920		Three-year certificate to possess with local police rejection without cause and "good cause" burden of proof, though "self-defense" was allowed.
1934	Transfer tax on machine guns, suppressors, short-barreled shotguns, and sundry destructive devices.	
1937		Added short-barreled shotguns to possession list, enacted transfer paperwork for machine guns, deleted self-defense as a "good cause."
1968		Added long-barreled shotguns and facilitated an amnesty turn-in for unlicensed guns.
1968	Required serialization of manufactured or imported guns, banned importing military style weapons, imposed 21 minimum age to purchase handguns from FFLs, prohibited selling of firearms to felons and the mentally ill.	

1986	Prohibited civilian ownership or transfer of machine guns made after May 19, 1986, redefined "silencer" to include silencer parts.	
1988		Prohibited semi-automatic and pump-action center-fire rifles, short shotguns that had magazines, pump-action and self-loading rifles, mandated "safe storage" for shotguns.
1993	Required background checks be conducted on gun purchases.	
1994	Federal assault weapons ban, banned magazines over 10 rounds.	
1997		Effectively banned private possession of handguns. 162,000 pistols were turned in.

A good place to start is the twentieth century. Though the Crown and Parliament always had some attitude about weapons and the masses (from hunting on royal properties to disarming Catholics) they had relatively little gun control in the first third of the twentieth century. In its earliest action, the British government required citizens to get a license to buy a pistol. But the license could be obtained at the post office and had no requirements other than the modest fee. A commoner could get a license from the post office, then get a gun from a hardware store all before getting to work in the morning.

The first real changes in the United Kingdom came in 1920 when the "right" to own a gun became a matter of subjective local decision. To get a certificate to own a gun, one had to get permission from the local constabulary, and show "good cause" for wanting or needing a gun. That being said, self-defense was considered a valid need and thus "good cause," and odds were if your local chief constable did not think you a loon or know you to be a criminal, a certificate would be issued.

Almost at the same time, the United States and United Kingdom made getting machine guns and other items a bit more cumbersome, though not illegal. In America, for example, the government added what was then a steep two hundred dollar tax every time ownership of a machine gun was transferred from one person to another. But on both shores, a citizen could still acquire machine guns, suppressors, short-barreled shotguns, and more.

The big change occurred in the United Kingdom under the same law that increased regulation of machine guns. In that act, "self-defense" was removed from the list of "good cause" criteria. As we saw in previous chapters, at least in America, self-defense is the top motivation for owning a gun. If we assume the same was true in 1937 England and Wales, the government legislatively negated the primary impetus for getting a certificate and a gun. Mathematically speaking, when the number one justification for obtaining a gun is removed from the list, the number of gun permits issued will naturally decline. Most people have an evening cocktail to help them unwind. If booze suddenly made everyone agitated, the gin industry would quickly die.

In both nations we have to fast forward to the end of the 1960s, a period of massive social upheaval in both lands, with bombs going off in cities and calls for armed revolution, though the political core of each eruption was fundamentally different. This led to what we'll call the "modern era of gun control" which lasted in the United States until 1994 (with the passage of the now expired Federal Assault Weapons Ban) and continually escalating restrictions in the United Kingdom with handguns effectively being outlawed in 1997.

This legal history primer behind us, the key question is if these separate and occasionally synchronous legislative undulations had any effect on violence. Luckily our British counterparts are even a bit more detail oriented with the record keeping that the FBI is in the United States. The British Home Office website, though not designed for the faint-hearted researcher, will eventually lead you to a repository of crime statics for England and Wales going back to the reign of Queen Victoria. The Yanks only started regimented crime statistics gathering in the 1920s, though we have from other

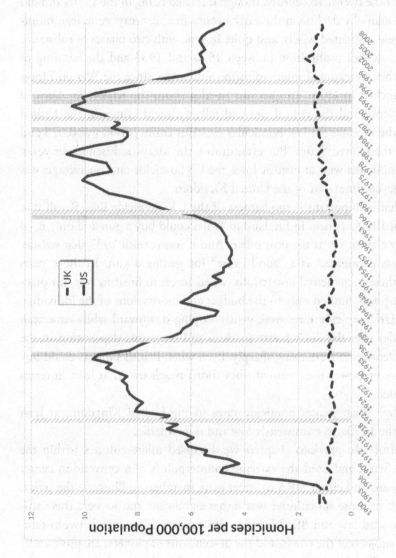

Homicides per 100,000 Population

British Data: Home Office, National Archives, police reported crimes. US Data: FBI Uniform Crime Reporting and National Center for Health Statistics, Vital Statistics; Vertical bars show years in which US (solid) or UK (hatched) laws were passed.

sources reliable summary stats predating the launch of the FBI's Uniform Crime Reporting system.

What we see right off is a bit confounding.

The United Kingdom had an admirably low and fairly flat homicide rate throught the twentieth century, though it started rising in the 1970s and did not substantially decline in the early twenty-first century. American homicide levels undulated wildly, and quite in sync with two phases of substance control, alcohol prohibition between 1920 and 1933 and the banning of most other recreational mind adjusting substances since the War on Drugs was launched in 1971. To give you an idea about the relative levelness of UK violence and the radical rise and fall of violent crimes in the United States, the variance for UK homicides over this entire period was 0.075 and 5.0 for the United States. But even during the idealistic Eisenhower years, when homicides were at historic lows, the US homicide rate, on average, was nearly seven times that of the United Kingdom.

What is important is the flatness of the UK homicide line. Recall that up until 1920 a person in England or Wales could buy a gun and only need first pay a small tax at the post office. And it wasn't until 1937 that self-defense was eliminated as a "good cause" for getting a gun. In those years before these incremental restrictions, when access to firearms was, for practical purposes, limited only to the budget and motivations of the individual buyer, UK homicide rates were gently sloping downward while American homicides over the illicit booze markets and economic deprivation in the Great Depression were rising sharply. Even when British subjects could buy whatever firepower they wanted, they didn't much use it, at least in terms of murder.

Why? What makes homicide rates in the United Kingdom, at least before the 1970s, so consistently low and non-volatile?

Culture. In previous chapters we discussed micro-cultures within the United States and used the extreme counterpoints of a convention center full of guns and either NRA or street gang members to illustrate the point. The gulf in those subcultures was rather significant and so were their attitudes toward law and life. Likewise, the cultural differences between rain-soaked subjects of the crown and the descendants of pioneers are profoundly different. Paraphrasing something said to me by a low-level chieftain in the organization called Sons of the American Revolution, "The conformist stayed in Britain."

That acerbic insight aside, there are likely a multitude of other social norms that define both countries. Attitudes toward one's place in the grand scheme of society, especially attitudes for a fellow citizen or to government authority, helps define a person or the subcultures in which they reside. These attitudes are on constant display and define both individual and collective actions, reactions, and interactions. Stereotypical "trailer trash" *culture* presented to a banker is just as financially debilitating as if someone displaying "gang banger" *cultural* attitudes asked for a loan on an Escalade.

Hence, it is culture that drives behavior and the general public reaction to those behaviors. The culture in the United Kingdom, even when guns were freely available, led to low homicide rates. American culture has produced different outcomes.

One aspect of American culture vis-à-vis guns is in the glorification of criminals, mainly latent overall, but overt in street gang communities. At the risk of stereotyping a nation, Americans generally frown upon subservience to authority, which explains much about those who fled to the new world and the subsequent revolution. Add to that attitudinal baseline a population that started off as, and at the time of the revolution was still heavily, pioneers or at least very rural residents largely dependent on themselves. Together, this lends itself to an early mass cultural disposition disdainful of authority, and as a byproduct creates a little passive fascination with or even glorification of criminals who so overtly defy the authority of law (both Bonnie and Clyde and 50 Cent had their fan base for their anti-authority attitudes). Many tales from America's pre-revolution era note that it wasn't just the King or Parliament that colonist held in low regard—often the local civic leaders were targets of insurrection, which was occasionally violent.

All told, Americans are more willing to stand ground than give it, be the opponent a belligerent neighbor, a rival street gang, or the government itself. British society does not, on an aggregate basis at least, indulge in such open cantankerousness (though one English comedian claims his nation to be the masters of passive/aggressive abuse). Summarized, when it comes to obedience to government or polite interactions, some countries maintain a stiff upper lip and others a stiff middle finger.

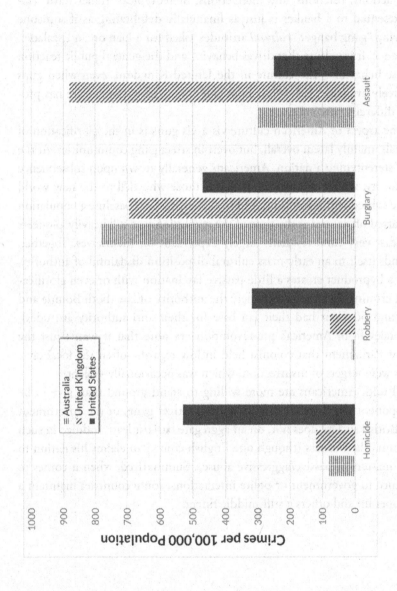

UN Office on Drugs and Crime, 2017. Burglary and assault per 100K population, homicide and robberies per 10M population

Crimes per 100,000 Population

Assault

Burglary

Robbery

Homicide

Australia
United Kingdom
United States

1000
900
800
700
600
500
400
300
200
100
0

But opportunity also factors into the equation, and one good way of demonstrating this is to look at the United Nations' tallies for various crimes in both countries, and we'll add in what they know about Australia as well.

In the previous graph, I scaled the homicide and robbery rates by a factor of one hundred in order to chart them, so divide accordingly (e.g., if the homicide rate is listed as a hundred incidences per hundred thousand population, it is actually only one instance). What we see is that the United States certainly has higher homicide rates, but lower burglary and assault rates. Recall in the chapter on crime that criminals disliked the idea of armed victims. Burglars don't like getting shot by homeowners and street toughs don't like the idea of armed retribution. If we were to weed out the homicides associated with America's 1.4 million gang members, the US homicide rate would shrink much of the gap in the left-side set of columns.

Indeed, very personal violence (assaults, rapes, robberies) is markedly different. Like the United Nations, the Dutch Ministry of Justice, at the turn of the century, normalized crime rates in one study via surveys in modern countries.[1] They ranked Australia (7 percent of the survey respondents claim to have been victimized in the year before) and the United Kingdom (5 percent) as the most likely countries in which to have your home burgled (USA 4 percent). They also scored them in the top ranks, along with Canada and Finland, for the most frequent contact crimes (assaults with force and sexual assaults against women—more than 3 percent, USA 2 percent). Poland beat out the United Kingdom and Australia in terms of robbery (1.8 percent, 1.2 percent, and 1.2 percent; USA was not even broken out in the report). And assault risk was top in Australia and the United Kingdom (6 percent) followed by Canada (5 percent, within the USA also not listed at all in the top-tier rankings).

Guns, their use, and misuse, play into two distinct camps: the average citizen and the criminal class. In the United States, both camps have guns and the defensive use of guns (see chapter 4) play into crime prevention. In other countries, the former group—non-criminal citizens—don't have guns and thus the other group—criminals—appear not to need them for very specific and very personal types of crimes. In the United Kingdom and Australia, it evidently is more fun to attack someone, and this may be in part due to the reduced likelihood of getting plugged in return.

The merry old land of Oz
The other common comparison that people make is between America and Australia. Some people prefer to contrast these two countries for their somewhat common stories, with settlers being outcasts and adventurers, and

Australia receiving its first permanent European immigrants around the time of ratification of the US Constitution. Others enjoy the gun control aspect since Australia has had a mixed history with firearms and their regulations in a nation of convicts and occasionally violent aborigines (and the massacres of the latter are sadly too similar to what happened with Native Americans).

For most of Australia's history, firearms were regulated in a reactionary mode. The convicts deposited Down Under were given guns to hunt with (since the government was not going to feed them) and to make exploring the new territory relatively safe. Some of these guns got stolen or were used in ways the government did not care for. The authorities of that time tried to collect all the guns they originally provided and were far from successful in the effort. By one account,[2] at most 25 percent of the guns found their way back to the crown, showing an early Australian inclination to keep a few guns "off the books," which continues to this day. After that, each of the Australian states devised their own rules about guns, and guns found their way into most every corner of the continent despite various rules, regulations, and restrictions. At one point after World War II, New South Wales effectively banned handguns, though this was not nationally replicated or even locally obeyed.

But most of the conversation concerning guns in Australia starts around 1996. It was that year when a disgruntled and fame-seeking man committed a mass public shooting at a popular tourist spot in Port Arthur. Though not previously immune to mass murder, against aborigines or others, this event launched Australia's modern gun control mindset. Political leaders (or opportunists, depending on your disposition) led efforts to heavily restrict firearm access and to get Australian citizens to turn in as many guns as possible. By orchestrating three agreements between the several states, Australia instituted more uniform laws and more restrictive ones at that.

There was no "gun ban" *per se,* as some pro-gun activists like to claim. From an American perspective, the combined Australian restrictions on gun ownership are, relatively speaking, rather severe and the mandatory turn-in was a shade shy of outright confiscation. Thus, some in the American gun rights movement used a bit of logistic shorthand in calling the 1996 gun control acceleration a gun "ban." But in the wake of the National Firearms Agreement (1996), the National Firearm Trafficking Policy Agreement (2002), and the National Handgun Control Agreement (2002), a new order was created. It also led to a pair of widescale "voluntary" gun turn-ins (I decline to call them "buybacks" as the government never held title to the guns before the events, and using that term proves that Australians can butcher the English language just as well as Americans can). By making certain guns illegal, then offering to pay people for turning them in, the goal was to reduce the number of guns in private hands.

For perspective's sake, about 650,000 guns were turned in to the government in the first and largest event. The government believes today there are over 260,000 unregistered guns in Australia.[3] The United Nations thinks it might be upwards of six hundred thousand unregistered firearms, and the Small Arms Survey thinks it is between four hundred and seven hundred thousand. That's in addition to the 816,000 gun licenses in Oz, and it is fair to think there is at least a one-to-one ratio of licenses to guns. So, 650,000 taken and between 1,076,000 and 1,516,000 remaining in private hands.

Perhaps the most interesting aspect is that despite new and nationwide restrictions on gun ownership, the number of illicit guns appears to be rising in Australia. In the year after the initial turn-in, the Australian government estimated there were fewer than forty thousand illicit guns still floating about. Today that estimate is 260,000. Australia is not alone in growing non-compliance. Among the hard numbers and estimates gathered by the Small Arms Survey, Australia pales in comparison to other countries with gun registration regiments and non-compliance rates. In their 2007 publication, the survey estimated there were about 0.2 unregistered guns for every one registered in Oz (averaging their high and low estimates for unregistered firearms). That same year the United Kingdom was a one-to-one ratio. Germany had 2.5 unregistered guns for each one on the books, and France was practically awash in unregistered guns with 5.7 kept in secret for each one that had government paperwork.

Regardless of nation, both the criminal and non-criminal classes understand the value of guns for their very different purposes, and like life, both groups find a way.

The obvious question is if the 1996-era change in laws and rather broad turn-in of guns had any affect, desirable or otherwise. This is both an easy and hard question to answer. Easy because the Australian government provided me with some hard numbers. Hard because nothing about Oz gun politics and statistics is entirely easy.

The first complication is that Australia is basically empty. In a continent the size of America's "lower forty-eight," there are about one-twelfth the number of people and thus, overall, a lower population density. However, that's cheating, as most of the Australian emptiness is in the middle, kinda like the United States, and many coastal regions are much more densely packed than the outback. Oz's biggest city, Sydney, has about 5.5 million people, which is well below New York at 8.4, and the comparative population density estimates are widely spread from 407 people per square kilometer to almost eleven thousand respectively. From this point alone, how Australians relate to one another and their opportunity and propensity for violence is going to make for apples-to-pineapples comparisons.

Further, the claims by Australian politicians about the purpose of the new gun laws is unforgivably flexible. Some claimed and still claim it was to reduce general violence. Others claimed it was to reduce mass public shooting such as the Port Arthur Massacre that precipitated the new laws themselves. To this day between the sundry and uncivil social media debating squads you can find both claims being made. Thankfully, the Australian Institute of Criminology (AIC), a branch of the government, provided some numbers when I asked for them. The AIC presents nice charts and recent data online, but with our interest focused on the 1996 change in law and national attitudes, I wanted a deeper data dump.

And on this point, a note of caution: The AIC was indeed responsive and helpful, but they sent me data only going back to 1989, which is sufficient for this review but might set off BS alarms for the more suspicious reader. Just know that the truncation of the analysis is not arbitrary on my part. Given that the AIC was not founded until 1973 and that the nation itself was not 100 percent free of legislative entanglement with the United Kingdom until 1986, clean and complete data from 1989 might be the best we can hope for. But I am troubled in as much as one of their publications[4] includes a chart of homicide statistics going all the way back to 1915, so AIC sending me abbreviated tables is a bit inexplicable.

The one clear measure we use as an acid test throughout this book is homicides. Since guns are used in the United States as the primary means for murder, and since Australia convulsively collected a large number of guns, the hypothesis is that homicides would be a primary category, if not *the* primary category, of crime to be affected with fewer guns in circulation.

That hypothesis does not test well.

The first noticeable aspect of Oz homicides is that they were on the decline before the 1996 gun turn-in program. If nothing legislative had changed, odds are the murder rate in Australia would have continued to decline. But of more interest is the rate of decline. Even if murders were decreasing, the hunch was that fewer guns would result in even fewer homicides. But the rate of decline in murders for seven years preceding the 1996-era change in gun availability, and for the same number of years afterward, was identical down to four decimal places, which means nothing changed, at least in the first seven years after the Port Arthur Massacre, which changed everything.

But starting in the eighth year, homicides started dropping more quickly. With some laws, there is a delayed effect due to the process of ramping up

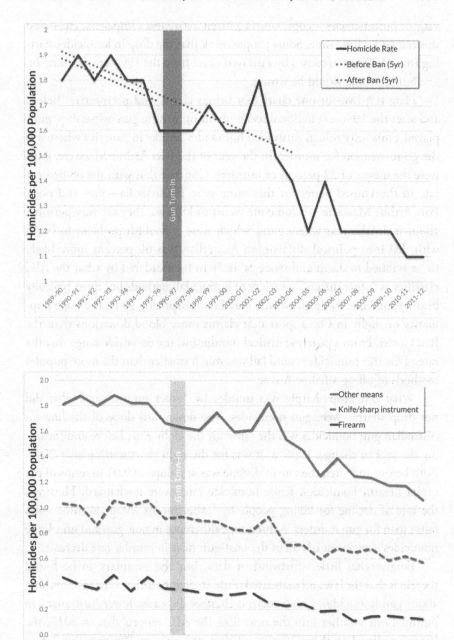

Australia Institute of Criminology, Australian Institute of Criminology, Nation Homicide Monitoring Program, 1989/90 to 2011/12

various bureaucracies—cops, courts, citizen awareness campaigns, etc.—and this can take a little time. Some people think that the drop in homicides starting around 2002 was caused by a delayed effect from the 1996-era gun turn-in.

Some people would be wrong.

Here is a two-for-one chart that brings clarity and perspective. Before and after the 1996-era national realignment on private gun ownership, guns played a minority role in Australian homicides, unlike in America where it is the go-to-weapon for murder. In the year of the Port Arthur Massacre, guns were the means of 22 percent of murders. Contrast that with the 68 percent rate in the United States for that same year. In Australia—pre- and post-Port Arthur Massacre—if someone wants to kill you, they are very personal about it. In the year where guns, which were a smallish problem to begin with, fell into political disfavor, an Australian was 60 percent more likely to be stabbed to death and twice as likely to be murdered by what the AIC classifies as "other means," a variety of homicidal methods but most typically beating someone to death (which may be unsurprising given the huge popularity of rugby in Oz, a sport that claims more blood donations than the Red Cross). From a purely statistical standpoint, the downside range that the rate of firearm homicides could fall was much smaller than the more popular methods of offing a fellow Aussie.

What did drop sharply was murder by "other means," and what did not drop sharply were gun homicides. The downward slope of the line for Australian gun homicides was the same for the eight years before and including the year of change, 1996, as it was for the eight years starting after 2002. Both before and after, the rate of decline was at a slope of 0.01 in terms of per capita firearm homicides. Knife homicide rates were unchanged. However, the rate of decline for killing people by "other means" dropped three times faster than for gun murders. A three-time difference in non-gun and non-knife homicides explains nearly all of the post-gun turn-in murder rate decrease.

Forgive that little whirlwind of data, but the summary to be found therein is that the law and mandated trade-in of guns did not change anything about gun homicides. Other societal changes did cause fewer Australians to pummel one another into the next life. The AIC reports that in 2017, the latest year listed on their "Victims of Violent Crime by Weapon Type," that 37 percent of all Oz murders involved "no weapon"—not a gun, not a knife, and no automobiles, hammers, or baseball bats, either—nada.

The other often made argument in favor of the government gathering up excess firearms was to prevent future mass murders. Recall it was thirty-five victims at Port Arthur that caused the nation of Australia to collectively

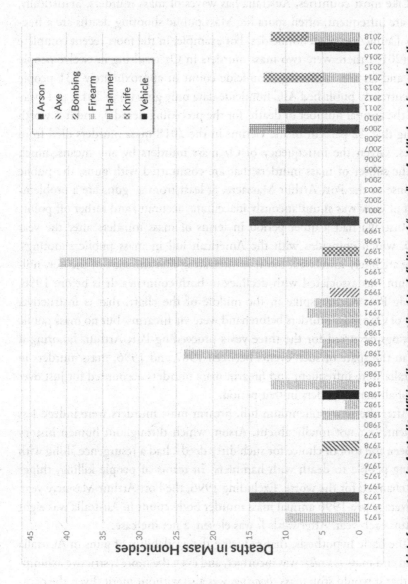

List of massacres in Australia, Wikipedia, normalized to definition of "mass" as 4+ killed, not including the perpetrator

recoil in horror and blame gun possession for the calamity. But this reaction had two significant errors in logic, namely the frequency and mode of mass murder.

Like most countries, Australia has waves of mass murders. Statistically, they are infrequent, often sporadic. Mass public shooting deaths are a fraction of a fraction of all homicides. For example, in the most recent complete year (2018) there were two mass murders in Oz resulting in twelve people dead and an annual average homicide count of approximately 231 people (the currently published AIC homicide data only goes up to 2014, so I averaged the annual number of deaths for the preceding decade), and it is worth noting that 42 percent of the victims in the 2018 mass murders died from knives. Given the infrequency of Oz mass murders by any means, much less the subset of mass murders that are committed with guns, the public response to the Port Arthur Massacre, at least from a "guns are a problem" point of view was simultaneously inaccurate, accurate, and rather off point.

Australia had a quiet period in terms of mass murders after the year 2000, which coincides with the American lull in mass public shootings. These are likely unrelated, but it is interesting that the start of the new millennium was associated with declines in both countries. It is before 1996, the big Port Arthur spike in the middle of the chart, that is instructive. Most of Oz's mass murders beforehand were via firearms, but no mass public shootings occurred for the three years proceeding Port Arthur. Ignoring if we can the spate of such events between 1987 and 1996, mass murders in Australia were infrequent and firearm mass murders accounted for just over half of all mass murders in that period.

After the new millennium lull, firearm mass murders were indeed less frequent, but not totally absent. Arson, which throughout human history has been the tool of choice for such dirty deeds, had a resurgence along with beating people to death with hammers. In terms of people killing, things have changed for the worse. Excluding 1996, the Port Arthur Massacre year, the average pre-1996 annual mass murder body count in Australia was eight humans each year. Afterwards it was eleven, a net increase.

The basic hypothesis, that reducing the availability of guns in Australia would end mass *murders* was incorrect, and even the more restrictive assumption that it would stop mass *shootings* was also without merit. Even the occasionally uttered opinion that the changes in Oz's gun laws would reduce the annual number of people killed either by guns or via mass murder is not substantiated by the numbers.

The spin

Though we used the United Kingdom and Australia as counter points to the United States, per the claims made by activist organizations and politicians, such comparisons are made with all sorts of countries. Though New York may be more culturally similar to London than Lisbon, they are still very different cultures. What passes for civil behavior or a social affront in Cardiff is very different from the same in Compton. And it is even highly variable within a country. I once had a pair of German lads stay at my home in central Virginia after routing through New York, and they commented that beforehand they thought all Americans were like New Yorkers. Definitely not the case!

Parties who compare the United States to other countries when it comes to guns and violence never dig below the surface. Yes, the gun murder rate in the United Kingdom is lower than in the United States in our modern age where guns are all but unavailable in Britain. But Britain's homicide rate was also lower when guns were readily available there. Hence, something aside from gun laws and gun availability is the controlling factor.

The other spin, mainly tied to the Australian experience, follows the same mode of not looking further than new data (post 1996) and older ways of killing. Aussies are rather adept with knives, fire, blunt objects, or their bare hands when they feel the need to kill.

Likewise, for spin comparing these countries, some politicos studiously ignore other crimes aside from murder. As we noted in the chapter on self-defense, guns prevent crime as well as being used to commit crime, and unsurprisingly they prevent specific types of violent crime more than others. Thus, honest assessments between US/AU/UK should include robberies, assaults, and other events that the Dutch Ministry of Justice classified as "contact crimes."

By the numbers: guns and violence in the United States, United Kingdom, and Australia

88, 6, 15	Per capita gun ownership in US, UK, and Australia (firearms per 100 people)
0.95:1, 0.32:1	Unregistered firearm ratio in UK and Australia (US is not applicable[5])
5.3, 1.2, 0.8	Homicide rates, 2017, US, UK, and Australia (per 100K population)
470, 694, 782	Burglary rates, 2017, in US, UK, and Australia (per 100K population)
250, 880, 298	Assault rates, 2017, in US, UK, and Australia (per 100K population)

CHAPTER 9
Other Aspects of Guns

Nobody except the police need guns.

Why do cops need guns?

ONE WEARYING ASPECT ABOUT GUNS is that for every predisposition, there is an equal and opposite predisposition and an endless number of topics for which a person can argue their case. It matters little if the person has any sound footing in the subject, they will scream their position loudly, or at least post it on Facebook in all caps.

With each topic there comes a small mountain of hokum.

Some of it comes from uninformed perspectives. For example, a pro-gun advocate once claimed that as a portion of the US population, mass public shootings were on the decline. I did not challenge him, but I did pull up the Gun Facts Mass Public Shooting database, added in population numbers from the Census Department, and concluded his statement was not true. Given the way his notion was presented I suspect it was more speculation on his part rather than a recycled sound bite. But it illustrates how one's attitudes can cause formation of perceived facts without the benefit of actual knowledge.

Any time someone makes a statement in generalities, odds are they have never looked into the data underlying the subject. Take as example the all too common phrase "we have an epidemic of gun violence." Foremost, as shown in previous chapters, firearm homicide rates have dropped from 7.0 to 3.5 per hundred thousand people between 1993 and 2014, though there has been an uptick to 4.5 since the multi-decade decline. And as we saw in the chapter on Guns and Crime, the gun violence that exists tends to be heavily localized, primarily in metropolitan areas and among the gang and crime communities. An *epidemic* is "a widespread occurrence of an infectious disease in a community at a particular time." Since gun violence is abating and isolated, it does not fit the definition of epidemic.

Some of the worst talking points come from various political factions. Both pro- and anti-gun camps create memes that are certainly emotive, but often have only the barest anchoring in statistically verifiable reality. For example, various cities are named as "the murder capital of the United States" by one or the other side depending on their agenda of the moment. One group will use the total body count in a given year (Cook County, IL—778 dead, rate of 15.0 murders per hundred thousand people) and the other team uses the gun homicide rate (Saint Louis, MO—128 dead, rate of 41.1). Both viewpoints may be mathematically correct, but neither side describes why they chose their definition of "murder capital" or switched from one to the other as political winds change. They may also aggregate multiple years of data or report from a year that most suits their propaganda goals (in my example, I used the CDC's most recent reporting year).

Yet more bad information comes via citing studies without actually reading them, and this sadly is very common in modern newsrooms. I recently engaged someone online who reacted (badly) to a chart I provided. In an attempt to prove me wrong, he sent links to Google Scholar, a place where I spend a lot of time and thus know how to scrutinize the contents therein. The links he lobbed my way were not to specific studies that disputed my point, but to a generic search for "gun availability on suicide rates." This person didn't bother to read any of the studies yet took great comfort in seeing that a few academics had studied the relationship between guns and suicides. He assumed, based on those efforts, that there was a relationship that proved his point, despite not reading any of those articles to know if his point was proven or denied.

To write about all the topics, subtopics, odd angles, and notions which are hurled past competing cabals in the gun control wars would take more time than I have left in the world, and I'm healthier than most horses. Here are some of those topic areas too narrow to pen an entire chapter about, but which you will encounter frequently and most often from people with fact-deficient opinions.

Children and guns

Nobody likes the idea of a child being hurt, regardless of how it happens. When it comes to guns, which are in the hands of alleged adults, we naturally perceive this to be an appalling and unnecessary outcome. The same can be said about a wide range of adult-inflicted disasters for kids, ranging from kids getting run over by a car to them not getting vaccinated. As always, perspective is a good starting point.

It is worth noting that a full 33 percent of the data points for the firearm deaths of children are listed as "unreliable" per the Centers for Disease Control database, due to there being so few instances that extrapolating the per capita rates is mathematically suspect. This is a first and fundamental clue for anyone serious about the topic. The CDC is not without statisticians. When they say "this happens so infrequently that our calculations are iffy," then you know the situation is not dire and is perhaps bordering on non-existent.

That precaution aside, and using the normal definition of child—that being someone who has yet reached puberty—we see that firearms nearly never figure into suicides (160 instances in the ten to fourteen age group). Indeed, suicides from firearms are below even intentional gun homicides of children. But when it comes to homicides, and to a lesser degree suicides, the rate jumps in the teenage years and continues upward into the young adult years. We'll cover that phenomena in a bit, but a little more perspective is necessary first.

Aside from diseases, children, not teens and adults, typically die by accident. Within the realm of accidental childhood deaths, firearms deaths are nearly negligible, with a rate that is 1.5 percent that of the leading cause, suffocation. It remains far down the list from the rate of motor vehicle deaths (4.8 percent as often) and drowning (8.3 percent). Even in the realm of homicides of children, the infamous "other" category is over four times as frequent a cause of death than guns. The sickening and sad side note behind this category is that year in and year out, parents are responsible for 60 percent or more of child homicides[1] using means ranging from shaking babies to beating preadolescents bodily. The "other" category for child homicides is thus a little vague because homicidal parents tend not to confess what they did, much less how they did it.

Then again, there are school shootings.

Guns at school are either a big problem or an unfortunate but infrequent occurrence, depending on how you define such things. If you look at just mass public shootings at K-12 schools, you see one perspective. If you include every incident where a gun is fired (including suicides, when a resource officer

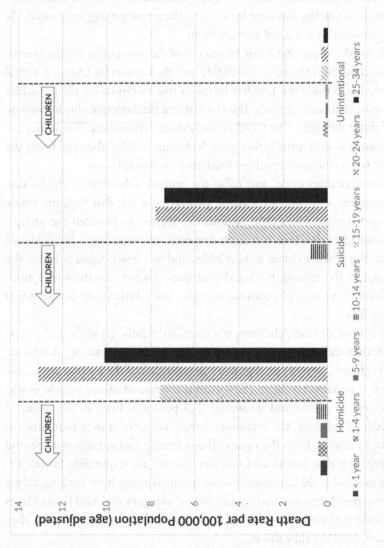

Firearm deaths, 2016, CDC WONDER database

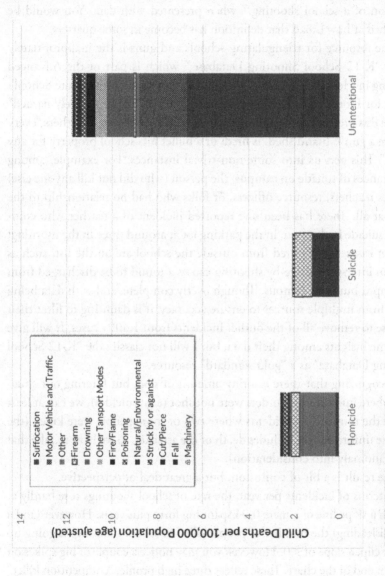

CDC WONDER database, 2016

shoots, and at least one case of the resource officer committing suicide) you get another perspective. And if you include every time a gun is used on campus, even simple brandishing and intimidation incidents, you get a third perspective. It is important for you, the intellectually curious, to ask "what is your definition of a school shooting?" when presented with data. You would be astonished at how broad that definition has become in some quarters.

One resource for triangulating schools and guns is the inappropriately named "K-12 School Shooting Database," which is part of the Advanced Thinking in Homeland Security program at the Naval Postgraduate School's Center for Homeland Defense and Security. I say "inappropriately named" because this project captures more than just school *shootings*. It gathers "every instance a gun is brandished, is fired, or a bullet hits school property for any reason." This gets us into some non-trivial instances. For example, among the instances of suicide on campus, the person (who did not kill anyone else) includes teachers, resource officers, or folks who had no relationship to the school at all. There has been one reported incident of a teacher who committed suicide in their car, in the parking lot at around three in the morning. In other cases, bullets fired from outside the school are on the list, such as when an inter-gang drive-by shooting causes a round to be discharged from off-campus but onto campus. Though overly complete, and with data being pulled from multiple sources to ensure accuracy, it is daunting to filter their database to remove all of the outlier incidents from 1,400+ cases. It will give you some insights among their data, but I will not classify the "K-12 School Shooting Database" as a "gold standard" resource.

Recognizing that there is a tiny amount of slop, but filtering out situations where innocent bystanders were not shot (e.g., suicides), we can at least look at the number of incidents where two or more people were killed (the database unfortunately includes death of the attacker, so we have to take that minor anomaly into consideration).

The result is a bit of confusion, but a great deal of perspective.

In terms of incidents per year, the rate of school shootings rose hardly at all, with a slope line of a mere 0.04 spanning forty plus years. However (and a little misleading) the number of people killed in school shootings is going up at a fair clip, a slope of 3.0. However, you may notice a couple of big spikes on the right end of the chart. These reflect three high profile, "competition killer" mass public shootings at schools, namely the Sandy Hook Elementary School massacre, the Parkland, Florida high school, and Columbine, with twenty-six, seventeen, and thirteen killed respectively. When we excluded these exceptional events, we see a less dramatic rise, though a rise none the less, in the slope for the number of people killed, a rate of 0.14. Stated a bit differently, if we remove these few pre-planned events from the category of "school shootings" to "mass public shootings," we still have a growing lethality situation, though not a growing incident frequency situation. For the 1980s, 1990s, 2000s, and thus far into the teens through 2018, the average annual number of school incidents were 1.6, 3.0, 2.0, and 3.0 in each decade, and the average number of people killed was 4.0, 7.1, 5.9, and 8.0 (both sets of stats exclude the classifiable mass public shootings).

Gun ownership rates

A common refrain made by anti-gun activists is that the household ownership rate is declining. The pro-gun faction claims it is steady.

Both are correct, believe it or not.

The household gun ownership rate is the common metric used by criminologists. The reason is that a gun in the home can be used by anyone who has access to the gun and thus can be used to either commit a crime or prevent one. This is why measurements of *household* gun ownership are important. Indeed, shortly before the manuscript deadline for the book you are reading, the US federal government issued a report on targeted school violence,[2] and noted that "the firearms were most often acquired from the home," including a surprising number of cases where the guns were "safely" stored in lockboxes and safes. Two examples help clarify why household gun ownership rates are the preferred mode of measurement for gun ownership. A typical husband and wife who keep a revolver in the nightstand have access to it and likely both know how to use it. It could be used to scare away a rapist or murder a cheating spouse. Thus, *estimating* the percentage of households that have one or more guns is important to proving or disproving certain statistical realities.

Estimate is a necessary word. People are, well, not always honest. When an unknown caller rings their phone and asks a person if they have a gun in the house, they might have multiple reasons to over- or under-report. This first came to light back in the 1980s when several criminologists were poring over ownership surveys. They discovered if you asked just women, the reported household gun ownership rate was near 30 percent. But if you asked men, it was commonly over 50 percent. Either women were lowballing, the men were bragging, or some women were unaware there was a gun in the house. Regardless of the "how and why" of this, survey estimates of household gun ownership rates need to be considered approximate numbers, especially state-by-state when some states have made gun ownership difficult and otherwise law-abiding types might want to keep their possession of a gun secret.

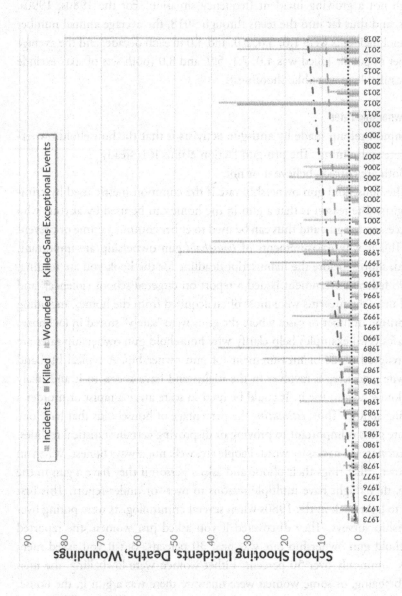

K-12 School Shooting Database, Naval Postgraduate School's Center for Homeland Defense and Security

Over time, there have been four surveys that were conducted with reasonable consistency. Two of the polls (ABC and Gallup) showed steady household gun ownership rates, ping-ponging around 44 percent, from the early 1990s on. Two other polls (Pew and the General Social Survey, or GSS) showed household ownership rates declining from approximately 44 percent down to 36 percent.

One of the agonizing side effects of perpetual curiosity is that when you see distinct patterns, you ask "why" and reach for a calculator. This is when a suffering spouse rolls their eyes and opens a bottle of wine, even if it is still before lunchtime.

The short explanation as to why two pollsters showed consistent ownership and two other surveys showed declining ownership comes down to who was asked the question. The ABC and Gallup polls asked registered voters the question about gun ownership. Voter registration roughly equates to American citizenship since citizenship is required to vote in state and federal elections. The other two polls (Pew and GSS) asked the gun ownership question of anyone who picked up the phone, regardless of their voting/citizenship status.

America is a nation of immigrants, and they continue to flock here. According to the Census Bureau, back in 1990 about 20 percent of the US population was immigrants (legal and otherwise). By 2010, it was 40 percent. Additionally, the range of non-citizen immigrants climbed from 12 percent to 22 percent. From this we can make some gross generalizations and assumptions. Foremost, people born in America and taking standard civics classes are likely to understand the nature of gun ownership as a right and as a reality, and thus are more likely than recent arrivals to legally acquire a gun. People with legally acquired guns are less likely to under report their ownership to surveyors. Illegal immigrants are highly unlikely to even try to buy a gun at a retail store. If they do acquire one underground, then they are not very well going to admit to a stranger on the other end of the phone that they did. Legal immigrants might buy a gun, but their cultural biases and uncertainty about the law might keep them from doing so.

The hypothesis at play is that as the percentage of the population composed of citizens declines, so would the reported rate of guns ownership among *all* residents including immigrants, not just citizens as proxied by voter registration. Though an imperfect fit, the trends are very close (R^2 of 0.81).

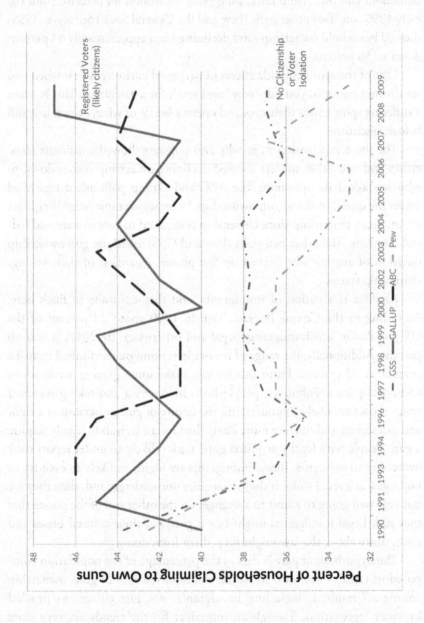

I and the Gun Facts project won't claim credit for what happened after we discovered the divergence, but within a couple of months of publishing our analysis, Pew released a new set of figures about household gun ownership and now claims that it is 42 percent (2017), which jives nicely with ABC reporting 47 percent (2018), Gallup at 43 percent (2019), and a Monmouth University poll at 46 percent (2018). Given all of these factors, we can safely say that among citizens, gun ownership rates have remained remarkably stable for a long period of time.

Score carding gun control strictness

A good question to ask is if a gun control law works. In this book, we have studiously avoided that question as we do not want to bias your perception about the underlying data and the realities that data exposes. There are plenty of gainfully employed people whose job it is to persuade you, one way or the other, that gun control laws either do everything or nothing at all, and I will leave it to them to drown you in rhetoric. I have discovered that a quality set of noise-canceling ear buds along with Led Zeppelin turned up to eleven helps a lot.

What is quite important to understand is that there is a horrid and recurring mishap with scorecards reporting state-level gun control laws. Loosely summarized, various policy groups define a state as having either "strict" or "lax" gun control based on the assortment of the laws each state has. These have been published as either score cards (rankings from highest to lowest) or using the familiar K-12 grading system of A-to-F.

All of it is poppycock, malarkey, balderdash, and other words unsuitable for publication.

For many years the anti-gun movement in the United States was centered around the Brady Campaign (now named the Brady Plan). They published one of the first gun law scorecards and did so for many years, finally stopping for unknown reasons. Since then, a different organization with ever changing names, which started life as the Community Against Gun Violence and is now the Gifford's Law Center, has picked up the process, though with changes.

The problem with these approaches is that they are not based on anything. The Brady Campaign, when they were ranking states, provided a numerical score for each of thirty-eight variations of laws. But there was no substantiation of why a particular value was assigned. For example, a state scored one point if they prohibited a mentally ill person from purchasing a gun, but deducted a point if the same state allowed people with concealed

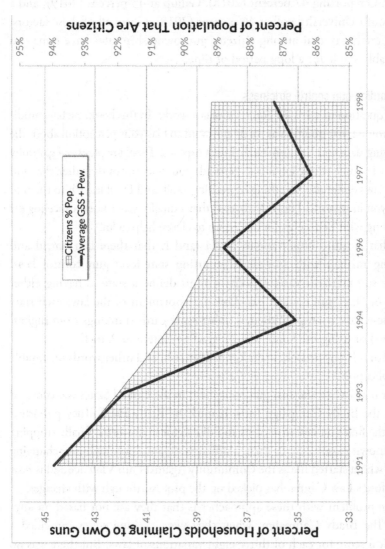

Self-Reported Household Gun Ownership and Citizen Status; Population data, US Census Bureau; Polling data, Pew Research Center, General Social Survey

carry permits to bring their guns into a church. I never found any publicly facing rationale for the Brady scoring system. It appeared, at least on the surface, to be scored in order to formulate a wish list. Some have claimed the scoring scheme was calculated to make certain laws look good or bad in order to drive legislative proposals currently in public or media favor.

What it really did was create mockery, and lots of it.

Every year, a few numbers nuts, including myself, would create a scatter chart like the one on the next page and evaluate the Brady scorecard against all variety of crime (and in passing, please note the "murder" scatter chart has the same outcome as the overall "violent crime" scatter chart above). On the far left is the state which Brady thought had the best selection of gun control laws and on the far right the state with the worst laws. From left-to-right, strict-to-lax. You will undoubtedly notice that California (the strictest state) had a violent crime rate nearly identical to the most-lax state, Arizona. In no form of violent crime, aside from rape which we have previously noted has a location and acquaintance peculiarity, did the Brady Score Card show alignment with violence (highest R^2 was 0.01) and was negatively associated with robbery rates (the stricter the set of gun control laws, the higher the rate of robberies).

I wish I could say things got better vis-à-vis gun law score-carding after the Brady Campaign got out of the business, but it didn't. The Gifford's Law Center, or whatever name they are using this week, switched from a numeric scoring and ranking to a school-like A through F report card, and in the process completely obfuscated how they came to assign the grades. I directly emailed the Gifford's Law Center and asked for a copy of their internal scoring system. I also asked friends not associated with the Gun Facts project or any other group to do the same. None of us received a reply from Gifford's, so how in the heck they come to choose their grading system remains a public mystery.

The point of this section is not to bash either Brady or Gifford, but to make you aware that the commonly reported ranking systems for aggregated gun laws have no observable basis for existence. They do not document established and controversy-free statistical evaluation of the effectiveness of any law. They merely denote which gun laws various groups want the public to believe are good and which are bad.

A bigger problem is that a tiny number of medical researchers have used the score cards to subjectively test gun violence. Herein is the problem. Since the scorecards themselves are rather fact-free in their creation, the subsequent medical school analysis is based on nothing as well. Garbage in, garbage out. Makes me wish pill pushers took a computer science class or two

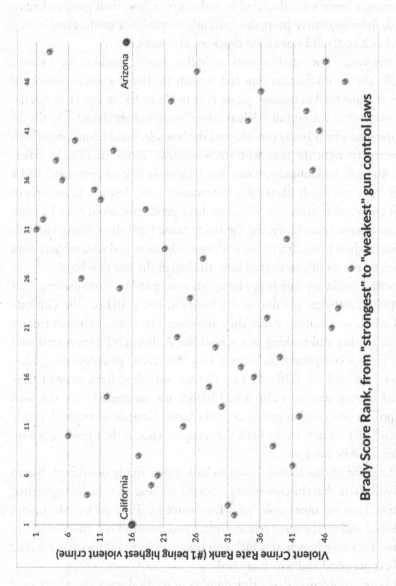

State law ranking, Brady Campaign 2013; Crime, FBI Uniform Crime Reporting, 2012

so that the GIGO theory would be in their minds before they dabbled in a field in which they are untrained.

Police catching bullets

I have a bit of interest in regards to the dangers police face. I grew up around cops. The father of my best childhood friend was the local police chief. As the town's teenage insomniac, I hung out with all the cops as they patrolled those corners of town where mischief tended to happen. Later in life I married into an Irish cop family (my father-in-law once had a rifle bullet zing past his skull, fired by a suspect wanted for arrest). And because of my studies, I have had many protracted conversations with beat cops, detectives, captains, and chiefs about their experience with armed people of both the civilian and criminal class.

Bluntly, cops get shot. It is an occupational hazard that they deal with criminals. As we saw in the chapter on Crime and Guns, your typical street gang member, robbery specialist, and Hell's Angel are more likely armed than not. Criminals desperate to avoid going to jail and fully steeped in their sociopathy shoot at cops. Hence, this is a bit of knowledge we need.

The National Law Enforcement Officers Memorial Fund keeps annual tabs about how on-duty officers die. In the most recent full reporting year, 94 percent of the deaths they documented were from four causes. In the order of their frequency, getting shot was the most common, followed closely by vehicle accidents (car and motorcycle), job-related illnesses, and getting run over.

What is of interest though is that the number and relative rate of cops getting shot to death is not rising, at least not according to long-term trends. On-duty police gun death rates are actually falling while the death rate from job-related illnesses now exceeds that from catching bullets. And the annual death rate by motor vehicle crashes is also dropping, which is amazing given how much of a shift a patrol officer spends in their car. Both of these data points fell while the ranks of sworn officers rose during the same period, with a small pullback starting between 2013 and 2016,[3] which, interestingly, was when firearm homicides began rising. One could, but I won't, hypothesize that fewer police on the streets provide criminals and gang members more unfettered opportunity to kill.

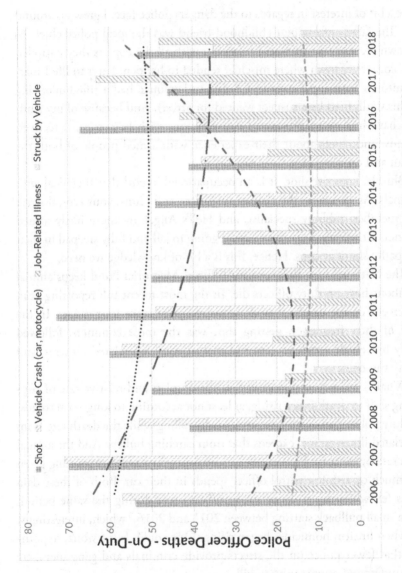

Police Officer Deaths - On-Duty

Shot   Vehicle Crash (car, motocycle)   Job-Related Illness   Struck by Vehicle

National Law Enforcement Officers Memorial Fund, Law Enforcement Fatalities Report, 2018

Social costs

There is a difference between the cost of something and the price you pay. The cost of a night of passion with someone you met in a bar might be three drinks, but the price might be a life-long disease.

This has not gone unnoticed by some of the warring factions in gun control debates who understand the overly flexible demarcation line between cost and price. One fundamental argument about gun control in general is whether public availability of guns is a good or bad thing. Some organizations and researchers have attempted to assign bottom-line costs to guns. Many of these analyses make for good reading if you are a fan of dramatic fiction.

Measuring the net value or cost has taken many forms. Though I make no claim either way, some politicos looked at the rate of defensive gun uses (DGUs) against the number of gun crimes to claim that private gun ownership is a net social gain. The opposing camp occasionally assembles models calculating the dollar cost associated with guns. My standard joke when speaking to an audience is that the societal costs of guns can be seen by the number of divorces filed when a husband spends the excess household cash on yet another scope for his hunting rifle.

Bad jokes aside, there are real costs from the misuse of guns and there are real benefits to DGUs. The problem is that the cost calculations are often based on some radical assumptions and the benefits cannot be calculated since there is a zero dollar cost to not being raped and murdered, made worse still by not knowing what the actual unarmed outcome of the crime might have actually been.

Where most of this discussion quickly goes haywire is on the cost calculations. What precisely is the "cost" of guns? I won't waste your bandwidth on all the different models that have been proffered in the past, but know that these calculations have included rational estimates of unpaid hospital bills compiled by gang members seeking treatment for gunshot wounds to completely irrational estimates of the lifetime lost income of gang members who did not survive.

One of the odder and more recent examples came from the Gifford's Law Center.[4] They present horrifically large numbers about the cost, in each state, wrought by guns and gun violence. Some of the measurements they choose are certainly acceptable, such as uninsured hospitalization of wounded gangbangers. But some of their data points are a mixture of necessary governmental expenses (courts and jails for whomever shot the indigent hospitalized gangbanger), others are unexplained and rather suspicious (costs to employers), and some are simply cockeyed (lost income of unspecified individuals).

But where it gets really squirrely is when the Gifford's Law Center includes the "reduced quality of life attributable to pain and suffering." It might be unsurprising that at birth this organization was called the Legal Community Against Gun Violence, and they no doubt had and still have a few lawyers on their staff. The dead giveaway (forgive the pun) is the raw numbers. In their home state of California, Gifford's estimated the direct cost of gun violence (even including some of the highly speculative and cross-sectional items) at $6.5 billion annually. But the headline number was $18.3 billion, the entirety of the difference being "pain and suffering," which can only be based on a hollow set of assumptions. In other words, that nearly tripled the alleged cost of gun violence (which incidentally included suicides in their formulas) based on pain-and-suffering guesswork.

What would be an interesting study, and one I'm happy to perform once you write me a check, would be to measure inarguable direct costs, but segregate those costs between the two primary criminal classes—gangs and career criminals—and the rest of the bad actors—terrorists, the mentally ill, and hotheads, plus the small amount of costs tied to gun accidents (for a little extra funding, I can even segregate costs for suicides). Since the former group (gangs and career violent criminals) create law enforcement costs, these expenses might be reduced through better policing, enforcing mandatory sentences for gun crimes, etc. This group is distinctly different than the second cluster because the first revolves in and out of the criminal system. The first group creates recurring and higher aggregate social costs, and thus a lack of access to guns might serve a measurable purpose.

CHAPTER 10
About Research

Peer review, on which laypeople place great weight, varies from being an important control, where the editors and the referees are competent and responsible, to being a complete farce.

SCIENCE ISN'T ALWAYS SCIENTIFIC. WHEN it crosses paths with politics, only forensics can identify its corpse.

In the world at large, and within politics specifically, people seek to influence your opinion. In the age of mass media, a single authoritative-sounding meme can persuade millions. If the pitch generates fear in the listener, then they are eased past critical thinking and into action, mainly passing along the meme. This is all well and good when someone yells "fire" in a crowded theater and there is actually a fire. It is dangerous to do so when nothing is ablaze.

One way in which people in politics attempt to persuade the populace is with research. Washington, D.C. is littered with the offices of sundry think tanks, centers, academics for hire, and policy groups armed with calculators and a smallish horde of people who invent "facts." As Todd Snyder famously said in his song "Statistician's Blues": "Eighty-two-point-four percent of people believe 'em/Whether they're accurate statistics or not."

As you can imagine, in the twenty-plus years I have been reviewing the intersection of guns, violence, and the effects of legislation, I have encountered hundreds of bad studies, often before breakfast. Not a single week in at least the last decade has passed without someone throwing me a link to a study along with a note that could be summarized as saying, "This proves you wrong!" So far, with three exceptions, nothing was proven except that the senders did not read and/or understand the study they hurled my way, much less identify the serious flaws therein. The situation for little-ol-me is so bad that I now reply with a copy/paste response where I make a bet with the sender; I'll read the study they likely only Googled. If it is of good quality and with accurate results, I'll write about it and thank them publicly for the new information. If I find two or more serious problems with the study they provided, they pay me my standard $250/hour consulting fee, minimum three hours.

I have had zero takers thus far.

The problem of horrific studies may be acute to guns and gun control, though I have little doubt other fields suffer as well. Because nobody likes the idea of getting shot, guns evoke a certain degree of fear and researching guns helps amplify these fears. Even NRA types I have met show a great deal of deference to guns, knowing that a lack of attention can result in catastrophe. The problem is that people of the political caste are very acquainted with the fact that fear is a short circuit to spark action. Take global climate change as an example. I won't debate the science, but politicians from nearly every country have used global climate change as a fear-based rallying cry to every proposal from cars that emit lower emissions to forced veganism. "Do this or you will die," is the unspoken underlying directive.

Data quality, methodology, assumptions, and those other pesky variables

However, what makes bad research is fairly simple. Detecting bad research involves reviewing merely three elements of any study, though admittedly this may lead to hour upon hour of digging in order to find where the flaws lie.

Dud data

Using the old computer sciences adage of "garbage in, garbage out", some bad research—be it about guns, global warming, or gum disease—is caused by lousy data. If you are measuring the rate of change in American firearm murders and your source data documents yogurt sales in Bavaria, odds are the results will be quite useless. However, this won't stop cable news networks from breathlessly reporting the headline conclusions of a guns-and-yogurt study.

In the world of guns and control, there was one shining example of a case where bad data generated a bad conclusion and the media broke bad reporting on it all.

A study by an enterprising medical student concluded that the rate of firearm deaths among children was rising. This summary was echoed by many of the major American news factories with great alarm. But those of us who live inside of the Centers for Disease Control mortality databases knew that this was not true. How could this budding but bungling student get the basic answer so very wrong?

Bad data, or more accurately, data he didn't understand fully. The student in question relied on the KIDS Inpatient Database, which gathers data about children being admitted to hospitals and why. This data included information about children being struck by bullets. Sounds good on the surface, but when it comes to research, nothing meaningful exits at the surface level.

The KIDS database is completely voluntary. Like any voluntary operation, it tends to start small and grow over time. For example, the first year that the Gun Facts project called for research volunteers, we acquired twelve. A decade later, we have several hundred. Likewise, with the KIDS database, in its early years, it received reports from a handful of hospitals around the country. Over time it had quite a few (4,200 according to their website), though not comprehensive enough at the time that the crippled research was performed. The student was, I assume, unaware that the number of participating hospitals had grown over the years and thus the number of reports had grown as a byproduct of that. This led to rising numbers of all childhood maladies, including getting shot. Thus, bad data (inconsistent measurement over time) led to a bad conclusion. This bad conclusion led to bad reporting.

Though bad data can exist on its own, more often researchers cherry pick data without appropriate cause. Once in a handful of blue moons there is a rhyme or a reason to carefully select certain subsets of data. For example, if one wanted to study specifically if gun shows near state borders, where one state had very strict guns control laws and the other did not, affected gun crimes in either location, looking at just two states *might* be appropriate. In gun policy research, cherry picking data is more the norm than the exception. I have seen a study where crime rates in a prosperous northeastern county were compared to an impoverished county in Texas. Bad data exists in terms of absolute quality (the Bavarian Yogurt Council has rather slipshod data collection processes), bad understanding of the source data (thinking the KIDS database was a constant, broad accumulation of data), or can be so hand picked as to make even good data meaningless.

There are a number of "gold standard" datasets. When it comes to crime data, the FBI has operated the "Uniform Crime Reporting" program since 1930. As unnavigable as the data often can be, it is the most reliable, robust, comprehensive data. This means that the FBI's data is very suitable for real insight into guns and crime, and completely unsuitable for politicos who wish to ignore the crime aspect of gun misuse. When this data is very inconvenient, researchers with a predetermined conclusion will often grab data from local authorities. Too often this data does not comport with Uniform Crime Reporting standards. But even with the FBI's data, precautions occasionally need to be taken. Some cities—often the ones with the worst crime problems—have failed to report their data. Others devised non-standard definitions for some types of crimes. Yet, despite these infrequent and isolated exceptions, the FBI's data is the best of the best. This in turn makes much of the research provided by the Bureau of Justice Statistics robust as well since they pull from the Uniform Crime Reporting system for many of their studies.

The Centers for Disease Control are good as well when it comes to collecting and providing access to raw numbers. They have two publicly facing portals (WISQARS and WONDER, known by their fuller names "Web-based Injury Statistics Query and Reporting System" and "Wide-ranging Online Data for Epidemiologic Research" respectively) where anyone can verify what is killing and injuring people. The United Nations' Office on Drugs and Crime has viable data, though we have to note that the data is only as reliable as each country's reporting, and many places may have political motives to lowball some estimates. This is especially true in countries where an oppressive government can command the killing—with guns—of multitudes, and the data is either unreported or misclassified (when you see that two hundred politically disenfranchised opponent tribesmen died from dancing the mohobelo, then you know something is up).

Often though, the inaccuracies cannot be helped. Throughout this book you have seen many disclaimers about data quality—low numbers from CDC extractions, the problems with estimating state-by-state gun ownership rates, and more. The problem that the public faces is that even when a researcher mentions data limitations, these disclosures are typically buried in small type toward the end of the paper. Reporters often skip over the study's abstract, racing on toward the "conclusions" section, and ignoring the rest (this assumes they are not working from just press releases, but please don't get me started on this ongoing debasement of journalism). Even an honest and scrupulous researcher who clearly documents the limitations of their data sources can create public misunderstanding, assisted by media and activist groups, who buy the study's conclusions without second guessing their own "confirmation bias." In other words, if the research report headline agrees with someone's preconceived notions, then it often is accepted blindly.

Selective omission of data is a research stunt worth watching for. In the world of American gun politics, the most often omitted thing is the nation's capital.

Washington, D.C. is its own sixty-eight-square-mile city-state. Beholden to neither of its neighboring states, D.C. has its own government with some degree of participation by the feds. This means it has its own laws and its own problems. For most of the latter twentieth century, D.C. had rather strict gun laws, including an outright ban on the sale and possession of handguns. Its problem was a very high violent crime rate, gun crime rate, and murder rate. How much higher was D.C.'s homicide rate than anywhere else? Check out the next chart.

It would indeed be curious if a bit of research investigating guns, violence, and policy were to omit the District of Columbia from any analysis. At the very worst, a report might appropriately segregate D.C. to study its peculiarities in parallel with the rest of the country. Dropping it from the mix, however, would be as odd as it would be criminal.

But that is precisely what many policy groups, medical researchers, and politicians did when they found the realities of D.C. violence inconvenient. Data quality in research then not only relies on the source data itself, but assurance that no important data has been absentmindedly or purposefully excluded. Sadly, this data exclusion tactic is so common that after a few years heading the Gun Facts project, it became the first thing I looked for in new cross-regional studies. Given the magnitude of the gulf in homicide rates—five times higher on average for all years and eight times higher for the worst year—ignoring D.C. in gun violence studies is likely intentional.

Another common research data problem is the pulling of incomplete timelines of data. A great example of this was a substandard analysis on California guns and murders. The study spanned 1993 through 2003. You may recall that starting year—1993—was the peak of violent crime in the United States, and that included California. It was also half a decade after states started switching over to "shall-issue" public carry. By starting with the peak year, the authors attempted to make certain laws look successful to the

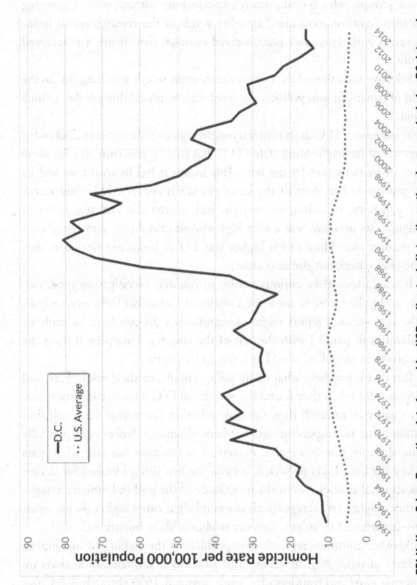

FBI Uniform Crime Reporting data from older UCR online tool. Note, the national average includes DC data and would be lower still were that removed.

exclusion of historical data. Though it is not always a problem beginning an analysis with incomplete data (see the chapter on the United States, United Kingdom, and Australia for an example of where back-data simply was not available), it does become a problem when older or newer data is available and might show longer term trends.

Madhouse methodologies

I can show, statistically, that the rate of rapes rises covalently with the rate of air-conditioning use in localized timeline analysis. But as you wisely suspect, air-conditioning does not cause rape. This is the old "correlation does not mean causation" reality.

Air conditioners and rapists, though, help prove a point—that the trip from raw data to published conclusion can introduce irregularities that hospital-grade laxatives couldn't address.

The next research calamity involves methodology, and on this one topic I could write endlessly (don't break into a cold sweat, for I will say as little as I can and still provide illumination). "Methodology" simply means "What work did you do to turn raw data into insight?" If that sounds vague, then you likely started getting a queasy feeling since this foreshadows the fact that methodologies are more varied than data and using the wrong methodology—intentionally or otherwise—produces bad results. These results may be exactly what the researcher wants, but that doesn't mean the results portray truth.

Sadly, the most frequent source for this malady is the medical field. I won't belabor this for long as entire books about how the medical community has committed criminology malpractice have been penned by people who held high positions within the Centers for Disease Control.[1] Unsurprisingly, we see a fair amount of suspect studies gurgling up from Johns Hopkins Bloomberg School of Public Health. If the "Bloomberg" in the school's name caught your attention, then yes—it is the same Michael Bloomberg who was the former mayor of New York, is the seventeenth richest person in the world, and is known as the gun control movement's private bank. Cynical people might think that Bloomberg's largess would influence the gun-centric criminology research conducted by Johns Hopkins doctors. All I'll say is that cynicism has value.

When it comes to inappropriate research methodologies, some doctors need to lose their licenses. At the Gun Facts project, we keep a page of *some* of the bad studies that have gotten media attention (there is a much longer list, but no public education value comes from documenting problems with papers nobody—except the Gun Facts volunteer researchers—ever reads). A full 59 percent of the bad studies we list came from medical journals. There is history behind why the medical community started dabbling outside their field of expertise, and I won't bore you with those horrid tales. But their assorted criminology misdeeds often provide textbook examples of how not to do research.

Core to good methodologies is to not use substandard data when gold standard data exists. Revisit for the moment the KIDS database example. The Centers for Disease Control provide a comprehensive, national database of data going back to 1981 for deadly things, and back to the year 2000 for non-fatal ones. With the major exception being datapoints where the numbers are so low that the CDC flags them as "unreliable," it would have been much better, and easier, to generate gunshot injury and death data, by age group, from the CDC, and not rely on the chronologically inconsistent KIDS database.

After "data selection as part of methodology" comes the more insidious sin of choice in statistical tools (worry not, my discussion of statistics will not make your head hurt . . . much). With large, consistent, and robust datasets from the FBI, CDC, and UN, elaborate statistical processes are unnecessary. Some of the tools used to create bad research when good data is available might well be the good tools to use when data is thin and flimsy. But they are inappropriate at best and misleading at worst when real data is in abundance. In the current era, several statistical stunts are used to get around relying upon abundant gold standard data, each of which would earn an "F" in a quantitative research college course.

Foremost is "synthetic modeling." If the name sounds icky, in the study of criminology, it is. The goal of synthetic modeling is to produce "data applicable to a given situation that are not obtained by direct measurement." As you know from above, when it comes to guns, crime, and injuries, we have a lot of gold standard data that comes from "direct measurement." So right from the start there is no need for synthetic anything. How this approach has been misused, mainly by the medical community, takes us a little deeper into this not-so-fresh hell.

Any statistical modeling relies on one or more assumptions. Bad research is loaded with assumptions (see the following section on the cascade effect of bad research to see the next step in creating bad "knowledge"). These assumptions might be right, they might be wrong, they might be fragile, or they might be fraudulent. This is important because the assumptions are never disclosed in the headlines or even the paper's abstract. Have you read through the list of assumptions in a study that a network news operation reported on? Well, neither have they.

The common objective of synthetic modeling is to create data where data does not exist, which is unnecessary given what the FBI, CDC, and UN provide. An example of this approach might be to create crime data (that never actually existed) for State-X derived from the crime data for State-Y based on the assumptions that State-X and State-Y have everything else in common, which is never the case. In effect, researchers are inventing crime data from something thinner than air. Using this approach, a researcher could "calculate" that the number of gun deaths in State-X would have been much lower than they were by comparing the artificially generated numbers with the real crime data.

A more common and statistically valid approach is to simply compare different places with different gun policies and include every variable that might conceivably cause gun crime or suicides to vary regardless of the law. For example, when measuring the effects of concealed carry laws between two states that passed their laws at the same time, you might include each state's poverty rate, educational attainment, degree of participation in religion, alcoholism, and the per capita consumption of Bavarian yogurt. These are called "confounding variables," which are streams of data about outside influences that can affect what is being researched (the *dependent* and *independent* variables that your long dormant "stats class" memory may be recalling at this moment). Via some basic statistical math, that relies on no assumption, invalid comparison, or tricks that create data, such multivariate analysis exposes which variables—alone or in combinations—explain the patterns in the FBI's, CDC's, and UN's data. For example, if State-X and State-Y both passed a concealed carry law the same year, you could take their FBI published crime data and then see if the law, local economic conditions, dropout rates, church closings, cocktail lounge openings, or a transient dearth of "double dark chocolate yogurt" explains the change in crime rates.

This is precisely what a lot of researchers avoid doing when it comes to guns.

One of the huge problems with research is assumptions. There is not enough paper in production today to document all the weird and horribly irrational assumptions exposed in peer-reviewed academic papers. Indeed, if you are ever so bored that reading the turbid prose in these papers is exciting by comparison to whatever else you could be doing, then start by scanning those papers for assumptions and then reject the paper if the assumptions are plentiful or absurd. Odds are your time investment will go way down.

Here is a favorite example of a bit of research that combined cherrypicked data with bad assumptions. The authors attended gun shows in two very different states with the intent of trying to document how many guns were illegally acquired from these events. They employed "observational evidence," which is a fifty-cent phrase for "what we saw." If they saw two people conferring about a firearm, and one person buying it, they assumed that this was a straw purchase, where the buyer was in fact acquiring the gun for the other person, presumably illegally. Alternative explanations, such as this being a case of two friends—one being more expert than the other—conferring on the relative quality and price of the firearm, were not considered. Occam's Razor teaches us all that "the simplest solution is most likely the right one." Likewise, the simplest explanation for any bit of "observational evidence" is likely the right one as well. It is also interesting that the authors of this particular paper neither validated their assumption (none of the alleged straw purchasers were proven or disproven to have done so), nor contrasted their data with the report produced every decade by the Bureau of Justice Statistics concerning how many crime guns are procured at gun shows (0.8 percent in the BJS's 2019 report[2]).

I hate to say it, but the degree of absurdity in assumptions made in research gets worse. Much, much worse.

Lastly, some researchers conflate the broad with the narrow and vice-versa. One review of guns and crimes amalgamated multiple countries from multiple continents, ignoring vast differences in cultures, wealth, education, and more. Way too many researchers extrapolate a small geography of data—one or a few counties—to the population at large. Knowledge can be gained from small scale studies that are applicable to the bigger picture, but not often. For example, the mechanics of how street gangs get guns will vary from city to city, but they won't vary radically since these are underground transactions with common modus operandi. This example might well be a valid projection of a small population to explain a larger one. However, applying the suicide data of young, urban adults to the overall population would be utter nonsense.

Collapsing mountains of equine effluvium

Recall that synthetic modeling requires at least one assumption. What if the core assumption is both wrong and yet presented as fact? The outcome would be wrong squared.

This is occurring in research, daily. At least in gun policy research.

In at least three papers that used synthetic modeling that I have reviewed in the last two years, all based their models on "facts" reported in other academic papers. Following the links for the most suspicious sounding "facts," I learned that nearly all of the conclusions of the cited papers ranged from debatable to demonstrably incorrect. In other words, the synthetic models were based on non-facts that were the basis of the assumptions used in the models. Garbage in, garbage out, but on the methodology side. And the more bad "facts" from incorrect papers, the more unreliable the outcome of the research itself. I have seen one paper where the "fact" used was not derived from the paper they cited, but in yet another paper that was cited in turn. In other words, a thirdhand "fact" which, upon examination, wasn't very factual either.

It is a given that the average voter lacks the time, skill, or inclination to dig into the study being reported on by their favorite evening news channel. They also lack the same resources and gumption to dig two, three, maybe four levels down through other papers to even begin to see if any of this chain of research is valid. Now contrast this with the work produced by most (but not all) criminologists. They rely on the aforementioned gold standard data sources and occasionally supplement it with survey work (which has its own set of problems, but at least surveys do not rely upon mathematical manipulations). This is one of the more obvious differences between works about guns and violence produced by criminologists and doctors and is worth paying attention to.

The problem with the cascade of citations is that nearly nobody checks them. Even editors and judges at peer-reviewed journals rarely delve past the top-level work being presented. There is no resource in which the papers, the source data, their methodology, and their conclusions are score-carded. There is no chain of authority for citations with bad research and data sources highlighted. In the absence of this, even the peer review process throws in its already threadbare towel.

But what about all these peer-reviewed papers?

Peer review, on which laypeople place great weight, varies from being an important control, where the editors and the referees are competent and responsible, to being a complete farce.

You might ask who made that claim. Some crank? Some political pundit? Someone who ran out of double dark chocolate Bavarian yogurt and was throwing a tantrum? No.

Robert Higgs penned that. Higgs has chops in this arena. He has spent a career in academia, and while doing so he has been a peer reviewer for more than thirty professional journals, and a research proposal reviewer for the National Science Foundation, the National Institutes of Health, and a number of private foundations. In other words, he has seen the peer review system from both the inside and the out, and what he saw wasn't pretty. Summarizing in one article he notes that "any journal editor who desires, for whatever reason, to reject a submission can easily do so by choosing referees he knows full well will knock it down; likewise, he can easily obtain favorable referee reports."[3]

And that's just one of the problems. There are many, many more. In brief, here are the plot points where the Italian opera of peer review litters the research stage with dead heroes and prosperous villains.

GETTING IN: Not all papers submitted to a journal get over the transom. If an author, the topic, or the headline conclusion are not to the journal editor's liking, the paper might not even be presented to a review panel.

FAST-TRACKING: However, if the paper agrees with the biases of the editor, it can go from submission to publication with numerous shortcuts provided, including bypassing some parts of the review process altogether.

STACKING DECKS: As Higgs said, if an editor wants a paper to have no chance to being peer reviewed, the editor simply selects judges who have previously published contrary conclusions.

EDITORIALIZING: Some papers are published with the editor providing unsolicited commentary, either in overzealous praise or condemnation. When in the negative, the editor provides their own mountain of citations which may or may not be worth consideration.

Now, lest you think the peer review process is a cesspool of anti-intellectual skullduggery (which it sometimes is), it is not completely unwholesome. Many good editors and honest peers judge papers with precision, respect, and commitment to honest enlightenment. But this is not universal, and I dare say growing less and less common. The problem, at least for gun violence studies, is that things have gotten bad enough to require many fine-tooth combs.

Some journals, where one would hope to find a minimum of reliability, are simply for-profit operations (visit some of these sites, as I do all the time, and notice how copies of papers from journals cost twenty-five to a hundred dollars each). For some of these operations, there is no real academic review at all. We know this because in 2018 a trio of academic hoaxers wrote twenty completely fake papers and managed to get seven of them published at peer-reviewed journals.[4]

One odd extension of this problem is in the arena of medical professionals publishing on gun violence in medical journals. Doctors, God bless their pill-pushing little hearts, are not criminologists, and thus their data sources and methodologies are often far off the mark. The peers who review their papers are unqualified for evaluating the criminology of the matter at hand, and thus do not second guess the work. It is a case of the blind optometrist judging the blind ophthalmologist.

What you, as someone wrapping your brain around guns or any other public policy topic for that matter, need to understand is that just because a talking head on TV, a pundit, a family member, friend or neighbor, or even an academic points to a "peer reviewed paper" as proof of their argument, they may be completely wrong because the paper they proffer may be completely wrong as well. Since you will not have the time to figure out if their cited source is credible or not, you can at least ask some basic questions; what was their data source, what was their methodology, what assumptions did the author make. If your talking head, friend, or academic nemesis cannot tell you up-front any of these things, then they have not read the paper and cannot verify its sanctity. At that point, feel free to change the subject since you would otherwise be discussing policy with an uninformed soul.

The amazing unpublished paper

One highly disturbing debasement of research, especially in the gun policy colosseum, involves the media citing unpublished papers. This regrettable trend started a few years back and appears to be increasing in frequency.

What happens is this: research is performed, occasionally with financing by a policy organization. The results are then privately shared with select media organizations, chosen I suspect due to the outlet's political alignment and biases. Headlines are splashed about the study's conclusions along with whatever plum-colored prose the reporter contributes. Time passes, the paper is never published (and likely was never submitted), the data and methodologies are never revealed, and the author's sobriety is never checked.

But headlines are made and they remain indexed by Google, and that is both the troubling intent and outcome.

In anything scientific, it needs to endure the "four eyes" principle, which means at minimum two unrelated people need to have access to all the data and all the computations. Otherwise, there is no validation. One of the great debates about guns and their control in recent times came when an American president cited a study about mass public shootings, echoing one study's conclusion that the United States was unique in the world for such events. But the author, at least as of when I penned this chapter and many years after he made headlines, has not shared the data with anyone. Even the rabble-rousing reporter John Stossel asked for a copy of the data and was denied, as was every academic who inquired. When another research group did a much larger study, using a wider array of native language speakers to seek info from most corners of the world (they may have missed Nauru), they not only found that the situation was very different than the president had said, but they made their datasets publicly available. In short, an unpublished, unsubstantiated, and non-reviewed paper influenced the "thinking" of an American president, and the conclusions therein were later debunked with transparent authority.

At least this form of bad research is easy for anyone to catch. Thus far most (not all) of the media outlets who have reported on unpublished papers mention this lack of public exposure and openness to critique, though that salient item is often buried far enough into the article that the vast bulk of readers never notice it. Even if the reporter fails to mention a lack of research paper publishing, they routinely mention the name(s) of the author(s) and a quick Google will confirm if the paper is published or not.

What is important for you is knowing this new shenanigan is regretfully routine. Keeping one eye open for disclosure about the paper's publishing status, or lack thereof, is wise.

A case study: the "forty-three times more likely" affair
In 1986, after disco had finally and thankfully died, a paper was published in the *New England Journal of Medicine* that was arguably the start of the ongoing problem of doctors dabbling in fields for which they are not educated. The conclusion of the study was that a gun in the home was forty-three times as likely to be used to shoot someone in the family as to shoot a criminal. The scintillating, yet positively erroneous meme, is still ricocheting in the political ether. That's one of the problems with bad studies; if they confirm someone's biases, they will be repeated in perpetuity.

I won't bludgeon the doctor who penned "Protection or Peril," for he has endured decades of verbal and digital abuse, though rightly so. Instead let's use his paper, the progenitor of bad-memes-about-guns, as a short case study in how limited data and bad methodologies can lead to total misunderstanding and an avalanche of bad citations.

The data
The data itself is not necessarily bad, just horribly limited and inappropriate.

All of the data came from one county, King County in Washington state, which includes Seattle as well as some long green past the city limits.

I have a friend who is a lifelong resident of that area, and one day on the phone I joked that there were only two kinds of people in Seattle; those who could deal with the rain and those who committed suicide. He didn't laugh, thought about it for a second, and said "yep." For reference, according to the CDC, the suicide rate in King County, Washington was about 33 percent higher than the national average for the year that the study was published.

The second problem with the study (the first being a single county with a known high suicide rate) was that they only collected reports of gun deaths. This is a twofer data defect, with two different data selection mishaps. First, as we have shown in previous chapters, over 80 percent of the time when a gun is used to stop a crime, the owner never pulls the trigger, and in another 9 percent of instances they shot to scare or wound, not to kill. Thus, potentially 92 percent of defensive uses of a gun were excluded from this study because the author only had data for gun deaths.

This bit is rather odd. The study itself plainly states that it does not "include cases where burglars or intruders are wounded or frightened away by the use or the display of a firearm." The authors were aware that this was a possibility, and that the "gun in the home" might have prevented serious injury or death. Hence, this exclusion is a methodology error.

In terms of gun deaths in the home (remember, the forty-three times meme was about being in the home), 83.7 percent of all the deaths were suicides. Do recall from our chapter on suicides and guns, there is no correlation between a gun being available and a successful suicide. Sure, Kurt Cobain shot himself in Seattle, but he had enough heroin around to kill an elephant, so he had options.

Is using only gun deaths a methodology problem or a data quality problem? In this case, it is a methodology error since data selection, as opposed to the quality of the numbers themselves, falls into the realm of study design. Regardless, the data itself was original sin as far as leading to polluted insights.

Delving deeper into the study under our microscope, there was no effort to test against other variables. King County covers a lot of turf, from Elliot Bay to the Cascade Mountain foothills. It goes from major metro regions where one might be killed by a thrown fish at Pike Place market, to nearly unpopulated and unforgivably beautiful forests. One would think testing the in-home and largely suicidal death rates against more localized rates of poverty, education, or chronic addiction to Dick's Drive-In hamburgers would factor into the analysis, but the authors did not, nor did they seem to understand that doing so is rather basic criminology, sociology, and economics practice.

Of the nearly 13 percent of King County gun homicides this study reviewed, nothing was explored about the relationship of the perpetrator and victim, aside from the fact that 57 percent of the victims had been drinking. Since we previously established that people who make bad life choices tend to make a lot of them, we have to question how booze, and I'm betting drugs (though this was not reported), factored in. Here is a hypothetical example, one where two drunk, drug-dealing thugs sharing an apartment get into an argument over a deal gone bad, and one shoots the other. This was not apparently considered in the forty-three times research.

Thus far we have bad data selection (which can be considered bad data itself), a methodology that faltered on several vectors, and a general sloppiness that would offend your garden variety criminologist. What is really concerning is not this study, for it has been savagely lambasted by people with real research chops. Nor is it that the forty-three times meme stumbles through the political landscape like a lost extra from the set of *The Walking Dead*. The big problem is that academics keep citing it to this day. I asked Google Scholar to show me all peer-reviewed papers published since 2017 that cite "Protection or Peril?" Among the two pages of results are citations in papers published by the *Journal of the American Medical Association*, the *American Journal of Forensic Medicine and Pathology*, and the *Journal of the American College of Surgeons*.

Seeing a pattern here?

What to do when a study is thrust at you

On guns and other topics, eventually someone will wave a ream of paper over their heads and frantically shout "studies show that . . ." Many of them claim to be journalists. How is the average Joe supposed to deal with these moments?

Step one, smile. Step two, breath deeply. Step three, prepare to lose a friend.

When confronted with a "this study says" claim, here are the steps perceptive adults should take.

SMELL TEST: Compare the claim against what you, friends, or family have encountered in real life. For example, a news broadcaster recently and breathlessly reported on the "growing epidemic of gun deaths among children." Think about all the kids in your neighborhood, your set of nieces and nephews, your local public schools, etc. If you cannot sense a pattern of increasing childhood gun deaths, then there certainly is no "epidemic," at least using the dictionary definition of the word ("a widespread occurrence of an infectious disease in a community at a particular time"). The study that the newscaster referenced was one of the many that defined "child" as people upward of age twenty-four, and as a byproduct included every young and now dead gangbanger. Incidentally, the CDC databases tell us that the childhood firearm death rate has been essentially flat for the past seventeen years, whereas actual epidemics grow rapidly.

ASK ABOUT THE DATA: If you encounter a paper-waving ideologue in a one-on-one exchange, ask the person making the claim, "What is the source data in the study and is it of high quality?" I've been doing this stunt for years, and the common answer is a sheepish facial expression followed by them mumbling, "Well, I didn't *actually* read the study." Even if they have read it, the key aspect is knowing if any of the accepted gold standard data sources—FBI crime, CDC mortality, etc.—underlie the methodology. If not, change the subject. I discovered that asking, "So, do you think the Dodgers will make it to the playoffs this year?" defuses everything . . . unless the acquaintance is also a Yankees fan, in which case the conversation gets rapidly less pleasant.

ASK ABOUT THE METHODOLOGY: "What was the study's methodology?" is another conversation stopper. People might have an answer about the data. Nearly nobody you meet will understand a methodology more complex than simple percentage calculations, and this assumes they read the study at all. If you add, "I hope they didn't use a synthetic modeling approach," the other person might actually excuse themselves from the table . . . and not return.

ASK ABOUT CRITIQUES: "What academic criticism has been made about your study?" One quirky manifestation of confirmation bias is that people tend not to look for disconfirmation. Once they find a study that agrees with their preconceptions, they quit searching. Follow up with, "Such comments are often on the same website that the paper was published," and you will demonstrate that knowing about criticism is as important as knowing about the study itself.

ASK ABOUT FUNDING: This gets a little too political, and you might want to dance lightly on this landmine. However, many advocacy groups with a mission fund research. This is not outright buying of results, but it commonly involves investing only in researchers who will likely produce results that the advocacy group desires ("Let's give Josh about two hundred thousand dollars. His last paper helped us a lot."). This is not to say active outcome-driven collusion purchases do not take place, but I'm loathe to publicly accuse the obvious suspects (buy me a burger and I'll privately dish on them). But the question is worth asking when confronted with any research. For a very long time, one outfit (who I choose to leave unnamed) has funded doctors doing criminology (bad), script writers pitching gun topics to Hollywood producers (bad), bankrolled advocacy groups (bad), and has teamed with crusading politicians (really bad). They have bought gun policy "research" by the freight load, and in the process cheapened American life. Some researchers do cite their funding in their papers, but others don't have to because the money goes to their parent organization, such as when an activist billionaire—with very publicly stated views about guns—funds a medical school, and people within that institution magically start churning out gun-related, piss poor research. These researchers are not obligated to disclose the original source of the money because the researchers get the laundered cash from the college, not the activist benefactor.

The short of this chapter is suggesting that you be skeptical. That includes being skeptical of me. Question everybody and everything, always.

CHAPTER 11

Putting a Ribbon around a Gun Barrel

DOES YOUR HEAD HURT? IMAGINE how mine feels.

The only pity I seek is for you to know that I have been at this for over twenty years. I have waded through collections of data that the FBI used to ship only on request and only via compact discs. I have read, dissected, and written about peer-reviewed papers that were either great, marginal, sloppy, or downright criminal in their delinquencies. I have sat in front of network news television cameras and caught talking heads repeating fables about guns and deaths from them. I have revived comatose audience members after diving a little too deeply into the arcane statistics. I have drilled into oddities of public surveying on gun ownership to identify obscure differences that made sense out of conflicting information. I have sat at meetings and held discussions at the offices of anti-gun groups and NRA conventions. I have found and combined arcane scraps of data that separately said one thing about guns, but together said just the opposite.

Yes, my head hurts too. A lot. Daily. Thankfully, Amazon now sells aspirin by the shipping container. I have two in my back yard.

But my biggest headaches don't come from data; they come from ideologues. Data, at least in its raw form from gold-standard sources, is pure and informative. Anything from ideologues requires weed whackers to level their underbrush. Sometimes it is a bad meme. The next day it is a paper that no self-respecting academic would publish, which says less about guns and more

234 • GUNS AND CONTROL

about the relative morality of some researchers. In a bad week it is a policy group proffering a factoid devoid of facts. And on any given day people from both the pro- and anti-gun camps feel obliged to read me their own riot act when the chart I prepared and shared on Facebook shatters their unfounded beliefs. In fact, I spent too much time this last week calming the agitation of a reader in Australia who did not appreciate a chart I made contrasting the rate of decline in homicides between Oz and the United States, despite the numbers being accurate and the visualization being commonplace.

And yet, I masochistically trudge on. After all, facts are important.

Now that I have spent many chapters flooding your cranium with a lot of info, I think it worthwhile to put a ribbon around what you have learned. To summarize and help prepare you for the rather tense discussions you are about to have with family, neighbors, and other people who may soon unfriend you on Facebook.

Go raw—with data, that is

Recall that research is not always what it appears to be. The political marketplace is filled with suspect calculations, assumptions-riddled analysis, and no end of utter hogwash. Be it either synthetic modeling that produces crime statistics that never occurred or a pack of lawyers who triple the alleged costs of gun violence in society by including highly speculative figures for "pain and suffering," your first assumption when someone says "research shows . . ." should be to ask for the raw data. This quite typically ends the discussion, which, if nothing else, adds to your free time.

Most people reading this book will not have the time or tenacity to download data and "run the numbers" in their favorite software. But you can get quick and meaningful glimpses into the reality of guns, violence, and suicides from the same gold-standard sources used by the pros. If you want crime data, ask Google for "FBI UCRdatatool" for the older online crime reporting services the FBI provides, or query "FBI crime data explorer" for the newer version. When suicide and accident data is of interest, Google will guide you to the "CDC WISQARS" (Web-based Injury Statistics Query and Reporting System) or "CDC WONDER" (Wide-ranging ONline Data for Epidemiologic Research) data exploration tools. The globe trotters among you may prefer to have Google drag you over to "UN drug crime statistics" to get your mitts on the United Nations' compilation of crime data from around the world. The nice thing about the internet is that it has democratized access to real information and made it easy to obtain. It also brought you Twitter arguments, so you have to take the good with the bad.

Earlier in this book I said not to take anyone's word about guns and crime, including mine. This glorious contraption called the internet has bypassed politicians and advocacy groups and is so simple to use that even a harried working mom can snoop some data in between dinner and the kid's soccer game.

There is no shortage of research

Despite my acerbic review of quality (or lack thereof) in modern gun research, not all of it sucks. You just have to be careful from whom you seek information.

Before I get into that briar patch, do take note of a currently popular but pitiful meme circulating around the political ether that claims there is a lack of gun violence research. This is poppycock that you can verify yourself. I mentioned Google Scholar, the website where Google has indexed academic papers, of which there are the good, the bad, and the butt ugly. In there you can find papers that will "prove" whatever you want to say about guns and gun play. You can also find some actual facts.

At Google Scholar, key in *"firearm violence" criminology* (the quote marks are important) and disable the tool from showing you citations and patents. What you receive are numerous pages with links to what criminologist have discovered about guns and violence (more or less criminologists—some doctors include the word "criminology" in their papers to get the attention of serious students like yourself and Google's overly generous indexing algorithms). Substitute "gun" for "firearm" for a few more, then replace "criminology" with "psychology" to see that head peepers have been very interested in this topic for quite some time. You can repeat the basic key phrase "firearm violence" at the Bureau of Justice Statistics website to see what relevant research the feds have found valuable.

If that is not enough, and you really want a deep dive, some criminologists have written entire volumes on the topic. One of the better books is titled *Targeting Guns* by Professor Gary Kleck. This book is not for the timid and covers nearly every aspect of guns and controls ranging from assault weapons to the impacts of some legislation, and does so with a stunning degree of mind numbing data, arcane abbreviations used in the trade, and enough tables to index it all. That the chapter following the introduction is titled "Illegitimate Practices in Summarizing Research" shows that I am not the only person discontented with what sadly substitutes for study and conversation about guns and violence. While you are on a book retailer's website, key in "gun violence criminology" and note that Professor Kleck is not alone in publishing at length about what I have tried to summarize in these pages.

Though the raw data is yours for the taking, it is important to know that criminologists and economists—two professions deeply acquainted with proper research methodologies and data analysis—have produced a boatload of insight using the same raw data I walked you through. And people in the mental health field have added to our knowledge from a "what makes shooters different" perspective. There is no shortage of research, despite what activists say. You just have to pay attention to the right type of researchers using the right data sources and employing the right methodologies.

The five bad actors are not you

You are not a murderer, rapist, bandit, gangbanger, or thug. If you are, put down this book and march yourself to the nearest police station. I'm sure the desk detective would love to have a chat.

The data shows that when it comes to gun violence, the five bad actors—criminals, gang members, terrorists, lunatics, and hotheads—cause most of the grief. The rest of gun owners do not, aside from those who cause the small and ever diminishing number of gun accidents.

You also saw that two of the five bad actors—career criminals and street gang members—are largely residents in bigger cities. This helps explain why over half of the counties in America have no homicides and why the top major cities have murder rates that outstrip their population levels.

What this all means is that gun violence is not universal. Thus, laws that are universal tend to miss the point and the opportunity to reduce gun violence by not specifically targeting those who misuse guns by choice. I once called such broad legislation "one-size-fits-all" to an audience, only to have a nice lady in the second row claim that "one-size-fits-all" was a fictional concept . . . just ask any woman who has tried "one-size-fits-all" pantyhose. On this, I'll have to take her word.

If I have explained things well to you, the question, "Who is committing gun violence?" is one that may well haunt you. As a thought experiment for audiences I address, I occasionally ask them to visualize the neighbors who live in the house on the left, and then the neighbors who live to the right. I then tell the audience that statistically one of those two houses has one or more guns in it. Then I ask them, "Which of your neighbors do you distrust?" The fact is that most people trust their next-door neighbors. They may not like those neighbors, especially if they have a teenage son with a car stereo so loud that it garners complaints from the residents of the local graveyard. But distrust? Typically not. This is a handy illustration that guns themselves lack any particular threat, nor does a typical neighbor. But somewhere (big cities) someone (criminal) is possibly misusing a gun as you read this because a gun crime is committed about every other minute in the United States. But it wasn't you, it wasn't your neighbor, it very likely wasn't in your neighborhood, and it was maybe not in your city or county. The who, where, and why are infinitely more important than the how.

Keep this in mind as you explore and debate guns and violence. If the societal goal is to reduce gun violence, applying attention to the bad actors—the who, where, and why—gets us to a solution faster, cheaper, and more reliably than any other approach.

We are not alone

Violence and gun violence are human problems, not American problems. They might even be Martian problems, but their crime data reporting system is indecipherable.

When it comes to murder, assault, rape, and other forms of uncivil behavior, we know it happens at differing levels everywhere, but it does happen everywhere, including in other advanced nations. But we know that in some countries with guns (either now or historically), crime rates can be low. We also know that in countries with few guns, certain categories of crime, including murder, can be high. Gun ownership rates are at best a weak variable when it comes to violence. Culture, though, is a strong one.

Aside from people being violent, we also know they want to be safe. In order to be safe from violent people, which can include their own government, they keep and use guns. This is reflected in estimates made by the Small Arms Survey that show massive non-compliance rates for gun registration in countries from England (95 percent non-compliance rate) to Mexico (223 percent). In some places it is so common that non-compliance enters into comedic social commentary. There is a joke told in the Ukraine about neighbors Ivan and Igor. One day Ivan sees Igor pouring motor oil in his flower bed. Ivan says, "Igor, you fool. That oil will kill your flowers!" Igor replied, "Yes, but my guns won't rust."

Regardless of the location, gun ownership, even if restricted to licensed and registered guns, makes zero difference in suicide rates. Gun ownership, or the lack thereof, has some odd and occasionally negative effects on some violent crime rates. But culture always affects violence, including gun violence. America, for all its positives, has a high cultural tolerance for violence in general, and in many inner cities, homicide is considered an honorable way to settle minor disputes. The American entertainment industry glorifies it and even the common suburbanite has an odd admiration for the bootlegger. In other places such as Somalia, violence is the ante just to get through the day. Without a guiding culture that disdains violence and marginalizes those who commit it, violence can be endured and even celebrated.

Accidents do happen . . . rarely

Murder and mayhem are one thing, assignable to bad actors. Gun accidents are tragedies and misfortunes caused and endured by good actors. They are also, thankfully, rare events.

This is not to discount the suffering that gun accidents bring. People die, and people are seriously wounded. But in terms of the number of people harmed, the danger from accidental gun injuries has been falling so much and is now so slight as to become a topic rarely discussed in the shouting matches between pro- and anti-gun sides. It even causes criminologists and public health researchers to yawn.

So many factors fall into this bucket of declining gun accidents that it is impossible to pinpoint the causes. But with household gun ownership rates steady and hunting licenses slipping only slightly, the causes for the steep decline in gun accidents likely come from better public education (which is a cultural element) and better firearm design. Regardless, keep up the good work.

Carry on?

Some people were traumatized when states began allowing any adult lacking a criminal record to carry guns in public. Over time however, it has become almost de facto, spanning forty-two states and the District of Columbia. Between public carry being nearly universally "concealed" carry (e.g., nobody sees that you have a gun on you) and the lack of public gun violence committed by people with carry permits, the initial trauma has all but evaporated. America has gotten used to the idea that people pack and they are not clamoring to reverse the trend. Indeed, only some states—talking to you California—have yet to recognize the lack of problems that expanded carry has caused.

One of the reasons that the initial reluctance has dissipated is that during the same period in which states one-by-one rolled out public carry, the crime rate in the United States fell like a bag of stones. The two may have limited cause and effect, but without there being any increase in violence caused by permit holders, people had nothing upon which to develop an adverse response.

America is now in what I'll call Phase-II of the process, where states are getting rid of the licensing process entirely and allowing any adult non-ex-con to carry guns as they wish. Though still early in this phase, we are not seeing any statistical negative effects. If history repeats itself—if the Phase-II of no-permit carry mimics Phase-I of "shall-issue" carry—then it may not be long before forty-two states repeal their permit systems.

You are so defensive

Numerous surveys by criminologists, pollsters, and media companies show that people use guns to prevent crimes, often and at multiples of the frequency for which guns are used to commit crimes.

We all would prefer to live in a world where self-defense, armed or otherwise, is unnecessary. But any world populated with human beings will be imperfect on its best day. And any day involving the Kardashians is positively bleak. Given this reality, we have to appreciate both the misuse and proper use of guns as they relate to crime and violence. We must examine both sides of the coin.

There are over 210,000,000 adults in the united states. The average of all defensive gun use (DGU) surveys is about two million DGUs a year. This roughly equates to about 1 percent of the American adult population using a gun every year to stop a crime. Are there a hundred houses in your subdivision? If so, then statistically speaking, one of your neighbors used a gun in self-defense. Either way you look at it—using the raw numbers of DGUs or the per capita rate of DGUs—that is a lot of crime that did not happen, and thus it has to be factored into the conversation.

Who should guns be kept away from and how?

All of this has led you to the key question: Who should or should not have access to guns? Some extremists think that everyone should own a gun and will even argue that ex-cons need guns, given that the company they once kept might have revenge motives in mind. On the opposite end of the extremism scale, some people think that nobody, including the police, should have guns, believing that the intended purpose of a gun is inherently undesirable. Both extremes are displays of absurdity, which is in keeping with modern politics.

On a slightly narrower footing, the pro- and anti-gun camps do not argue for totality, but for major expansions or restrictions on the ability to own a gun. Interestingly, the five bad actors—criminals, gangs, terrorists, lunatics, and hotheads—don't really voice an opinion because the laws really don't apply to them. While the NRA and Everytown argue about the retail availability of guns, members of the Crips and sundry untreated psychotics go about their days unworried about anyone's legislative agenda or what laws are currently in force.

The key question about gun misuse is who, where, and how. The "who" and "where" questions are easy to answer. Data shows that the average gun owner—the estimated fifty-eight million American households with guns, covering more than 134 million people—are not causing much grief. The "who" then devolves toward the five bad actors with gangs and career criminals leading the pack. And since their gun misuse is statistically logged in the throat of bigger cities, the where—though not universal—is also fairly easy to address.

So, the "who" and "where" are easy. The "how" is hard.

It is different elsewhere, in nations that either were never interested in guns or had severe restrictions on them so that fewer guns were "free floating" in underground marketplaces. But America has a written policy that people get to own guns, and as such some of those guns leak into the underground markets and have for nearly 250 years (if you see someone holding up a liquor store with a musket, make sure to post the video on YouTube, though such retail establishments have actually been robbed with swords, weapons that predate guns by quite a while). The logistics in absorbing that excess supply of underground is beyond practical and maybe beyond possible. Criminals are unlikely to obey gun turn-in programs, and having attended a few so-called "buy backs," I can attest that the types of guns brought in are not those used by criminals, and are more likely being traded for cash by your aunt getting rid of her late father's rusting hunting rifle that was up in her attic. Also, finding that stockpile of underground guns likely could not be accomplished without door-to-door sweeps and digging up a lot of oily flowerbeds, an approach that presents a whole other set of problems.

That leaves culture and targeting bad actors as key alternatives, and this gets me to the perspective that is guaranteed to aggravate everyone.

Passing laws is relatively easy. Changing culture isn't. Laws are largely ineffective vis-à-vis the five bad actors. Cultural changes would produce results.

As you learned when I covered the underground markets for crime guns, as you saw with cross-national estimates on non-compliance for gun registration, and as was demonstrated for the kinds and rates of gun used for committing crime, existing laws are ignored. Bypassed. Considered optional by many. This does not mean we should not pass laws, for if nothing else they provide tools for eventually taking some bad actors out of the public for a while—prosecutors love stacking every charge they can atop a defendant who has been in court one too many times. But we should also not assume yet another law is going to make a major change in the attitudes of these five bad actors, nor in the levels of gun violence. The get-tough-on-crime laws enacted in the 1990s have had great effect but diminishing returns this century.

Yet, the criminal element in America's major metropolitan areas account for most of the gun play and the least respect for laws. Since any intelligent person (i.e., you) would want to attack the biggest source of a problem, that is where you would start and where most laws would fail.

Culture, on the other hand, changes everything. Recall the absurdist comparison I made between a convention center full of NRA types and the same arena full of gang members. Different cultures, different outcomes. Misuse of guns (we don't really find a problem with the proper use of guns) for nefarious purposes is a symptom of a disorder, a disease if you will. We can try to legislatively treat the symptom called gun violence, or we can treat the disease that makes a person willing to shoot another human for anything other than self-defense.

But Lord, that is a tall order. Cultural change is a slow-moving train. Changing even a micro-culture, such as a gang-infested neighborhood, is not easy by anyone's triangulation. But without a shift in culture, we can expect the disease to persist, if not actually grow, and for gun violence to continue.

Acknowledgments

Writing a book is like getting pregnant. Sure, it sounded like a good idea when the notion struck you, but as the process drags on and on, you begin to have doubts.

Thankfully, I had more than a few midwives for this book, and I am grateful for their patient assistance, perpetual indulgence, and for not having me involuntarily committed for taking on this project.

Dave Grossman: It may be impossible to overstate the colonel's contributions to our understanding of the psychology of violence. His work has been of great help in understanding both the trajectory of mass shootings and some of the underlying process that leads a person to mass murder.

Professor Gary Kleck: Kleck is the most knowledgeable man I know when it comes to gun criminology. His books (*Targeting Guns* and *Point Black*) and his academic papers have been a wellspring of insight and endlessly helpful. The good professor also patiently answers my inquiries and, without much bugging on my part, expounds on key points to deepen my understanding.

The Gun Facts Research Volunteers: As of the Fall of 2019, there are almost three hundred volunteer researchers in the Gun Facts projects database, and I'm grateful for their pitching in whenever I ask. Often there is a great deal of heavy lifting that needs doing, being it normalizing data, scraping stats from non-exportable sources, and other tough work. For this book, there were several requests sent to do unlovable jobs, and they—as always—came through.

Professor Henry Schaffer: Henry is a godsend. Ensconced in academia, he likes to explore topics of interest and pull exotic papers and data from dusty archives. When I lacked access to some obscure stuff, Henry waved whatever magic wand they issue geneticists and made information appear.

Jason Goertz: My longtime and slightly anal-retentive friend Jason read the book and identified many places where, had I not added endnotes, amplified statements, or explained things better, I would have caused your B.S. detectors to register false positives. Jason is the only private pilot I have ever flown with (those small planes terrify me) and I did so because I knew his nature for leaving nothing to chance. True to form the day we rendez-voused at the air strip, despite many, many air hours, Jason extracted from his bag a ringed set of laminated cards that had his pre-flight check list, and he went through every bullet point. I slept better knowing he would likely find lapses that I, in the flurry of writing, would not myself recognize.

Notes

Chapter 1

1. "Civilian Firearms Holdings, 2017," Small Arms Survey, http://www.smallarms-survey.org/weapons-and-markets/stockpiles/civilian-inventories.html.
2. "Country Socioeconomic Status Scores: 1880–2010," Shawn Dorius, Iowa State University, 2017, https://www.kaggle.com/sdorius/globses.
3. Gary Kleck, *Targeting Guns* (New York: Walter de Gruyter, 1997), 187.
4. "Murders in US very concentrated," Crime Prevention Research Center, April 25 2017.
5. Tom Smith, "Gun Ownership in the United States: Measurement Issues and Trends," University of Chicago, January 2014, 4.
6. Bindu Kalesan, "Gun ownership and social gun culture," Injury Prevention, June 29 2015, – 2013; "BRFSS 2002 Survey Data and Documentation," Centers for Disease Control, Behavioral Risk Factor Surveillance System (BRFSS), 2002, https://www.cdc.gov/brfss/annual_data/annual_2002.htm.
7. Angela Ruggiero, "Reputed gang member held to answer on three Oakland cold case murders," *East Bay Times*; March 15, 2018, https://www.east-baytimes.com/2018/03/14/reputed-gang-member-held-to-answer-on-three-oakland-cold-case-murders/.
8. Philip J. Cook, "Underground Gun Markets," *The Economic Journal* (November 2007): 117.
9. P. J. Cook, H. A. Pollack, and K. White. "The Last Link: from Gun Acquisition to Criminal Use," *Journal of Urban Health* 96, 784–791 (2019).

10. "Intimate Partner Violence: Attributes of Victimization, 1993–2011," Bureau of Justice Statistics, November 27, 2012, https://www.bjs.gov/index.cfm?ty=pbdetail&iid=4536.

Chapter 2

1. "CDC WONDER," Centers for Disease Control, 1999–2016, https://wonder.cdc.gov/.
2. Erminia Colucci, David Lester, *Suicide and Culture: Understanding the Context* (Boston: Hogrefe Publishing, 2013).
3. "America's Complex Relationship With Guns," Pew Research Center, June 22 2017, https://www.pewsocialtrends.org/2017/06/22/americas-complex-relationship-with-guns/.
4. P. Cummings et al. "The association between the purchase of a handgun and homicide or suicide," *American Journal of Public Health*. 1997;87(6):974–978. doi:10.2105/ajph.87.6.974;
5. Jeffrey W. Swanson et al., "Implementation and Effectiveness of Connecticut's Risk-Based Gun Removal Law: Does it Prevent Suicides?" *80 Law and Contemporary Problems*, 179–208 (2017).

Chapter 3

1. James Alan Fox, Jack Levin, "Multiple Homicide: Patterns of Serial and Mass Murder" *Crime and Justice* 23 (1998).
2. John R. Lott, "How a Botched Study Fooled the World About the U.S. Share of Mass Public Shootings: U.S. Rate is Lower than Global Average" (August 25, 2018).
3. "Country Socioeconomic Status Scores: 1880–2010," Shawn Dorius, Iowa State University, 2017, https://www.kaggle.com/sdorius/globses.
4. "Guns and the City: Civilian firearm ownership for 178 countries," Annexe 3, The Small Arms Survey, August 2007, http://www.smallarmssurvey.org/publications/by-type/yearbook/small-arms-survey-2007.html.
5. We are using the Gun Facts Mass Public Shooting database. This database was created by combining the *Mother Jones* and Crime Prevention Research Center databases for American MPSs, normalizing the data for the original definition of MPS, improving the data hygiene, and adding columns of data not previously available.
6. Semiauto reload time estimates derived by reading entries on gun enthusiast online conversation groups.
7. James D. Wright, Peter H. Rossi, *Armed and Considered Dangerous: A Survey of Felons and Their Firearms*, (New Jersey: Aldine Transaction, 1986).

8. "School Shootings: Evil or Drug-Induced Behavior?" *Dr. Whitaker's* 23 no. 2, February 2013.

9. N. Mikita et al. "Irritability in boys with autism spectrum disorders: an investigation of physiological reactivity." *Journal of Child Psychology and Psychiatry.* 2015; 56(10).

10. Jennifer Johnston, Andrew Joy, "Mass Shootings and the Media Contagion Effect," Western New Mexico University (2016).

11. Dave Grossman, *Assassination Generation* (Boston: Little, Brown and Company, 2016).

12. Peter Langman, "Role Models, Contagions, and Copycats: An Exploration of the Influence of Prior Killers on Subsequent Attacks," June 22, 2017, SchoolShooters.info.

13. Jennifer Johnston, Andrew Joy, "Mass Shootings and the Media Contagion Effect," Western New Mexico University (2016).

14. "Annual Gun Law Scorecard: Giffords Law Center to Prevent Gun Violence, December 2018, https://lawcenter.giffords.org/scorecard2018/.

Chapter 4

1. "Key takeaways on Americans' views of guns and gun ownership," Pew Research; June 22, 2017, https://www.pewresearch.org/fact-tank/2017/06/22/key-takeaways-on-americans-views-of-guns-and-gun-ownership/.

2. Gary Kleck & Kovandzic, Tomislav & Saber, Mark & Hauser, Will. (2011). "The effect of perceived risk and victimization on plans to purchase a gun for self-protection," *Journal of Criminal Justice.* 39. 312–319. 10.1016/j.jcrimjus.2011.03.002. 1.

3. Rachel E. Morgan, Barbara A. Oudekerk, "Criminal Victimization, 2018," Bureau of Justice Statistics (September 2019).

4. Gary Kleck, *Targeting Gun,* (New York: Aldine de Gruyter, 1997), 187–188.

5. James Wright, Peter Rossi, "The Armed Criminal in America, A Survey of Incarcerated Felons," National Institute of Justice, July 1985.

6. Gary Kleck, Marc Gertz, "Armed Resistance to Crime," *Journal of Criminal Law and Criminology,* Vol 86 (Fall 1995).

7. Michael Planty, Jennifer L. Truman, "National Crime Victimization Survey, 1993–2001," Bureau of Justice Statistics, (May 2013).

8. M. Joan McDermott, "Rape Victimization in 26 American Cities," US Department of Justice (1979).

9. Gary Kleck, Marc Gertz, "Armed Resistance to Crime," *Journal of Criminal Law and Criminology,* Vol 86 (Fall 1995).

Chapter 5

1. Stephen J. Subner, "Abortion and Crime, Revisited" *Freakonomics Podcast* (Ep. 384), Produced by Zack Lapinski, July 10, 2019, https://freakonomics.com/podcast/abortion/.
2. Mariel Alper, Matthew R. Durose, Joshua Markman, "2018 Update on Prisoner Recidivism: A 9-Year Follow-up Period," Bureau of Justice Statistics (May 2018).

Chapter 6

1. "Elusive Arsenals, Gang and Group Firearms," Small Arms Survey 2010, Chapter 4; Gun Facts web search of local criminologist estimates.
2. "Measuring the Extent of Gang Problems," National Gang Center, https://www.nationalgangcenter.gov/survey-analysis/measuring-the-extent-of-gang-problems.
3. "Recidivism Release Cohort Datafile," U.S. Sentencing Commission, 2005; "2018 Update on Prisoner Recidivism: A 9-Year Follow-up Period (2005–2014),"Bureau of Justice Statistics, May 23, 2018; FBI Uniform Crime statistics, 2018.
4. M. DeLisi et al. (2019). "The Past Is Prologue: Criminal Specialization Continuity in the Delinquent Career," *Youth Violence and Juvenile Justice*, 17(4), 335–353. https://doi.org/10.1177/1541204018809839.
5. Jessica Saunders, Gary Sweeten, Charles Katz, "Post-Release Recidivism among Gang and Non-Gang Prisoners in Arizona From 1985 through 2004," Arizona Criminal Justice Commission, 2009.
6. J. C. Barnes, Kevin M. Beaver, J. Mitchell Miller, "Estimating the Effect of Gang Membership on Nonviolent and Violent Delinquency: A Counterfactual Analysis," *Aggressive Behavior*, 2010.
7. James D. Wright, Peter H. Rossi, "The Armed Criminal in America, A Survey of Incarcerated Felons," National Institute of Justice, July 1985.
8. Beth Bjerregaard, Alan J. Lizotte, "Gun Ownership and Gang Membership," *Journal of Criminal Law and Criminology*, Vol 86, Issue 1 (Fall 1995).
9. George W. Knox et al. "Gangs and Guns," *American Jails* Volume:9 Issue:2 (May/June 1995).
10. Clare S. Allely et al. "Neurodevelopmental and Psychosocial Risk Factors in Serial Killers and Mass Murderers," *Aggression and Violent Behavior*, 19 (2014).
11. A. Valdez, C. D. Kaplan, and E. Codina, "Psychopathy Among Mexican American Gang Members: A Comparative Study," *International Journal Of Offender Therapy And Comparative Criminology*, 44 (2000).
12. P. J. Cook, H. A. Pollack, and K. White, "The Last Link: from Gun Acquisition to Criminal Use," *Journal of Urban Health*, 96, (2019).

Chapter 7

1. Randall T. Loder, Neil Farren, "Injuries from firearms in hunting activities," *Injury*, Volume 45, Issue 8, August 2014.
2. Gabriel B. Eber et al., "Nonfatal and Fatal Firearm-Related Injuries Among Children Aged 14 Years and Younger: United States, 1993–2000," *Pediatrics*, Vol 113, No. 6 (June 2004).
3. Marc Caplan, Jolene Hernon, "Equipment Performance Report: 9mm and 45-Caliber Autoloading Pistol Test Results," *National Institute of Justice*, August 1987.
4. "Gun Product Safety Notices," Violence Policy Center, November 2019, https://vpc.org/regulating-the-gun-industry/gun-product-safety-notices/.
5. S. E. Parks et al., "Surveillance for violent deaths—National Violent Death Reporting System, 16 states, 2010," (January 2014).
6. Julian A. Waller and Elbert B. Whorton, "Unintentional shootings, highway crashes and acts of violence—A behavior paradigm," *Accident Analysis & Prevention*, Volume 5, Issue 4 (December 1973).
7. *Targeting Guns*; Kleck; Aldine De Gruyter.
8. "Homicide Trends in the United States, 1980–2008," *Bureau of Justice Statistics*, (November 2011).
9. Gabriel B. Eber et al., "Nonfatal and Fatal Firearm-Related Injuries Among Children Aged 14 Years and Younger: United States, 1993–2000," *Pediatrics*, Vol 113, No. 6 (June 2004).

Chapter 8

1. John Van Kesteren, Pat Mayhew, Paul Nieuwbeerta, "Criminal Victimisation in Seventeen Industrialised Countries. Key findings from the 2000 International Crime Victims Survey," 10.15496/publikation-6595.
2. Christopher Halls, *Guns in Australia*, (London: Hamlyn 1974)
3. "Illicit firearms in Australia," Australian Criminal Intelligence Commission, October 21, 2016, https://www.acic.gov.au/publications/intelligence-products/illicit-firearms-australia-report.
4. "Australian crime: facts and figures 1998," Australian Institute of Criminology, https://www.aic.gov.au/publications/facts/1998.
5. There is no national firearm registration in the United States.

Chapter 9

1. "Homicide Trends in the U.S.," Bureau of Justice Statistics, November 16, 2008, https://www.bjs.gov/index.cfm?ty=pbdetail&iid=2221.
2. "A U.S. Secret Service Analysis of Targeted School Violence: United States Secret Service, National Threat Assessment Center," 2019.
3. "Local Police Departments, 2016: Personnel," Bureau of Justice Statistics, October 15, 2019, https://www.bjs.gov/index.cfm?ty=pbdetail&iid=6706.
4. "The Economic Cost of Gun Violence," Gifford's Law Center, November 2019, https://lawcenter.giffords.org/resources/the-economic-cost-of-gun-violence/.

Chapter 10

1. Dr. Miguel A. Faria, *America, Guns, and Freedom,* (Herdon, VA: Mascot Books, 2019).
2. "Source and Use of Firearms Involved in Crimes: Survey of Prison Inmates, 2016," Bureau of Justice Statistics, January 9, 2019, https://www.bjs.gov/index.cfm?ty=pbdetail&iid=6486.
3. "Peer Review, Publication in Top Journals, Scientific Consensus, and So Forth," Robert Higgs, The Independent Institute, May 7, 2007.
4. "What the 'Grievance Studies' Hoax Means," *Chronicle of Higher Education*, October 9, 2018, https://www.chronicle.com/article/What-the-Grievance/244753.